Just Right

Jeremy Harmer
& Carol Lethaby

FARNHAM COLLEGE

Morley Road • Farnham • Surrey • GU9 8LU

Student's Book

MC ELT Marshall Cavendish London • Singapore • New York

Text acknowledgements

p.8 Dream or Nightmare, based upon articles by Dan Kennedy and Mark Meltzer; p.13 Google search engine, reproduced kindly by Google; p.28-9 How could we get it so wrong based upon an article by Jonathan Glancey, ©The Guardian; p.43-44 Based upon an article by Tim Adams; p.44 Based upon an article by Ed Douglas, © Ed Douglas; p.50 The Anger Page, based upon various articles; p.52 How to Teach Writing, Jeremy Harmer © Jeremy Harmer; p.66 Based upon article by John Gibb and various others; p.73 Article 1 by Sarah Wilkin, ©Adhoc Publishing; p.73 Article 2 based upon an article Max Luscher; p.73 Article 3 by Victoria Moore, ©The Independent on Sunday 6.05.01; p.73 Article 4 based upon article from, The Observer; p.81 Article 1 granted by kind permission of the Vegan Action Group; p.81 Article 2 granted by kind permission of the Greenpeace Organisation; p.81 Article 3 granted by kind permission of Dr Mercola; p.81 Article 4 based upon an article by Monsanto; p.84 Longman Dictionary of Contemporary English 4, ©Pearson Education; p.87 Statistical Table based upon information from The Vegan Research Panel; p.87 Pie chart based upon information from Balwynhs School, Australia; p.93 Based upon an article by Brian Bates, ©Brian Bates; p.101-2 Notes by Elenor Coppola published by Simon and Schuster, © Faber and Faber; p.108 Adrian Mole The Wilderness Years by Sue Townsend, © Sue Townsend 1993. Permission granted by Curtis Brown Group Ltd; p.115 Based upon a story by Edward De Bono; p.125 About a boy by Nick Hornby, ©Penguin Group USA; p.126 Paula by Isabel Allende, ©HarperCollins; p.126 The Green Mile, by Stephen King, ©Stephen King; p.127 White Teeth by Zadie Smith (Hamish Hamilton, 2000, ©Zadie Smith, 2000; p.139 Based upon an article by L.D. Meagher; p.140 Based upon an article by Lisa Margonelli; p.145 Midsummer, Tobago from Sea Grapes by Derek Walcott, published by Jonathan Cape. Used by permission of the Randon House Group Limited; p.145 Like Beacon by Grace Nichols, ©Grace Nichols. Permission granted by Curtis Brown Group Ltd; p.145 Handbag by Ruth Fainlight, ©Ruth Fainlight; p.151 Small Boy by Norman MacCraig, ©Birlinn;

Audio acknowledgements

p.5 Little House on the Prairie, by Laura Ingells Wilder, reproduced by kind permission of HarperCollins Children's Books (USA); p.16 Stormy Weather, lyrics by Ted Koehler & Harold Arlen reproduced kindly by Fred Ahlert Music. Performed by Billie Holliday reproduced kindly by Universal Music; p.22 White Teeth by Zadie Smith, reproduced kindly by AP Watt on behalf of Zadie Smith; p.26 Midsummer, Iobago from Sea Grapes by Derek Walcott, published by Jonathan Cape. Used by permission of the Randon House Group Limited; p.26 Like Beacon by Grace Nichols, ©Grace Nichols. Permission granted by Curtis Brown Group Ltd; p.26-7 Handbag by Ruth Fainlight, ©Ruth Fainlight; p.27-8 Interview between Jan Blake & Presenter, ©Jan Blake; p.29 Small Boy by Norman MacCraig, ©Birlinn; Beanfields (Live) by Penguin Café Orchestra, reproduced kindly by Penguin Café Orchestra and Virgin Music; Debussy: String Quartet 3rd Movement, reproduced kindly by EMI Music.

Photo acknowledgements

p.6: 1, ©Inmagine/Alamy, 2, ©Toshihide Gotoh/Dex Image/Alamy, 3, ©Royalty Free/Corbis, 4, ©Russell Underwood/Corbis, 5, ©Rob Gage/Photo Network/Alamy; p.11:Bottom right, ©Dynamic graphics Group/IT Stock Free/Alamy; p.17: Top left, ©Arkansas Democrat-Gazette, Top right, ©Rene Burri/Magnum Photos, Bottom left, ©Associated Press, AP, Bottom right, ©Corbis; p.24: a, ©Luca I. Tettoni/Corbis, b, ©Jeremy Harmer, c, ©Hulton-Deutsch Collection/CORBIS, d, ©Jeremy Harmer; p.29: Main, ©Royalty Free/Corbis, Insert, ©Royalty Free/Corbis; p.35: Left, ©Ingram Publishing/Alamy, Right, ©Royalty Free/Corbis; p.36, Bottom left, ©Paul Joynson Hicks/Jon Arnold Images/Alamy; p.39: a, ©Scott Hortop/Alamy, b, ©Alan MacWeeney/Corbis, c, ©Brand X Pictures/Alamy, d, ©Buzz Pictures, e, ©Royalty Free/Corbis, Danny, ©Royalty Free/Corbis, Carmen, ©Ron Chapple/Thinkstock/Alamy, Jack, ©Royalty Free/Corbis, Marcus, ©Royalty Free/Corbis, Ellie, ©Bob Thomas/Alamy; p.40: a, ©Royalty Free/Corbis, b, ©ROB & SAS/Corbis, c, ©Don Mason/Corbis, d, ©Ron Chapple/Thinkstock/Alamy; p. 43, Bottom left, ©Tom Jenkins, Top right, ©UNKNOWN, Bottom left, ©PA Photos/EPA; p. 47: Bottom background, ©John Lawrence Photography/Alamy, Insert, ©NANO CALVO/VWPICS/Visual&Written SL/Alamy.com; p. 50, Bottom right, ©Anthony Redpath/Corbis; p.52: Shark, Brandon Cole Marine Photography/Alamy; p.58: Top, Comstock Images/Alamy, Centre Bananastock/Alamy, Bottom, Comstock Images/Alamy; p.69: Left, ©Royalty Free/Corbis, Centre top, ©Joe Sohm/Alamy, Centre bottom, ©Michael Saul/Brand X Pictures/Alamy, Metropolis, ©Michael Saul/Brand X Pictures/Alamy; p.71: Nataraja by Bridget Riley, ©Tate Gallery; p.84: a, ©Shout/Alamy, b, ©Owen Franken/Corbis, c, ©Owen Franken/Corbis, d, ©Steve McDonough/Corbis, e, ©Royalty Free/Corbis, Chris, ©Image 100/Alamy, Jed, ©ImageState/Royalty Free/Alamy, Julia, ©Image100Alamy, Martin, ©Cameron/Corbis, Naomi, ©Royalty Free/Corbis; p.92: Gandalf, ©New Line/Everett (EVT), Bridget, ©Corbis Sygma, Amelie, ©Steve Sands/New York Newswire/Corbis, Rocky ©Everett Collection/Rex Features, a, ©Big Cheese Photo LLC/Alamy, b, ©Royalty Free/Corbis; p.93: Top left, ©Gregory Pace/Corbis, Top right, ©Gregory Pace/Corbis, Bottom left, ©CinemaPhoto/Corbis, Bottom right, ©Photo Japan/Alamy; p.101: Top right, ©SIPA Press/Rex Features; p.105: Top, ©Royalty Free/Corbis; p.106: Left, ©CSU Archv/Everett (EVT)/Rex Features; p.111: Left, ©Reuters/Corbis, Centre, ©Eyebyte/Alamy, Right, ©London Weekend Television (LWT/KMK)/Rex Features; p.114: a, ©Neal Preston/Corbis, b, ©Rufus F. Folkks/Corbis, c, ©Corbis; p.115: d, ©Bettmann/Corbis, e, ©Reuters/Corbis, f, ©Reuters/Corbis, g, ©Reuters/Corbis, h, ©Manuel Blondeau/Corbis, i, ©Mitchell Gerber/Corbis; p.118: Bottom right, ©Jean Pierre Amet/Corbis; p.120: Jackie Chan, ©Kevin Lock/ZUMA/Corbis, Shakira, ©Reuters/Corbis; p.123: Stephen King, ©John-Marshall Mantel/Corbis, John Grisham, ©D. Herrick/DMI (DMW)/Rex Features, Zadie Smith, ©MC Pherson Colin/Corbis Sygma, Amy Tan, ©Reuters/Corbis, Alice Walker, ©Roger Ressmeyer/Corbis, Nick Hornby, ©Rune Hellestad, Danielle Steel, ©Matt Baron/BEI(BEI)/Rex Features, Isabel Allende, ©AP Photo/Eric Risberg; p.124: Bottom right, ©Sam Barcroft (SFT)/Rex Features; p.135: Bottom right, ©Roger Vaughan Picture Library; p.136: Al Capone, ©Bettmann/Corbis, Bonnie and Clyde, ©Bettmann/Corbis; p.138: Mona Lisa, ©Gianni Dagli Orti/Corbis; p.145: Derek Walcott, © Brooks Kraft/Corbis, Grace Nichols, ©Paul Taylor, Ruth Fainlight, ©David Sillitoe; p.147: Jan Blake, ©Jan Blake, used with kind permission; p.152: Top left, ©Tim Clark used with kind permission, Top right, ©The artist/Courtesy the artist and Jay Jopling, Bottom, ©PA Photos; p.156: Top, ©Buddy Mays/Corbis

© 2005 Marshall Cavendish Ltd

First published 2005 by Marshall Cavendish Ltd

Marshall Cavendish is a member of the Times Publishing Group

Marshall Cavendish ELT
119 Wardour Street
London W1F 0UW

Designed by Hart McLeod, Cambridge
Editorial development by Ocelot Publishing, Oxford, with Geneviève Talon
Illustrations by Yane Christiansen, Francis Fung, Dylan Gibson, Cathy Dineen and Ella Tjada

Printed and bound by Times Offset (M) Sdn. Bhd. Malaysia

Contents

Skills		Language

Skills		Language

UNIT 1
Winning, hoping, giving

Vocabulary: money words and sayings

1 a **Look at the following sayings. What do you think they mean?**

b **Answer these questions in groups.**

• What is your attitude to money? Which proverbs do you agree or disagree with? Why?
• Do you have any similar sayings in your language?

> Money can't buy you love.
> Money makes the world go round.
> Money is the root of all evil.
> Money doesn't grow on trees, you know!
> A fool and his money are soon parted.

2 **Read each of the statements a–e. Match each one with a picture of the person who said it (1–5).**

a 'Listen to me, son. I had a lot of credit cards, and I took out loans to pay my debts. Now I'm bankrupt. Money has ruined my life. Don't let the same thing happen to you.'

b 'I've just been collecting my winnings. That's £7,000! Fantastic!'

c 'I've saved a lot of money and I've invested in successful companies, that kind of thing. So I guess you could say I was pretty well off.'

d 'Money? It just slips through my fingers. I'm permanently broke! But hey, who cares. I'm happy!'

e 'Since I lost my job, I find it really hard to make ends meet. At the end of each month I'm broke!'

Explain the meaning of the words and phrases in blue.

3 **Role-play** Student A takes on the personality of one of the speakers (a–e) from Activity 2, but doesn't tell the other students which one.

The other students interview Student A about any subject except money. The students have to guess who Student A is.

Example: STUDENT B: Have you got a big house?

STUDENT A: A big house? I have got three big houses!
(Student A is role-playing the rich woman.)

4 The verbs in the box can all be used with money (e.g. *to borrow money*). Copy and complete the table with as many verbs from the box as possible. Use a dictionary if necessary.

blow	borrow	donate	earn	gamble
get	give	invest	lend	lose	make
pay	put	save	spend	take	win

What a wise person does	*earn, ...*
What a foolish person does	
What a kind person does	

Compare your table with a partner's. Are there any words which you can't put in the table? Which ones can fit into more than one category?

5 Read the following phrases. Look up the meanings of any words you do not know.

a .... a little money every month

b .... a couple of pounds from a friend

c .... a pay rise to the employees

d .... about £80 a week on clothes

e .... away all my savings

f .... £50 to cancer research

g .... money into a new music company

h .... money on an expensive new camera

i .... money out of a cash machine

j .... my debts

k .... my savings in a new company

l .... ten pounds to my brother

m .... £30 a week

n .... £2,000 on the last race

Complete the phrases with verbs from Activity 4. Sometimes more than one verb is possible.

Example: a *save / spend / invest a little money every month (There are other possibilities.)*

6 Tell the class about someone real or imaginary, using as much language as you can from Activities 4 and 5.

Example: *I knew this man who gambled all his money away on horse-racing. He never invested any money, never paid his debts and was always broke. And then one day he won a lot of money, put all his money into a friend's company and now he's a millionaire!*

7 **Money in phrases** Using a dictionary or some other source, find definitions for the following phrases.

a not for love nor money

b a waste of money

c let's see the colour of your money

d to be a little short of money

e to be rolling in money

f to give somebody a run for their money

g to have money to burn

h to marry into money

i to put your money where your mouth is

j to throw money at something

Student A gives the definition, Student B gives the phrase.

Example: STUDENT A: *A spoken way of saying 'I want to know that you can pay for this!'*

STUDENT B: *'Let's see the colour of your money!' (c)*

Reading: lottery dreams

8 **Discussion** Answer these questions with a partner.

a Have you ever bought a lottery ticket?

b Have you, or anyone you know, ever won anything?

c If you won a lot of money, would you do any of these things?
  • go crazy and buy lots of expensive things
  • buy gifts for your family
  • give up work
  • move to a more expensive neighbourhood
  • invest your money carefully
  • donate money to good causes
  What else might you do?

9 Read the article *Dream or nightmare?*, on page 8, quickly. Where do sentences *a–f* fit in the article? The first one is done for you.

a Lynette Nichols was a bookkeeper before she won about $17 million in the lottery. **2**

b So why does a sudden win cause so many problems?

c Brett Peterson was just 19 and working as a busboy in a small restaurant in California.

d So, do you still want to win the lottery?

e On top of this, big winners are not prepared for the new expectations that people now have of them.

f John and Sandy from Ohio won about $12 million and almost immediately the letters and phone calls started.

DREAM OR NIGHTMARE?

Have you always dreamed of winning the lottery? Everyone does, don't they?

After reading Janet Bloom's article, you might change your mind.

For many, a big win in the lottery is their dream and so they buy tickets every week hoping for 'a dream come true'. When they win, they think, they will be able to stop doing their boring job and live a life of luxury. But if their numbers really do come up, that dream often becomes a nightmare.

(1) .... When he found out he was going to receive a $2 million payout in the lottery, he immediately gave up work, lent money to all his friends, whether or not they would be able to pay it back, and went out on a wild spending spree. Within months he had huge credit card debts and no money left to pay them. A year later, he had taken a job as a sales clerk to try to make ends meet.

(2) .... Did it bring her happiness? Not exactly. She and her husband immediately started fighting over money. She couldn't believe that he was wasting it on electronic toys for himself, while he objected to her buying expensive cars for her family. They ended up in court in a trial that cost them both hundreds of thousands of dollars and, of course, they're now divorced.

(3) .... Everyone, from crazy inventors to people needing help putting their kids through college, wanted a donation from them. Their own kids lost all their friends when they moved house to a more expensive neighborhood and they spent way too much time and energy worrying about their own safety. And to make matters worse, they both lost their jobs as accountants.

(4) .... Well, it seems that a large win can put enormous stress on people who are not prepared for it. The majority of people who win are people who did not have a lot of money before. They tend to come from blue-collar backgrounds and have been used to working full time and living 'pay-check to pay-check'. When they get this unexpected windfall, they don't know how to cope. Very often they stop working and they move house. But these are probably the two worst things they can do. Who lives in wealthy neighborhoods? Wealthy people of course – people who are used to having and spending money. Moving to these areas alienates lottery winners from their familiar world and friends. From one day to the next, they lose the structure that the working day offers and they no longer have the support system of neighbors who come from similar backgrounds around them. They find themselves surrounded by strangers from a different world with different life experiences, and on top of that, they have plenty of free time on their hands.

(5) .... Their friends expect them to be generous and pay for everything and they receive requests from strangers asking them to donate money to a particular cause. Very often, lottery winners do not have much experience in investing money wisely and end up making disastrous financial decisions, which quickly eat up their winnings. Many past lottery winners have commented on how easy it is to spend a lot of money very quickly once they started to believe, on a daily basis, that 'money is no object'.

(6) .... If you do win, the best advice is probably to get yourself some good, independent financial advice and, more importantly, to be aware that becoming rich overnight could radically change your life – and not necessarily for the better.

We want to hear from YOU. How do you handle money? What would you do if you won the lottery? Would you save or spend? Write and let us know.

10 Fact check Read the article again. Copy and complete the table with information about Brett, Lynette, and John and Sandy. The first one is done for you.

	Brett	Lynette	John and Sandy
Job(s)	a ......busboy...... b	f	j ....
How much did they win?	c	g	k ....
Main problems	d .... e	h .... i	l .... m .... n ....

11 Match the two parts of the sentence according to what you read in *Dream or nightmare?*

a People who win money unexpectedly
b They can feel separated from
c They receive letters and phone calls from
d They don't know how to

1 ... invest money well.
2 ... people who want money.
3 ... are not usually prepared for it.
4 ... their family and friends.

Do you agree with these statements? Look for evidence from the text and give reasons for your answers.

Example: a Yes, it's true. In the text, there are examples of people who spend their new money unwisely, or who start arguing because they don't know how to handle it.

12 Varieties of English The text is written in a US variety of English. Look at these words and expressions from British English. What is the US word or expression used in the text to mean the same thing?

British English	US English
a a wealthy area	
b neighbours	
c working-class backgrounds	
d pay-packet to pay-packet	
e supporting their children while they are at university	

13 Vocabulary Explain the meaning of the following words as they appear in the text.

a objected to (paragraph 2)
b windfall (paragraph 4)
c alienates (paragraph 4)
d wisely (paragraph 5)
e disastrous (paragraph 5)
f eat up (paragraph 5)
g overnight (paragraph 6)

Language in chunks

14 Look at how these phrases are used in the text and then use them in the sentences which follow. You may have to change them to make them fit.

a dream come true   to end up (doing something)
(to have) time on one's hands
to make matters worse   money is no object
way too much (of something)

a That girl is never at school and when she has .... she gets into trouble.
b They spent all their money and .... they then borrowed money to buy a car.
c The cost of the project doesn't matter at all. ....

d We didn't know what to buy with the money we won and we .... depositing it all in a bank account that gives high interest.
e Kevin had .... money as a kid – his parents gave him everything he wanted – and now he doesn't know how to manage his own financial affairs.
f Getting this new job was .... for me. I really enjoy it, the hours are great and the pay is good.

15 Write questions using the phrases in Activity 14. Interview a classmate and tell the other students what they said.

16 Noticing language There are seven questions in the text. Are they all the same kind? What is the difference between them?

17 Discussion Answer these questions in groups.

a Do you think it would change your life if you won a lot of money? Why? Why not?

b What things in your life would you change? Why?

c What things would you keep the same? Why?

Grammar: question forms

18 Find questions that have the same grammatical form as the four examples below (the verb tense is not important). Copy and complete the table.

a Did you spend all the money you won?
b Do you like gambling?
c Does she spend a lot of money on computer equipment?
d How many people came?
e How often does someone win?
f I'm on time, aren't I?
g Is it going to rain tomorrow?
h It's not very likely, is it?
i She's been here before, hasn't she?
j That's never going to happen, is it?
k What took three hours?
l What did you do when you found out you'd won?
m Which team won?
n Who called you on the phone?
o Why did they buy such an expensive car?
p You can't retire from work yet, can you?

Question type 1 (yes / no)	Did they win the lottery?
Question type 2 (question tag)	They won the lottery, didn't they?
Question type 3 (open-ended question)	What did they win?
Question type 4 (question about the subject / agent)	Who won the lottery?

Look at 1A in the Mini-grammar. Do you want to change any of your answers?

19 Write down the names of two people and two places that are important to you. Give the names to a partner. Your partner asks questions about the names, using each of the four question types from Activity 18 at least once.

Examples: STUDENT A: Who's Pieter?

STUDENT B: He's the man who taught me to play the guitar.

STUDENT A: Did you find it easy?

STUDENT B: Not at first. But when I joined a group I learned fast.

STUDENT A: How did you get on with the people in the group?

STUDENT B: Quite well, most of the time.

STUDENT A: You had some disagreements, did you?

STUDENT B: One or two!

20 Spoken questions Read questions *a–i* and then listen to the conversations on Track 1. Say which of the following functions (*1–6*) the questions correspond to (B's questions in the case of dialogues). The first one is done for you.

1 'asking' to try and get someone to agree with us
2 asking because we don't know the answer
3 asking to confirm what we think we know
4 asking to make sure we heard correctly (or because we want to question what we heard)
5 asking to make sure we heard the question correctly (or because we want to 'question' the question)
6 exclamations

a A: I love this restaurant.
   B: Me too. Isn't this food great?
   6 – exclamations
b A: I lost the money.
   B: You lost the money? Oh no.
c Aren't you the person who called last night?
d We're never going to win the lottery, are we?
e A: I bet $1,000 on a horse-race.
   B: You did what?
f We're not going bankrupt, are we?
g A: Why are you so unhappy?
   B: Why am I so unhappy? I just am.
h A: I'm writing a book.
   B: You're writing a book, are you?
i A: There were 200 people at the party.
   B: There were how many?

Look at 1B in the Mini-grammar. Do you want to change any of your answers? What different question forms are used for each function (*1–6*)?

21 Conversations Have conversations which start with the following statements. Use question functions 4 and 5. Use as many different question types as possible. The first one is done for you. You can use **1B in the Mini-grammar** to help you.

a I never want to see you again! *You never want to see me again? Why not? – Because of what you said.* etc.
b I'm late for work!
c It's going to be a busy day at the office tomorrow.
d She gave all her winnings to a dogs' home.
e She invested $20,000 in the stock market.
f We won $500!
g They finished dinner at 2 in the morning.
h They invited 14 people for dinner.
i We waited for six hours.
j Why are you investing all your money?
k Why don't you like buying lottery tickets?

22 In groups Each student chooses one of the following topics. Use the questions to make notes so that you can tell the others about it.

a
A day when you or someone you know won something

What did you / they win? What did you do after? How did you feel?

b
A party you went to

How did you get there? How many people were there? What kind of people were they? What happened? How did you get home?

c
A sports event you saw or played in

What happened? Who was playing? What were the most memorable moments? Who did what?

d
An extraordinary journey you went on

Where were you going? What happened? Why extraordinary? What did you do?

Tell your story. The other students interrupt you as often as possible using question functions *1–6* from Activity 20.

Functional language: expressing sympathy

23 Read the statements in the box. How many can you use for each situation (*a–h*)? The first one is done for you.

I'm so sorry to hear that. **a**
I'm really sorry about that. **a**
That's such a shame. **a**
That's so sad. **a**
What a pity.
It's a real shame that things didn't work out for you.
It's a pity that you're not feeling up to it.
That's a shame. **a**

a Your friend has lost her cat.
b Your friend lost all the money from her investments.
c Your friend loses her job after 10 years.
d Your son studied hard, but failed his maths test.
e The weather is not good and your partner wanted to go away for the weekend.
f A guy you know didn't get the job he wanted.
g Your friend's daughter didn't win the prize she was expecting to win.
h Your daughter is not feeling well and doesn't think she will be able to play in a game.

24 Listen to Track 2. Copy and complete the table. Match the conversations *1–8* to the statements and the situations *a–h* from Activity 23. The first one is done for you.

Conversation	Statement		Situation
1	I'm so sorry to hear that.		c
2			
3			
4			
5			
6			
7			
8			

25 Copy and complete this table with different ways of expressing sympathy. The first one is done for you.

Using a clause

a I'm (so) .....sorry......... that you are having financial difficulties.

b It's (such) a .... that you didn't talk to someone before it happened.

c It's a (real) .... that your family is not supporting you.

d It's (really) .... that you will have to sell your house.

Using an exclamation

e What a ....!

f What a ....!

g That's (such) a ....!

h That's a (real) ....!

i That's a (real) ....!

j That's (so / really) ....!

k I'm (so) ....!

What is the effect of using *so / such / real / really*?

● ● ● Pronunciation: stress

26 Listen to Track 3 and underline the stressed syllables in the sentences. Then circle the word that is stressed most of all.

Example: That's <u>such</u> a (shame!)

a I'm so sorry that you lost your job!

b It's so sad that he lost all the money.

c It's such a shame that they had to leave that beautiful house.

d It's such a pity that you didn't save the money.

e That's such bad luck!

27 Now practise saying the sentences with the same use of stress.

28 Pair work React to these situations. Use *so* and *such* with appropriate stress.

a Your sister lost her wallet and all her money on the first day of her holidays.

b Two of your friends lost a lot of money at Las Vegas in a casino.

c The house of a family in your neighbourhood caught fire and burned down last week.

d A colleague of yours lost her job at the office two weeks ago.

29 In pairs Imagine you are in these situations (a–e) and take turns reacting to them using the expressions in the box in Activity 23. You can invent the details.

a You didn't pass your English test after you studied hard.

b You had an argument with one of your friends about what to do at the weekend.

c You have a terrible cold and you don't feel like doing anything.

d You have had a terrible day. Everything that could go wrong has gone wrong.

e You lost a lot of money.

Example: STUDENT A: Guess what? I didn't pass my English test. I worked really hard for it.

STUDENT B: What a shame. What are you going to do?

30 Think of two disappointments in your life or the life of someone you know. Tell your partner about them.

Example: STUDENT A: I was disappointed when I didn't pass my driving test.

STUDENT B: Oh, that's a shame. What happened?

Speaking: making a decision

31 In groups Re-write the following sentence so that it reflects the group's opinions.

People shouldn't give money to charities.

32 Choose one of the following five charities and read the information about it.

a **Adopt a minefield** (www.landmines.org) raises awareness and funds to clear landmines and help survivors of landmines around the world.

b **Médecins Sans Frontières** (www.msf.org) provides emergency medical assistance in over 80 countries where healthcare is insufficient or non-existent.

c **WaterAid** (www.wateraid.org.uk) provides clean water and sanitation for the millions of people who have no access to this vital resource.

d **Stop Global AIDS** (www.stopglobalaids.org) raises money to fight the disease with prevention measures, care for victims, providing affordable medication and influencing political opinion.

e **The WWF** (www.panda.org) helps to conserve the world's biological diversity, ensure renewable natural resources, and promotes good consumption policies.

In your own words, and without looking back at the book, explain what the charity you have selected does, and say why it might be a good idea.

Listening: money advice

35 Why might people at different ages visit a financial advisor? Would you visit a financial advisor? Why?

36 Listen to Track 4. Choose the best answer.

Don wants to:

a ... learn how to invest money.
b ... talk about how to pay his debts.
c ... find out how to make more money.
d ... manage his money better.

37 Listen to Track 5. Copy and complete Suzanne Moore's notes about Don.

33 In groups You have some money that you wish to donate to a charity. Choose one of the charities in Activity 32. Compare your choice with another group.

Speaking and writing: ellipsis

In writing, we generally make complete questions and sentences. In informal speech, however, we often leave out all but the most important words.

Examples: 'Nice day!' instead of 'Isn't it a nice day?' or 'It's a nice day, isn't it?'
'Coffee?' instead of 'Would you like a coffee?'
'Raining.' instead of 'It's raining.'

34 What might be the full (written) form for A's utterances in the following exchanges?

a A: Surprised?
  B: Yes, just a bit.
b A: Difficult exam?
  B: No, not too bad.
c A: Biscuit?
  B: No thanks. I've just eaten.
d A: Nice car.
  B: Thanks. Glad you like it.
e A: Going to rain.
  B: Yes, I think you're right.
f A: Drink?
  B: Yes, let's.
g A: Starting a new job tomorrow.
  B: You're doing what?
h A: Hot!
  B: Yes it is.

Can you think why / where the conversations took place?

Suzanne Moore – *Independent Financial Advice*

Spends now	Ways to save
Spends (a) $............ per week on food.	Shop at (b) ....
Goes to (c) .... four times a week.	Go (d) .... a week.
Spends (e) .... on rent.	Maybe find somewhere cheaper.
Buys (f) .... a week.	Only buy one.
Goes to the movies once a week.	Go (g) ....
Eats in the (h)	Make a sandwich at home.

38 Listen to Tracks 4 and 5 again. Complete these sentences with the words you hear.

a I'm not a big ...., but I just can't seem to make ends meet.
b I'm an English lit .... so I have a lot of work.
c Hmmm – that's a ...., isn't it?
d You're going to have to make a .... …
e … whatever you spend your money on – your ....
f And then on the other side, you write down what you could change and .... on to save money.
g How much money do you spend on .... per week?
h It .... from one week to the next, but I'd guess about $100.
i They often have good prices and ....
j … and try to share the expenses with your ....

What do these words and expressions mean?

Writing: mind maps

40 Mind maps can be used to help you to brainstorm and organise your ideas before you start a piece of writing.

Look at this mind map. Which one do you think is the central theme, *a*, *b* or *c*?

a winning the lottery
b seeing a financial advisor
c investing for the future

Compare your answer with a partner and give reasons for your choice.

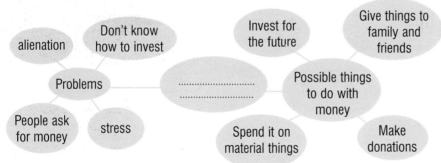

41 Copy and complete the mind map below with your own ideas and associations. Then show your mind map to a partner and explain it. How similar is your partner's map?

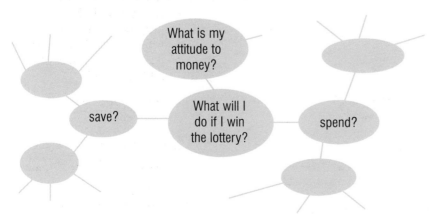

39 Answer these questions in groups.

a Do you think the financial advisor gave Don good advice? Explain your answer.
b What things do you typically spend your money on?
c Are you good at budgeting? Why or why not?
d How do you save money?

42 Writing Look at the end of the article from page 8.

> We want to hear from YOU. How do you handle money? What would you do if you won the lottery? Would you save or spend? Write and let us know.

Write a short letter in answer to these questions in the article.

Divide your writing into three paragraphs and use your mind map to help you.

Paragraph 1: my attitude to money.

Paragraph 2: why I would spend some money and what I would spend it on.

Paragraph 3: why I would save some money and how I would save it.

43 Compare your letter with other students. Have you written similar things?
What are the main differences?

Review: grammar and functional language

44 Imagine you were going to interview this woman who has just won the lottery. What questions would you ask her?

Example: How much did you win?

45 Read this interview with the woman. Based on her responses, what are the interviewer's questions? You can look at Activities 18–22 for help.

INTERVIEWER: So, (a) how do you feel ?
MAUREEN: I feel great. This is the most amazing feeling.
INTERVIEWER: So, tell us your story. (b) .... ?
MAUREEN: No, this is the first time I've ever bought a ticket.
INTERVIEWER: (c) .... ?
MAUREEN: Well, things were not going too well in my life. I lost my job, first.
INTERVIEWER: I'm sorry to hear that. (d) .... ?
MAUREEN: Then one of my children was ill and needed a lot of care.
INTERVIEWER: That's very sad. I'm so sorry. (e) .... ?
MAUREEN: Well, I had to borrow a lot of money and use credit cards and I just found it so difficult to make ends meet.
INTERVIEWER: That's such a shame. (f) .... ?
MAUREEN: Well, yes. My friend, Emma – she was great, but she was short of money herself, so she couldn't really help me there.
INTERVIEWER: So, you live in London, (g) .... ?
(h) .... ?
MAUREEN: In the corner shop. I was in there buying some milk and something made me buy a ticket for the first time in my life.
INTERVIEWER: And (i) .... ?
MAUREEN: Well, we were watching the television and they were reading out the winning numbers and I had a look at my ticket and I saw that I had those numbers.
INTERVIEWER: (j) .... ?
MAUREEN: Well, I called Emma straight away.
INTERVIEWER: (k) .... ?
MAUREEN: She came round and we had to call to claim the prize.
INTERVIEWER: (l) .... ? Was it you or Emma?
MAUREEN: She had to do it. I was shaking all over.
INTERVIEWER: So, (m) .... ?
MAUREEN: Well, the first thing is to get proper care for my little boy and then I want to pay off all my debts and start working again.
INTERVIEWER: You're not going to work, (n) .... ?
MAUREEN: Oh, yes. I want to set a good example for my kids. I plan to go back to school and study to be a nurse. That's my dream.

Was there anything in Maureen's story that surprised you?

46 Look at these situations. In pairs, imagine the conversation between the people in the pictures. You can look at Activities 23–25 for help.

Example:
STUDENT A: I failed my maths test, mum.
STUDENT B: That's such a shame, Charlie, but did you study for it?

47 In pairs Think of a famous person that you both know. Imagine you are going to interview her / him. Write down at least ten different questions you would like to ask.

Role-play the interview.

Example:
STUDENT A: Mr Mandela, how long did you spend in prison?
STUDENT B: 27 years.

Review: vocabulary

bankrupt broke credit card
disastrous loan objected to
overnight to alienate
to blow to borrow to donate
to earn to eat up to gamble
to get to give to invest (in)
to lend to lose to make
to pay to put to save
to spend to take to win
windfall winnings wisely

a dream come true
'A fool and his money are soon
   parted.' *
a waste of money
let's see the colour of your
   money
'Money can't buy you love.'
'Money doesn't grow on trees,
   you know!'
money is no object
'Money is the root of all evil.'
'Money makes the world go
   round.'
not for love nor money
to be a little short of money
to be rolling in money
to end up (doing something)
to find it hard to make ends
   meet
to give somebody a run for their
   money
to have money to burn
(to have) time on one's hands
to make matters worse
to marry into money
to put your money where your
   mouth is
to throw money at something
way too much (of something)

*Phrases in inverted commas are
conversational phrases.

48 **Answer these questions about the Word List and Word Plus.**

a Which is your favourite new expression and why?
b Which is the expression that you think is the most useful?
c Choose five words that you can associate and explain why you
   chose those five words.

Example: 'blow', 'waste', 'spend', 'throw', 'lose': these are
all words about spending money.

Pronunciation

49 **Copy and complete the table with as many words as you can from
the Word List and Word Plus.**

/ʌ/ – money	/æ/ – gamble	/e/ – get

Check your answers by listening to Track 6.

Add more words of your own to the list.

50 **Listen to these sentences on Track 7. What do you notice about
the stress of the word *object*?**

Money is no object for my brother.
I object to people who waste money on gambling.

**Practise saying these sentences with the correct pronunciation of
object.**

a That's a very strange object.
b Did she object to the bank charges?
c When he said he was going to gamble with our money, I
   objected.
d Those objects over there are very rare and precious.

Find other pairs of words like 'object and ob'ject.

51 **Tell one story about someone you know using as many of the
expressions in the Word List and Word Plus as you can. See who
can use most expressions.**

Example: My friend, Rick, finds it hard to make ends meet.
He spends all the money he earns and then he uses
his credit cards. I always tell him that money doesn't
grow on trees, but he throws his money at ridiculous
things and does not invest wisely ...

UNIT 2
Photographs

→ *used to* and *would*
→ photography
→ asking for help

Speaking: choosing a photograph

1 Find out the following information about your partner.

  a Do you have a camera? If so, what kind is it?
  b What do you take photographs of?
  c Do you 'photograph well'? (Do you like yourself in photographs?)

2 **In groups** You are going to judge the finalists in a photography competition on the theme of 'the most powerful black and white images of the 20th century'. Agree on at least five criteria you will use to make your judgement.

Examples:
- the picture is interesting
- the picture tells us something about the person (or people)

3 Use your criteria to choose a winner from the following photographs.

4 Choose one of the photographs and try to answer the following questions.

  a When was the photo taken?
  b Where was the photo taken?
  c What is the relationship between the people?
  d How do they feel?
  e What happened before the photo was taken?
  f What happened after the photo was taken?
  g How important are photographs like these? Why?

Reading: more than a moment

5 Read the text in Activity 6 quickly; don't study it in any detail. Which of the four photos (*a–d*) in Activity 3 is being talked about in the text?

6 Read the following sentences and then decide where they should go in the text. There is one sentence too many. The first one is done for you.

a And because of this black children were finally admitted to whites-only schools.
b The first test case of this ruling occurred in Little Rock, Arkansas, in 1957 when nine black students tried to attend classes at the Central High School. **1**
c Finally, at the ceremony 40 years later, she and her victim met face to face.
d He called for greater understanding between races, a call which echoes down the years in the wake of misunderstandings between different peoples and religions of the world.
e The photographs Counts took that day were soon published all over America and the world.
f William Counts had been a student at the Central High School himself.
g And so there was.

MORE THAN A MOMENT

Some photographs, like the one taken by photographer William Counts outside the Central High School in Little Rock, Arkansas (USA) all those years ago, are so powerful that they help to change the course of history.

In 1954 the Supreme Court of the United States of America decided that segregated education (previously accepted as 'separate but equal') was unconstitutional.

1 **b** But racism was a fact of life in those days, and many white Americans were bitterly opposed to multiracial schooling. The governor of the state of Arkansas, Orval Faubus, sent soldiers of the National Guard to the high school to stop black children from attending classes there, and to 'maintain order'.

2 Now 26 years old, he arrived at the scene with his camera after only a few days as a photographer with the Arkansas Democrat newspaper. Nobody paid him too much attention because he was a local man. As a result he was not attacked by the angry crowds as many photographers from out of town were that day, and he was able to take his famous picture.

Counts had recognised immediately that the moment the black students tried to get to the school there would be trouble. **3** Elizabeth Eckford, the first of the nine, was turned back by the soldiers, and Counts, running backwards in front of her, started taking his pictures. And that was how the world saw a picture of a 15-year-old white girl, Hazel Bryan, shouting abuse at the black student. 'The crowd were right in her ear,' Counts recalled many years later, 'they were yelling their hate, but she [Eckford] never lost her composure, she just remained so dignified, so determined in what she was doing.'

4 They caused outrage. Dwight Eisenhower, the president of the United States, saying how moved he was by pictures of the 'disgraceful occurrences', took control of the National Guard and ordered federal troops to escort the 'Little Rock Nine' to school despite the objections of the Arkansas governor. Desegregated education had begun.

Forty years later, the nine black students were awarded the congressional medal of honour by American president Bill Clinton in a ceremony at the Central High School. In his speech, he said, 'Like so many Americans, I can never fully repay my debt to these nine people. For with their innocence, they purchased more freedom for me, too, and for all white people.' But he was far from optimistic about the future of race relations: 'Today, children of every race walk through the same door, but then they often walk down different halls,' he said. 'Not only in this school, but across America, they sit in different classrooms, they eat at different tables. They even sit in different parts of the bleachers at the football game. Far too many communities are all white, all black, all Latino, all Asian. Indeed, too many Americans of all races have actually begun to give up on the idea of integration and the search for common ground.'
5

And what of Hazel Bryan Massery, the girl with her face screwed up in anger and hatred? Five years after the photograph was taken she rang up Elizabeth Eckford to apologise. 'I am deeply ashamed of the photograph,' she said later, 'I was an immature 15-year-old. That's the way things were. I grew up in a segregated society and I thought that's the way it was and that's the way it should be.'

6 'I wanted to end my identification as the poster child for the hate generation, trapped in the image captured in that photograph. I know my life was more than a moment.' And William Counts was there to take a new photograph of another moment – of reconciliation.

7 **Discussion** What is your reaction to Hazel Bryan's actions as a 15-year-old and as a 55-year-old?

8 **Fact check** Who were the following people, what did they do, and when did they do it? The first one is done for you.

Name	a Who?	b What?	c When?
Hazel Bryan	– white student at Little Rock's Central High School	– shouted at a black student – apologised – reconciled with the black student	– 1957 – 1962 – 1997
William Counts			
Bill Clinton			
Dwight Eisenhower			
Orval Faubus			
Elizabeth Eckford			

9 Which words from the text in Activity 6 tell you that the following statements are true? The first ones are underlined for you.

a Education was not integrated in 1953.
b Separate education for black and white children was not in agreement with the laws of the country.
c A white girl was rude to Elizabeth Eckford.
d The crowd were making a lot of noise.
e Elizabeth Eckford behaved in a way that should have made people respect her.

f People were very upset by the photograph.
g The governor of Arkansas did not agree with the president's actions.
h The 'Little Rock Nine' did not have much experience of life.
i Hazel Bryan looked very angry in the photograph.
j Hazel Bryan was not very grown up.

Language in chunks

10 Match the phrases in italics from the text (a–g, on the left) with their explanations (1–7, on the right).

a *a fact of life*
b *bitterly opposed to*
c *I can never fully repay my debt to*
d *in the wake of*
e *she never lost her composure*
f *there would be trouble*
g *to change the course of history*

1 after (and as a result of) an event
2 make things different for ever
3 something that is or was always true
4 in strong disagreement with
5 something bad was going to happen
6 stopped looking calm
7 give someone what we think we owe them

11 Use the words in brackets to rewrite the following sentences so that they mean more or less the same. Use the phrases in italics from Activity 10.

a She didn't seem to be upset when the police arrested her. (composure)
b Everybody gets colds and flu from time to time. (fact)
c Nothing was ever the same after the Industrial Revolution. (course)
d It is impossible to thank you enough. (debt)
e I am totally against your plan. (bitterly)
f They built new flood defences after the terrible storm. (wake)
g When he saw the people in the stadium, he knew things were going to go wrong. (trouble)

12 Noticing language Find at least one more example of the following verb tenses in the text.

- past simple of the verb *to be* (example: *racism was a fact of life*)
- past simple with other verbs (example: *the Supreme Court decided*)
- passive sentence (example: *he was not attacked*)
- past continuous (example: *they were yelling*)
- past perfect (example: *William Counts had been a student*)

13 Discussion Bill Clinton said, 'I can never repay my debt to these people.' Can you think of two other people in history who we should be grateful to? Compare your choices with other students.

Functional language: asking for help

14 Listening Look at the Fowler family. Now listen to Track 8. What is the mistake in the picture?

15 Complete the following requests with *stand over there* or *standing over there*.

a Can you .... ?
b Could you .... ?
c Do you think you could .... ?
d I'd like you to ....
e I wonder if you would mind .... ?
f Would you mind .... ?
g You couldn't .... , could you?

Which of the requests *a–g* are more formal / polite than the others?

16 In groups Take turns to decide where the other members of your group should stand or sit for a photograph. Now get them into the right positions.

Example: STUDENT A: Where do you want us to go?

STUDENT B: Well, I'd like Tom to sit down here.

STUDENT C: OK.

STUDENT B: And Mary, could you ...

17 Use words from two or three of the boxes to ask for a favour. Consult a dictionary if necessary.

do give help lend	me	a favour a hand out

Example: Could you help me out?

18 a Copy and complete the table with expressions from the box. The first one is done for you.

> Certainly.   I can't really.   I'd rather not.
> I'm afraid I ...   No problems.
> Of course I could / would.   OK.   Sorry, but ...
> Sure.   That depends on what it is.   Well ...
> Why should I?   Yes, of course.

1 Agreeing to a request
Certainly.

2 Could be either 'yes' or 'no'

3 Saying 'no' to a request

b How many ways can you say 'yes' to the following request?

Would you mind giving me a hand?

◐ ◑ ● Pronunciation: intonation clues

19 Read the conversations and listen to the people on Track 9 saying 'no'. Should the first speaker ask them again? Why? Why not?

a SPEAKER A: Would you answer the door?
SPEAKER B: I can't really.

b SPEAKER A: Could you lend me some money?
SPEAKER B: I'd rather not.

c SPEAKER A: Can you help me tidy this room?
SPEAKER B: Sorry, but I've got a lot to do.

d SPEAKER A: Would you collect my film when you're in town?
SPEAKER B: Why should I?

e SPEAKER A: You couldn't help me paint this wall, could you?
SPEAKER B: I'm afraid I can't.

20 Have the conversations in pairs. Student A makes the request and Student B says 'no', choosing an intonation. Should A continue the conversation or not? Does Student B agree?

●●

21 Say 'no' to the following requests using the word given, and adding an excuse. The first one is done for you.

a Could you help me with my homework? (really)

I can't really. I've got to wash my hair!

b You couldn't give me a lift to the shops, could you? (rather)
c Can you help me tidy the darkroom? (afraid)
d Do you think you could lend me your camera? (sorry)
e Would you mind giving me a hand with this painting? (why)
f I wonder if you'd mind giving me a hand with this photographic equipment. (really)
g Could you lend me a hand with my shopping? (afraid)
h You couldn't help me deliver these letters, could you? (sorry)
i Do you think you could give me a hand with the washing up? (rather)

Are the replies polite, neutral or quite strong?

22 Conversation writing In pairs, choose one of the following situations.

a You are on holiday with a friend. You ask a stranger to take a photograph of you both.
b A number of friends have turned up unexpectedly. You want your friend to help you to cook them a meal.
c You are moving into a new office. You ask someone you do not know very well to help you unpack boxes of files and books.
d There's a storm outside. You want your friend to give you a lift to college in their car.

Write your conversation and act it out for the class.

Vocabulary: photography (compound nouns)

●●

23 Look at the pictures and answer the questions.

Which camera:
a ... has a *flash*?
b ... has a *viewfinder*?
c ... has a *zoom lens*?
d ... is a *digital camera*?
e ... is a *throwaway camera*?

a

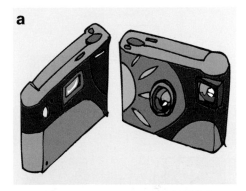

b

24 Match the words with the best definitions.

photo
photograph
snap

a a picture not taken by a professional, but taken quickly and informally, often of a place you visit
b a picture taken with a camera
c an informal word for a picture, especially of you, your friends, your family or places you have visited

25 Look at the diagrams. Match the pictures with the following phrases. The first one is done for you.

- buy a film   *a*
- collect the photographs
- finish the film
- get some copies made / have some enlargements made
- put the film in the camera
- take the film out of the camera
- take the film to be developed
- take pictures

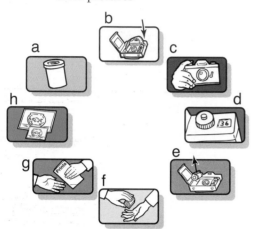

- put the disk in the camera
- upload the pictures to a computer
- take pictures
- view pictures on the screen
- buy a disk

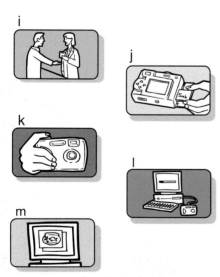

26 **Writing** Describe a photo which you like and which was taken by you or someone you know. What kind of picture is it? What kind of camera was it taken with? What was the procedure (traditional or digital)?

27 **Compound nouns** Use the clues (a–h) to make compound nouns. The first one is done for you.

What is a/an:

a ... booth where you get a photo for a passport?

1 a photo booth

b ... man who works with a camera?
c ... photograph taken at a wedding?
d ... photograph taken for a passport?
e ... opportunity (for a politician or film star, etc.) to have their photo taken?
f ... room which is dark (for developing films)?
g ... frame to put a photo in?
h ... recorder for video?

What do the following mean?

- photofit
- photo finish

28 a Match the nouns in box 1 on the left with the appropriate nouns in box 2 on the right. Some words from box 2 may be used more than once.

1	alarm	mother
	birthday	newspaper
	contact	race
	credit	shopping
	greenhouse	steering
	heart	washing
	human	windscreen

2	article	machine
	attack	relations
	bag	rights
	card	tongue
	clock	wheel
	effect	wiper
	lens	

b Test your partner, using the words from boxes 1 and 2.

Example: STUDENT A: *What do you call a clock with an alarm?*
STUDENT B: *An alarm clock.*

c Copy and complete the description of compound nouns with further examples from Activities 27 and 28a.

> Some compound nouns are one-word only (examples: *tablespoon, homework, ...*). Some are two separate words (examples: *town hall, sitting room, ...*) and some, which are very common, are joined by a hyphen (examples: *decision-making, roller-coaster, ...*). There are no rules for this. If in doubt, use two words without a hyphen, but check with your dictionary.

29 **In pairs** Choose one of the following and tell your partner about it.

- a photo album belonging to you or someone in your family
- a photograph album you'd like to have or make
- pictures in frames in the place where you live
- the best photographs you've seen (in a book, in newspapers, etc.)
- the last film you took
- the last time you got a passport
- wedding photos you know or would like to see

Grammar: the past (tenses and habits)

30 Read the sentences. What is the correct sequence of events (*a* is first)?

a I was driving home when it happened.
b I didn't mind what they had done.
c I had been to a party with my friends.
d I had only drunk orange juice at the party.
e I was listening to the radio in my car.
f I was relieved that nothing terrible had happened.
g My brake light was not working and so they followed me.
h The police stopped me two miles from home.
i Then they drove away.
j They had seen me two minutes before.
k They made me breathe into a breathalyser.
l They warned me about my brake light.
m They were only doing their job.

Look at 2A–2D in the Mini-grammar. Do you want to change your answer?

31 Without looking at Activity 30, tell the story in your own words.

32 Work it out Look at the examples and answer the questions which follow.

Examples: He used to play tennis when he was younger.
I used to live in a house. but now I live in a flat.
We would go to the seaside every July when we were young.
~~I would have a red bicycle when I was a boy~~.

a How do we describe habits in the past?
b When we describe past states with verbs like *be, believe, have, live, think,* etc., can we use *used to*, or *would* or both?

Check your answers by looking at 2B–2C in the Mini-grammar.

33 Replace the verbs and phrases in blue with phrases using *used to* or *would*. Remember that sometimes *would* is not possible.

Example: They used to live in a small terraced house.

Things have changed since my grandparents' day. They were poor working-class people. They lived in a small terraced house with no bathroom and an outdoor toilet. It was quite a hard existence and people got ill all the time. There was no National Health Service in those days so they had to pay for a doctor to come and see them.

Every morning my grandfather walked three miles to work. He worked eight hours a day in a steel factory. He complained about the noise all the time but no one really listened. Everybody complained about the noise. While he was at work my grandmother looked after the children and used what small money she had to try and clothe and feed them. Often she didn't have enough money for the food she needed and so she took in washing from rich families to earn some extra money.

When I think of those two people I don't know how they did it. Life was a real struggle for them, but when I think back, all I can remember is how happy I was when I went to visit them.

34 Compare your lives (and the way you travel) with your grandparents' lives when they were your age.

Example: My grandfather used to live on a farm in the country but I live in an apartment in the city.

Word choice: *remember, remind* and *forget*

35 Look at the Word Choice notes for *remember, remind* and *forget* on page 56 in the booklet. Complete the following sentences with the most likely verb. You may have to change the tense.

a Did you ... to turn off the light?
b I'll never ... the first time I saw Mount Fuji.
c I ... to post the letter and so I missed the entry date for the competition.
d I ... getting home late, but I've completely ... what we talked about all night.
e ... me to call him when I get home.
f Don't ... to take your notes to the lecture.
g I ... her taking the photograph, but I can't ... why we were in London.
h If you ... I'll never forgive you!
i If you don't ... him he'll ... to do it, I assure you.

36 Complete the sentences with *didn't, use, used* or *wouldn't*.

a I didn't .... to take photographs when I was younger, but I do now.
b Didn't you .... to be a professional photographer?
c We'd meet in the evening, ... we?
d You used to play football, ... you?
e I am not .... to living in a flat. It's strange.

• How do we usually make negative sentences and questions with *used to*?
• How do we make tag questions for *used to* and *would*?
• Which sentence is about present habits?

Check your answers by looking at **2E–2F in the Mini-grammar.**

37 **Interview** How much can you remember about life at your primary school? Interview a partner and find out:

• ... how they got to school.
• ... what they did there.
• ... what happened at different times of the day.
• ... if they had any special friends and what they did together.
• ... if they had any teachers with special habits.
• ... anything else they remember especially well.

Example: I think I used to walk to school with my father. Sometimes, when it was raining, he took me in the car, but mostly, yes, we just walked.

Listening: what our photographs remind us of

38 Listen to Track 10. Match the photographs with the speakers. The speakers are in the right order.

Peter   Jane   Kate   Betty

How old do you think the speakers are? Why?

39 **Fact check** Who:

a ... learnt to ski when he was young?
b ... once had a box camera?
c ... has a mother who teaches?
d ... has lived in various different countries?
e ... visited Bolivia?
f ... went to a place that looked better than pictures of it do?
g ... didn't enjoy school in Johannesburg very much?
h ... used to go for long walks?
i ... had a seaside holiday every summer?
j ... has a sister who went to Chile?
k ... acted like a tourist guide?

40 History and places Listen to Track 10 again. What do the speakers say about:

a ... Peru, the Spaniards, Cuzco and Machu Picchu?
b ... The Grand Palace in Bangkok?

41 Words and phrases Listen to Track 10 again or look at the Audioscript. Match the words and phrases in italics in the first column with their equivalent meanings in the second column. The first one is done for you.

a	*diplomat*　10	1	a path, usually in the wilderness
b	*fabulous*	2	as if we were
c	*I'd so like* to go back	3	died
d	*it dates back to* the 18th century	4	enjoyable
		5	I would very much like
e	*it's not a patch on the real thing*	6	it happened / was built in
		7	it is not as good or impressive as the thing itself
f	*kind of like* tourist guides	8	really fantastic
g	*primitive*	9	sides of mountains that people ski down
h	*scenery*		
i	*slopes*	10	someone who works for their government, but in an embassy in a different country
j	Thailand was *really cool*		
k	the dog *passed away*	11	the countryside (mountains, rivers, etc.) that you see before you
l	*trail*	12	very old-fashioned, unsophisticated

42 In pairs Discuss one of the following topics.

a Tell your partner about a photograph from your past that you really love. Perhaps it's a photograph of you, or one that you took. Better still, bring it to class.

b Jane says, 'There are places like that, aren't there? You know, no matter how often you've seen photographs, it's just not a patch on the real thing.' Do you agree with her? Have you ever been to a place like that?

Tell the class what you heard from your partner.

Writing: headlines (précis)

43 Look at the following newspaper headlines and answer the questions.

a What is the story behind the headlines, do you think?
b What, typically, is left out in newspaper headlines? What verb?

Shake-up in car-parking fees

Family 'owe lives' to smoke detector

Little Rock photographer dies at 70

Photo booth murder suspect arrested

Queen's horse in photo finish win

44 Summary writing Read the following story. How many headlines can you write which summarise the story using some of the words in blue? (You may have to change some of the words, e.g. from verbs to nouns, etc.)

A mother of three escaped injury when the car she was driving plunged into a river. She had been driving home after dropping her children at school. She was rescued by a passing cyclist who dived into the river and pulled her from the car. 'I owe that man my life,' said Mrs Martha Galvan, 'he's a hero, but his identity is a mystery. He ran off after he had rescued me so I don't know who he is.'

Example: River plunge mother escapes injury.

45 Read the following stories and note the words you may want to use in headlines which will summarise them.

When James Knight, a university student, went to collect his photographs at Boots 24-hour developing centre on Thursday, he got the shock of his life. Two of the photographs showed his girlfriend standing in a street in London. But behind her were two robbers running out of a bank. 'I didn't notice them at the time,' Knight said, 'but when I showed them to the police they were very excited.' The police have since made two arrests.

The Swedish singer Carla was making no comment yesterday after an incident at Mexico City Airport in which she hit out at a press photographer, breaking his nose. The attack took place as the singer was arriving from Sweden for a countrywide tour. Witnesses said that Carla posed for the waiting photographers with her 6-year-old daughter who is accompanying her, but when one photographer, American Brad Puttnam, kept taking photographs of the mother and daughter, the singer lashed out. Puttnam is threatening to sue. The singer's publicity aide says that Carla regrets the incident and just wants to be left alone.

Write as many headlines as you can for the stories. Get as much information in the headlines as possible. Compare the headlines. Which are the most successful?

Review: grammar and functional language

46 Favourite things Try to remember what it was like when you were a child. What were your three favourite activities or experiences? You can look at Activities 32–33 for help.

a at home
b during the holidays
c at the weekend

47 Match the following requests (*1–6*) with the correct answers (*a–f*). The first one is done for you. You can look at Activities 14–22 for help.

1 Do me a favour and make me some coffee.
2 Do you think you could help me with the washing up?
3 I wonder if you'd be good enough to help me.
4 Would you mind getting me a film when you go to town?
5 Would you mind giving me a hand with this table?
6 You couldn't help me with these boxes, could you?

a I wonder if you'd be good enough to help me. (3)

  – It depends on what you want. I can carry your suitcases if that's your problem.

b ....

  – Not at all. Where do you want it to go?

c ....

  – Of course I wouldn't. What kind does your camera take?

d ....

  – Of course. Where do you want them to go?

e ....

  – Sorry. I'd love to, but I've got to go. Brad's waiting for me.

f ....

  – Why should I? I'm working just as hard as you.

Review: vocabulary

Word List

alarm clock   birthday card
cameraman   contact lens
copies   credit card
darkroom   digital camera
diplomat   enlargements
fabulous   film   flash
greenhouse effect   heart attack
human rights   mother tongue
newspaper article
passport photograph
photo booth   photo finish
photofit   photo frame
photo opportunity   primitive
race relations   really cool
scenery   shopping bag
slope   snap   steering wheel
throwaway camera   to develop
to pass away   trail
video recorder   viewfinder
washing machine
wedding photograph
windscreen wiper   zoom lens

Word Plus

a fact of life
bitterly opposed to
in the wake of
to be kind of like
to be not a patch on the real
  thing
to change the course of history
to date back to
to know there will be trouble
to never be able to repay a
  debt to
to never lose your composure

48 Which five words from the Word List would be the best / most useful ones for you if you were:

a ... a backpacker?
b ... a politician?
c ... a housewife or householder?
d ... an actor?

Give reasons for your answers.

Example: a a credit card – I
wouldn't have to carry
cash with me.

● ● ● **Pronunciation**

49 Copy and complete the table with as many individual words as you can from the Word List.

/θ/ – thin	/ð/ – the	/f/ – five	/v/ – very

Check your table by listening to Track 11. Then add more words to your table and answer the questions.

a Which parts of the mouth do we use to make the sounds?
b What is the difference between /θ/ and /ð/? What is the difference between /f/ and /v/?

50 **Sound chains in teams** How many words from the Word List or Word Plus can you say in 60 seconds? Student A says a word, Student B has to say a new word which has at least one sound from Student A's word. Student C has to say a new word with at least one sound from Student B's word. Student D's word must have a sound from Student C's word.

Example: STUDENT A: copies
STUDENT B: cool (/k/ from 'copies')
STUDENT C: develop (/l/ from 'cool')
STUDENT D: primitive (/p/ from 'develop')

51 **Newspaper headlines** Use as many words from the Word List as possible to write imaginary headlines. You will have to use other words too.

Example: Zoom lens snaps credit card cameraman

Invent a story to go with the headline.

Example: Someone with a zoom lens who was taking a picture
of a street caught (on film) a cameraman, John
Smith, taking money from a credit card machine.

52 Take one of the phrases from Word Plus and think of a situation to use it in. Tell your partner about it. Start with a sentence using the phrase. Your partner has to guess the situation.

Example: STUDENT A: I am bitterly opposed to all those digital
machines. The quality isn't as good as film
and now everybody thinks they can do a job
that it has taken me 50 years to learn. So
if you want to work here, you'd better be
prepared to use some of the old ways.
STUDENT B: Maybe you are a photographer giving a young
apprentice a job.

UNIT 3
Wolf

→ adverbs and adverbial phrases
→ metaphor (animals)
→ warnings and threats

Reading: wolves

1 **Metaphor and idiom** Complete the sentences with a word or phrase from the box. Consult a dictionary if necessary.

> crying wolf   keep the wolf from the door
> lone wolf   wolf   wolf in sheep's clothing
> wolf (down) your food   wolf-whistle

a A man who actively pursues different women used to be called a ....

b A person who seems pleasant but is really rather horrible is sometimes called a
....

c If you earn just enough money to survive, you ....

d If people call for help when they don't really need it, we say they are ....

e Someone (usually male) who likes to live or work alone used to be called a ....

f When some men see an attractive woman, they make a loud sound called a ....

g When you eat too quickly, we can say that you ....

2 Answer the following questions.

a What impression of wolves is given by the sayings in Activity 1?

b Do you have any 'wolf' sayings in your language?

c How would you describe the same ideas in your language?

3 One of the following mini-paragraphs represents the view of the writer Peter Hedley about wolves. Which do you think it is?

a Wolves are savage predators who attack human beings. They hunt on their own and abandon their young at an early age.

b Wolves are hated by most humans, but in reality they are sociable animals who love singing, playing and dancing.

c In stories wolves are always portrayed as dangerous and bad (as devils and werewolves) because of the way they behave in the wild.

d Wolves are beautiful beasts, but they make a terrible noise when there is a full moon.

Now read the text. Were you right?

How could we get it so wrong?

Recent controversies over the reintroduction of wolves to parts of the United States and Scotland yet again focus on one of nature's most misunderstood beasts.
Peter Hedley **takes up the story.**

Once upon a time, much of the world was populated by wolves. They ranged all over the United States and Canada, Siberia and much of mainland Europe, as well as Great Britain, and if humans hadn't come along, they would still be there in great numbers. But man did come along, farmed the land, objected to the wolves killing their livestock and so gradually drove them out of the homes that had once been theirs.

Wolves are not victims in our language and our literature, however. In fairy stories, they are seen as evil and dangerous, always ready to eat people. Remember the time when Little Red Riding Hood thinks that a wolf is her grandmother? 'What big teeth you've got, grandmother!', she says, and the wolf, disguised as her grandmother, growls back sadistically, 'all the better to eat you with, my dear!' In Prokofiev's musical fable *Peter and the Wolf*, the old grandfather speaks for us all at the end when he says, 'Ah, but if Peter hadn't caught the wolf, what then?!'

In medieval times, the devil was often portrayed as a wolf, and the concept of a werewolf – the man who turns into a savage monster on the night of the full moon – is still a popular figure in both books and films.

If you really want to see how English-speaking humans think of the wolf, just look at the language! 'A wolf in sheep's clothing' is not a pleasant person and a 'wolf-whistle' is not a pleasant sound!

Yet wolves are totally unlike the image we have of them from legend and language. For a start, they don't usually attack humans; indeed they do their best to keep out of our way. They are very sociable animals, living in packs and looking after their young with a fondness that should make some humans ashamed of themselves. Far from wolf music being ugly, the howl of the wolf – the cry of the whole pack – as the full moon rises in a star-bright sky is one of the most beautiful sounds in nature. Wolves dance and play games like frisbee and tag with bones and twigs. They are beautiful creatures which can run at speeds of up to 65 kph if they have to. They can jump vertically and run up rock faces like a cat. And when they do kill, their 42 large teeth, exerting a pressure of 1,500 lbs per square inch, are fearsomely effective.

But the fact remains that we love the lion, the king of the jungle, another killer that spends much of its time asleep and often practises infanticide, while we demonise the wolf, one of the most beautiful animals in the world. Only occasionally do writers treat them nicely; for example, a she-wolf is supposed to have suckled the twins Remus and Romulus, who went on to found the city of Rome. If only the boys had stayed with her, perhaps they would have learnt to love and respect each other. But instead they went back to the human world, Romulus killed his brother and Rome was founded in rivers of blood.

And so, while man kills animals in their millions, often just for the fun of it, the wolf on the mountain, out in the wilderness, running over the Siberian wastes, represents a state of natural grace that we do not know and can never obtain, even though we dream of it in our hearts. Perhaps that's why, in the end, we hate the wolf so much – for having something we can never get our hands on.

4   **In pairs** Discuss the following questions.

- What, if anything, surprised you in the text?
- Why do we hate wolves, according to Peter Hedley? Do you agree with him?

5   **Fact check** Who or what:

a   ... was the reason farmers didn't like wolves?
b   ... is Little Red Riding Hood?
c   ... is *Peter and the Wolf*?
d   ... was the image of a wolf used for many years ago?
e   ... do wolves use instead of frisbees?
f   ... sometimes kills their own or their partner's children?
g   ... killed his brother?

6   **Vocabulary** Explain the meaning of the following words as they appear in the text.

a   ranged (paragraph 1)
b   victim (paragraph 2)
c   fairy story (paragraph 2)
d   sadistically (paragraph 2)
e   portrayed (paragraph 3)
f   legend (paragraph 5)
g   sociable (paragraph 5)
h   demonise (paragraph 6)
i   Siberian wastes (paragraph 7)

Language in chunks

7 Look at how these phrases are used in the text and then use them in the sentences which follow. You may have to change them a little to make them fit.

> ashamed of (themselves)   for a start   in the end   just for the fun of it
> to do (their) best   to get (your) hands on   to keep out of (our) way

a Don't come anywhere near me. Just ....
b I didn't come yesterday because .... , after a long day, I just didn't have the energy.
c I don't mind if I pass or fail. I just want to ....
d I've always wanted to own one of Picasso's paintings. I'd love to .... one.
e Bungee-jumping isn't good for me or useful or anything. I do it ....
f Why do I want to leave my job? Well, ... , I'm not enjoying it any more.
But there are many other reasons too.
g Why did you cheat in your exam? You should be ....

8 Choose two of the phrases and write sentences in which you use them as naturally as possible.

9 Noticing language Label the following words and phrases from the text according to which of the questions in the box they answer. The first one is done for you.

> How?   How often?   When?   Where?

a once upon a time (paragraph 1)   When?
b all over the United States (paragraph 1)
c out of (their) homes (paragraph 1)
d sadistically (paragraph 2)
e in medieval times (paragraph 3)
f vertically (paragraph 5)
g only occasionally (paragraph 6)
h nicely (paragraph 6)

Are the eight words / phrases *adverbial* (= they describe verbs) or *adjectival* (= they describe nouns)?

10 In pairs Copy the table and add one more question of your own. Interview your partner and complete the table with his or her answers.

Questions	Answers
a What is your favourite wild animal?	
b What is your favourite domestic animal?	
c What animal would you most like to be? Why?	
d What animal would you most like to study / photograph / know more about? Why?	
e ...	

Tell the class what your partner said.

Vocabulary: animal metaphors

11 In groups Look at the picture. Describe one of the animals, saying what they do, where they live, etc. The other students have to guess which animal it is.

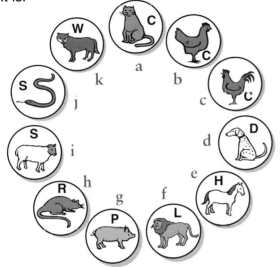

12 Find creatures from Activity 11 which make the following noises (one animal makes two of the noises).

bark   bleat   cluck   crow   growl   grunt
hiss   howl   neigh   purr   roar   squeal

13 Listen to Track 12 and choose one of the verbs (in the past tense) for each gap.

a 'Turn that music down,' he ....
b 'Get out of my house,' he ....
c 'I'm not really sure I want to do this,' he
....
d 'Why should I care?' he......................... .
e 'Don't expect to get away with this,' she
....
f 'That was so lovely,' she ....
g 'I've just been given a fantastic mark for my composition,' she ....

14 Language research Find out what you would expect or understand if:

a ... someone had a sheepish grin.
b ... someone was being really catty.
c ... someone had made a real cock-up.
d ... someone was really cocky.
e ... something was dog-eared.
f ... someone's determination was really dogged.
g ... something was really fishy.
h ... someone was rather mousy.
i ... someone's room was a real pigsty.
j ... someone was really ratty.
k ... someone's new invention turned out to be a real turkey.

15 Animal idioms Complete the following sentences with an animal idiom from the box.

fishing for compliments
from the horse's mouth
going to the dogs
hold your horses
in the doghouse
kill two birds with one stone
let the cat out of the bag
making a real pig of
smell a rat
the lion's share

a ....! We haven't decided whether to go to the cinema yet and you're halfway out of the door.
b He contributed most of the money for the costs of the concert so he gets .... of the profits.
c I know the story's true because I heard it .... I mean he's the one who's most involved.
d Let's .... We can go to the supermarket and fill up with petrol right next door.
e I can't help it. I .... There's something wrong with his plan.
f She's really cross with me because I left the freezer door open. I'm really ....
g He's really .... He just doesn't seem to care about himself anymore. He spends all his time wasting money at parties.
h Sheila's 'surprise' party isn't a surprise any more. Someone ....
i Stop .... You know we all think you are a brilliant cook, so you don't need to get us to tell you all the time.
j Stop eating so much, Michael. You're .... yourself.

In pairs Choose any three of the animal idioms and use them in sentences. Explain who is saying them, in what situation and why.

16 Test items Write five gapped sentences, to be completed with words or phrases from Activities 12–15.

Example: I'm really hungry. I'm going to make a real .... of myself.

Give your sentences to other students. Can they complete them successfully?

Grammar: adverbs

17 Adverbs and adjectives Read the following story. Are the words which follow the letters a–t adjectives (describing nouns) or adverbs (describing verbs)?

I was in a hurry. I was going to meet my girlfriend at 6 o'clock (**a**) sharp. I'd had a (**b**) late meeting and so I got to the bus stop (**c**) late and missed my bus. I decided to walk home the short way.

In most big cities you can see people sleeping (**d**) rough, and my route took me past a very (**e**) rough area where there were lots of dangerous-looking people. I had chosen (**f**) wrong. My fault.

Someone started shouting at me. I looked around. A man with an (**g**) extremely (**h**) ugly face was shouting at me, and many of his friends were getting up. The situation was turning (**i**) ugly. One of the men put his foot out and I fell (**j**) flat on my face. I was in (**k**) deadly danger.

At that moment a car roared round the corner and stopped (**l**) short. My grandmother (who had never driven in her life) called out my name. I'm a (**m**) cowardly kind of guy, so I jumped up and got into her car. We roared away. She drove (**n**) fast. She was driving a (**o**) fast car.

'I haven't seen much of you (**p**) lately,' she said. I said nothing. I wasn't feeling too good.

'Can I talk (**q**) freely?' she said, and when I agreed she went on, 'you've learnt your lesson the (**r**) hard way. Don't go to that area again.' At that moment, we reached the crossroads and she hit the brakes (**s**) hard, and turned to tell me off a bit more. But I could (**t**) hardly hear her. Her voice was disappearing into the distance ...

Then I woke up. It had all been a terrible dream.

Find examples from the text for each of the following explanations.

1 Some adjectives look just like adverbs (e.g. ...) and some adverbs look just like adjectives (e.g. ...). You can tell which is which by seeing whether they are describing a noun or a verb.
2 Some words can be both adjectives and adverbs (e.g. ...).
3 Some adverbs can have more than one form (e.g. ...).

18 Word formation Read **3A in the Mini-grammar** and make the adjectives in the box into -ly adverbs.

basic calm chronic clear definite extreme
fantastic funny futuristic happy possible
sadistic terrible tidy vertical

19 Adverbs of manner In pairs, choose a verb from the verb box and two adverbs from the adverb box to make two-line exchanges.

VERB BOX	ADVERB BOX	
argue	fast	quiet
criticise	intelligent	rude
drive	loud	slow
eat	messy	soft
run	nasty	stupid
speak	nice	tidy
talk	noisy	untidy
write	polite	

Example: STUDENT A: *Please don't argue so loudly.*
STUDENT B: *All right, I'm sorry. I'll talk quietly, OK?*

20 Adverbs and adverbial phrases Copy and complete the table with the adverbs and adverbial phrases in the box.

a lot   angrily   at 6 o'clock   before   certainly
clearly   daily   eventually   every evening
finally   from time to time   hardly ever
in a friendly way   in my room   in the park
never   next week   noisily   now and then
often   on April 30th   out of the window
probably   soon   twice a year   upstairs
very well   with great patience

Type of adverb	Examples
Manner *how is / was it done?*	
Place *where is / was it done?*	
Time *when is / was it done?*	
Indefinite frequency *how often, more or less, is / was it done?*	
Definite frequency *how often is / was it done?*	
Certainty *How sure are you?*	

Look at **3B in the Mini-grammar**. Think of two more adverbs or adverbials for each category.

21 Word order Are the following sentences correct, wrong or borderline (= not wrong, but not very natural)? The first one is done for you.

a Always I try to watch wildlife films on the television.   *wrong*

b I go only a few times a year to the cinema.

c I haven't seen often television programmes about wolves.

d I might possibly have seen that film – I can't remember.

e I saw on January the 23ʳᵈ my first wolf in the wild.

f I will have almost certainly finished reading this wildlife book before I see you.

g Never trust a lone wolf!

h She talked enthusiastically in the sitting room this evening.

i She went this evening enthusiastically to the party.

j The programme will probably start at about 6 o'clock.

k They did quietly not go home.

l Through the window she could see the wolves.

Now look at 3C in the Mini-grammar. Do you want to change your opinion about any of the sentences? Can you correct or improve the sentences that are wrong or borderline?

Example: *a I always try to watch wildlife films on the television.*

22 Tell your partner about the following things.

• a hobby (e.g. playing the guitar)
• a regular activity (e.g. studying, working)
• something you may or may not do next week (e.g. going to stay with your brother)

Use as many adverbs or adverbials as possible from the box in Activity 20.

Example: *I play the guitar every evening in my room. I don't play it very well.*

23 Expand the following sentences using as many adverbs or adverbials as possible.

a She got home.
b She heard a noise.
c She went to investigate.

How does the story end, do you think?

Functional language: warnings and threats

24 Where might you hear or see the following?

a Come any closer and I'll shoot!
b Danger – Keep away from skin and eyes.
c I wouldn't go in there if I was you ...
d Never talk to me like that again, do you understand!
e Warning – Smoking can cause heart attacks.

25 Listen to Track 13 and the way the people speak. Are the sentences warnings or threats? The first one is done for you.

a Do that again and I'll get really angry.   *threat*
b Don't ever take my things without asking again, do you understand!
c Don't move! There's a wolf behind you.
d I would think very carefully before I said another word.
e I wouldn't go swimming there if I was you.
f I'm warning you not to drive that fast again.
g If you talk like that you'll be in serious trouble.
h Never talk to me like that again.
i Speak to me nicely or I'll cry.
j Watch out! There's a bear behind you.

26 Which kind of warnings or threats are the sentences in Activity 25?
Match the letters *a–j* with the descriptions *1–6* in the table below.

Example: *a   2*

Description	Examples
1 Warnings with exclamations (imperatives, affirmative and negative)	*Be careful! Look out! Don't move!*
2 Threats with the imperative	*Say / Do that again and ... Stop that, or ...*
3 Threats with negative imperatives	*Never do that again!*
4 Threats with *If + will* sentences	*If you don't finish your homework on time, you'll have to leave the class.*
5 Threats / Warnings with *If + would* sentences	*I wouldn't go in there if I was you.*
6 Threats with the present continuous	*I'm telling you ...*

27 Where would you put the main stress in the following sentences? Underline the syllable. The first one is done for you.

a Don't ever criticise me in public again!
b Look out!
c I would think very carefully before I tried that again.
d I'm warning you. Don't do it.

e Never do that again.
f Stop. Right now.
g Watch out! Behind you!

♪) **Listen to Track 14. Did the speakers agree with you?**

28 Say the sentences in the same way as the speakers.

29 What would you say in the following situations?

a A friend is about to dive into a swimming pool.
You know the water is very cold indeed.
I wouldn't go in there if I was you.

b A wolf has just attacked one of your animals.
You talk to it as if it was human.

c An English friend has threatened to tell your best friends something bad you said about them.

d Someone has just said something nasty to you and you don't want them to do it again.

e Someone is about to step on a banana skin.

f You are a traffic warden. You have just let someone off a parking ticket, but ...

g You are furious with someone who has just borrowed your laptop computer without asking you.

h You are teaching someone to drive and they've just scared you half to death. Now they've switched off the engine.

i Your boss is about to pick up a very hot plate.

j Your English cousin (who you don't like very much) has just spilt coffee all over the book you're reading.

30 a Choose one of the pictures and write a short scene to accompany it in which one character warns or threatens the other, and their reply.

b **Rewrite your conversation like a film script and add adverbial directions saying how the characters should speak and move. You can look at the box in Activity 20 for ideas.**

Example: 1

Lecturer (with great patience): Don't ever hand in work late again, do you understand?

Listening: a story about wolves

31 Listen to Track 15 and say which of these three books the extract comes from.

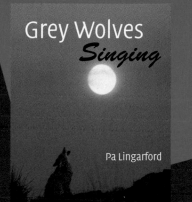

A study of wolf behaviour in the wild, discussing how man has tried hard to eradicate them. Written by a British author, published in 2002.

Grey Wolves *Singing*

Pa Lingarford

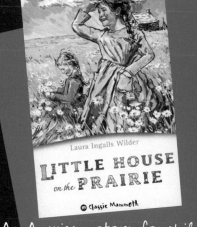

Laura Ingalls Wilder

LITTLE HOUSE *on the* **PRAIRIE**

Classic Mammoth

An American story for children about a family who build their own log cabin in the wild before the days of cars, telephones and electricity. Published in 1935.

From log cabin to *luxury penthouse*

Sasha Kleinstock

The autobiography of the American Sasha Kleinstock, telling how a girl from a poor family ended up one of the richest women in the world.

What helped you make your decision?

32 Listen to Track 16 and then answer these questions.

a What woke the girl up?
b What did she see?
c What did she hear?
d Who protected her?
e What stopped the girl being frightened?

33 Think of three things (or events) in your childhood which were similar to the girl's experiences and three things (or events) which were different.

Example: Once, when I was 10, I went out and I saw ...
But we didn't live ...

34 **Work it out** Answer the questions a–d.

a What is a quilt and how many are mentioned in the extract?
b Who or what is Jack?
c Why does the writer talk about window-holes instead of windows?
d Who is Mary?

Word Choice: *hear* and *listen (to)*

35 Look at the Word Choice notes for *hear*, *listen* and *listen to* on page 56 in the booklet.

Complete the gaps in these lines with a form of *hear*, *listen* or *listen to*.

a I can .... a noise coming from those woods, but I don't know what it is.
b There's no point in talking to me, I'm not ....
c When he's alone, he likes .... his old jazz CDs.
d I looked over at Ruth. She was .... intently with a look of complete concentration.
e There's no point in talking to me. With all this noise, I can't .... a thing.
f Laura could .... the wolves' breathing all round the house.
g I'm prepared to .... your point of view, but I don't expect to agree with it.
h Be quiet! I'm trying to .... their conversation.
i Go on! I'm ....

36 Listen again to Track 16 and complete the following extracts from the story with between one and five words.

a Jack .... his teeth.
b She wanted to go to Pa, but .... bother him now.
c He stood his gun against the wall and .... to the window-hole.
d Laura lifted her toes into a crack in the wall and she .... on the window slab, and she looked and ....
e When they saw Pa and Laura looking out, the middle of the circle .... way.
f Go to sleep. Jack and I will ....
g She lay and listened to the breathing of the wolves .... the log wall.

37 What was your favourite story when you were a child? Tell your partner about it.

Speaking: comparing pictures

38 **Differences and similarities** Student B, turn to Activity Bank 1 on page 156. Student A, look at the picture on this page. Find five similarities and differences between your picture and Student B's.

39 **Discussion** Ask your partner the following questions.

a Ivory sales (from elephant tusks) have been declared illegal, yet poachers still kill elephants secretly so they can sell ivory. What is the correct punishment for ivory poachers, do you think?
b Elephants are used for work in some countries. Do you agree with this?
c Elephants are shown in circuses around the world. How do you feel about this?
d Recently an elephant charged into a crowd at a circus and killed a spectator. What should happen to that elephant?
e Some elephants are kept in zoos. Do you agree with this? Why? Why not?

Do you agree with your partner?

Writing: linking words and phrases

40 a Read the question and the student composition which answered it. Is the student generally in favour of zoos or not?

Write a composition discussing the following statement.

Nobody should enjoy going to zoos which keep animals in cages.

I'd like to start this composition by saying that I have enjoyed going to zoos and looking at animals in the past. It's always very exciting to look at creatures you have never seen before. But many people say that zoos are not pleasant places and the animals are in cages and don't have their freedom. And if you deny animals their freedom and keep them in enclosed spaces, they become ill and psychologically disturbed.

But people who support zoos say that the animals are well looked after and fed, something that does not always happen to them in the wild. And zoos have started many breeding programmes to save endangered species. So many animals that might have become extinct are now still alive.

If I had thought about it when I first went to see a zoo, I would have been unhappy about animals in cages, and I now think that is wrong. But some of the wildlife parks in various countries in the world give animals both security and freedom. So those are the ones I approve of.

So I think that zoos are often cruel places. Proper wildlife parks are a better way for man to preserve species while, at the same time, giving us all a chance to see animals in a natural habitat. But I am sure many families will still take their young children to visit zoos.

b In formal writing, we use more sophisticated words than *and*, *but* and *so*. Replace the words in blue in the student's composition with the following words and phrases. Use each one once only.

as a result   and furthermore   however
in conclusion   therefore,   in contrast   moreover
not only that, but   nevertheless
on the other hand

Notes:
- *However* is always followed by a comma. When it occurs in the middle of a sentence, it has a comma before it too.
- *Moreover* generally occurs at the beginning of a sentence or a clause (e.g. after a semi-colon). In the middle of sentences, it usually occurs with *and* and has commas before and after it (... *and, moreover, ...*).

Now check your answers with the text in Activity Bank 2 on page 156.

41 Read the following composition question.

Zoos are absolutely vital for the protection of various animal species.

Make notes in English for and against the opinion given.

42 Plan your own composition (three or four paragraphs).

Paragraph 1: introduce the topic. (*I'd like to start by ...*)
Paragraph 2: set out arguments / give reasons.
Paragraph 3: set out more arguments / give more reasons.
Paragraph 4: draw your own conclusion. (*In conclusion therefore ...*)

43 Write your composition, using some or all of the linkers from Activity 40b.

Review: grammar and functional language

44 Write sentences using some of the following words as either adjectives or adverbs.

Read your sentences to your partner. Can they say whether it is an adverb or an adjective? You can look at Activity 17 for help.

| dead | fast | hard | late | loud | pretty | rough |
| slow | tight | ugly | well | wrong | | |

Example: STUDENT A: *That was dead funny!*
STUDENT B: *Is 'dead' an adjective?*
STUDENT A: *No.*

45 Make sentences about yourself using the verbs below. Add adverbs or adverbial phrases of manner, place, time, definite / indefinite frequency and certainty. You can look at Activity 20 for ideas.

Things I do:
- eat
- feel nervous
- feel regret
- feel tired
- like reading books
- sing
- sleep
- stay silent
- study
- talk to animals
- watch people

Example: *I frequently eat noisily in restaurants at about 7 o'clock!*

46 What are the people saying? What words can go in the speech bubble in each case? Add a threat or a warning. You can look at Activities 24–30 for help.

Review: vocabulary

Word List

catty   cock-up   cocky
dog-eared   dogged
fairy story   fishy
mousy   pigsty
portrayed   range   ratty
real turkey   sadistically
sheepish grin   (Siberian) wastes
sociable   to bark   to bleat
to cluck   to crow
to demonise   to growl
to grunt   to hiss   to howl
to neigh   to purr   to roar
to squeal   victim   wolf

Word Plus

ashamed of themselves
for a start
from the horse's mouth
in the doghouse
in the end
just for the fun of it
lone wolf
the lion's share
to cry wolf
to do their best
to fish for compliments
to get (your) hands on
to go to the dogs
to hold your horses
to keep out of our way
to keep the wolf from the door
to kill two birds with one stone
to let the cat out of the bag
to make a real pig of
to smell a rat
to wolf (down) your food
wolf in sheep's clothing
wolf-whistle

47 What are your two (a) favourite and (b) least favourite animals? Are there any words or phrases in the Word List or Word Plus that can be used with your animals? Can you find any more words or phrases about your animals in your dictionary?

●●● Pronunciation

48 List words (including compound nouns and adjectives) of two syllables or more in the Word List and complete the following tasks.

a Which is the stressed syllable?
b What is the vowel sound in the stressed syllable? Underline it.
c Can you find other words with the same stressed vowel sound?

Example: fishy – victim

Listen to the words on Track 17 and check your answer.

49 Say the words of the following phrases as separate words. Then say them as phrases. How does the pronunciation of the individual words change, if at all?

a ashamed of themselves
b for a start
c from the horse's mouth
d in the end
e just for the fun of it

Listen to Track 18 and repeat the phrases like the speakers.

50 In pairs Choose one of the animal metaphors from the Word Plus box. Without looking at a dictionary, write your own definition for the expression, and then include the phrase in two example sentences.

Example: from the horse's mouth – from the person who knows most about the subject

I heard the story in the canteen, but then I asked my boss, because I wanted to hear it from the horse's mouth.

51 Game List the animals from the picture in Activity 11. Team A says the name of an animal. Team B gets one point for a word associated with the animal, and two points for any metaphorical phrase that includes the animal.

Example: TEAM A: cat
TEAM B: purr (= 1 point)
Don't be so catty! (= 2 points)

UNIT 4
Just for fun

→ present perfect continuous
→ hobbies and activities
→ asking for clarification /
  buying 'thinking time'

Listening: things people do for fun

1 What are the people doing? Would you like to do it yourself?
  Why? Why not?

2 Look at the people. Which of the activities from Activity 1 do you think they do just for fun?

Danny   Carmen   Jack   Marcus   Ellie

Listen to Track 19. Were you correct?

3 Listen again. Who says ... ?

  a It gives you time to think.
  b I've begged her to stop.
  c And that's the truth.
  d I've never had any trouble.
  e I'll take your word for it.
  f The only downside is that it can be
    pretty cold.
  g I'm not addicted to it or anything.
  h You can't be serious.
  i It's not for everybody.
  j People call us nerds and anoraks.

4 Which of the phrases in Activity 3 mean ... ?

  a I've asked as strongly as possible. I've begged.
  b I could easily stop doing it.
  c I believe you, but I don't want to try it.
  d Only some people enjoy it.
  e very boring people who are interested in silly little
    details (slang)
  f the one disadvantage
  g That's a ridiculous suggestion.

5 In pairs Student A asks Student B about the five people in
  Activity 2. How many questions can A think of, and how many
  answers can B give?

  Example: STUDENT A: How does Danny spend his spare time?

  STUDENT B: He goes fishing. He's an angler.

Vocabulary: hobbies and activities

6 What do we call someone who ...

a ... arranges flowers?
flower arranger

b ... plays golf?

c ... climbs mountains?

d ... climbs rocks?

e ... collects stamps?

f ... dives through the sky?

g ... fishes?

h ... goes down potholes?

i ... keeps bees?

j ... makes models?

k ... skis on water?

l ... spots (watches) trains?

m ... dives (swims under water) with a scuba tank?

n ... uses a skateboard?

o ... uses a snowboard?

p ... walks up and down hills?

q ... watches birds?

7 a Look at the names you've found in Activity 6: which are compound words and which are words with different forms (e.g. verb + -*er* = noun)?

Example: *compound words:*
flower arranger
verbs + '-er': skier

b What do we call the activity?

Example: *flower arranging*

8 **Language research** Using a dictionary or any other source, find out what activities you might use the following objects with. The first one is done for you.

a album   *stamp collecting*

b binoculars

c gloves

d glue

e goggles

f helmet

g magnifying glass

h mask

i money

j net

k notebook

l oxygen tank

m rod

n skis

o torch

p vase

q wetsuit

9 Where would you put the phrases on the following line?

hate | ———————————————————————— | love

a I am addicted to

b I am keen on

c I am mad about

d I am not crazy about

e I am not really into

f I am not very interested in

g I am not very keen on

h I am obsessed by

i I am really into

j I do not enjoy

k I do not like

l I get a kick out of

m I really enjoy

n ... doesn't do much for me

o ... turns me on

p ... doesn't really turn me on

10 Say how you feel about the activities mentioned in the unit so far.

Example: *I'm really keen on water-skiing, but skiing on snow doesn't do much for me.*

11 **In groups** Write questions for the people in the pictures. Ask about their hobby, their lives, their daily routines, their likes and dislikes, etc.

A student chooses one of the four characters. The other students in the group have to interview the student as if he / she was that character. The student should answer any question in the way he / she thinks the character would.

Example: *c*

STUDENTS: *Aren't you frightened of bees?*

BEE-KEEPER: *Not really. But I have to be careful.*

STUDENTS: *What do you do when you are not with your bees?*

BEE-KEEPER: *Umm, well I like scuba-diving!*

Speaking: making a presentation

12 Preparation Complete the following tasks.

  a Choose a hobby or an activity that you would like to talk about, either because you do it just for fun or because you would like to do it.

  b Make notes in answer to the following questions.

> Why do you want to talk about it?
>
> What is special about it?
>
> Have you ever done it and what was it like?
>
> OR Would you like to do it and why?
>
> What kind of person does this activity?
>
> When and where is the best place or time to do it?
>
> Who is the best person to do it with?
>
> What would you say to encourage other people to do it?
>
> What does it feel like?
>
> What else would you like to say about it?

  c Use your notes to plan your talk. You can follow this outline plan.

what you're going to talk about and why
↓
what it is
• what it's like
• how you do it, etc.
↓
conclusions

13 Giving a presentation in groups

Stage 1
Student A: give your presentation.
Student B: you are a kind critic. Write down any examples of good English that you hear.
Student C: you are a harsh critic. Write down any mistakes you hear.
Students D, E, etc.: write down questions you want to ask when Student A has finished.

Stage 2
In groups, Students D, E, etc. ask their questions and Student A answers them.

Stage 3
Students B and C give their kind critic / harsh critic reports. The group discusses the reports.

Grammar: present perfect continuous (and simple)

14 What's the problem with each of the following sentences?

  a I have lived in London since a long time.

  b I haven't seen him yesterday.

  c I've just only realised who you are.

  d I've tried never slack-lining and I don't think I want to.

  e I have tried a couple of times cliff diving but it frightened me so I'm not going to do it again.

  f I have watched freediving on the television last night and it was very boring.

  g I have forgotten already the name of the world cliff diving champion.

Look at 4A–4D in the Mini-grammar. Do you want to change your answers?

15 In which <u>one</u> of the following situations is the present perfect simple (*has done* / *have done*) NOT used?

  a when we want to talk about a recent past action with present consequences

  b when we want to talk about a completed / finished action in the past (and we don't want to make any connection with the present)

  c when we want to talk about an action which started in the past and is still continuing

  d when we want to talk about general experiences that have affected us in our lives

16 Choose the simple (*has done*) or continuous (*has been doing*) form of the present perfect for the following sentences. The first one is done for you.

a Bruce (skydive) __has been skydiving__ for three years and he wants to keep doing it.

b He (make) .... 60 jumps in competitions so far this year.

c For the last four months, he (see) .... a girl he met in Greece. She's a nurse in a hospital casualty department.

d He (ask)............................ her to marry him and she (agree) ....

e He (buy) .... a beautiful ring for her. She loves it.

f His fiancée (never jump) .... because she doesn't like heights.

g She (go) .... to Bruce's skydiving competitions for the last few months.

h She (not enjoy) .... a single one of them.

i He (promise) .... to give up his hobby, but she won't believe him until he does.

j He (watch) .... her at work twice, but he's not going to do it again.

k He (never be able) .... to stand the sight of blood!

Look at 4A–4F in the Mini-grammar. Do you want to change your answers?

17 Use **4A–4F in the Mini-grammar** to decide whether the following sentences are correct or wrong.

a I've been taking tennis lessons for a few weeks now.

b I've been having six tennis lessons so far.

c This is only the second time I've been seeing a cliff diving competition.

d I've been understanding most of his lectures.

e She's been visiting her grandmother on Sundays for the last year and a half.

f He's gone to English classes for the last two months.

g This mountain has been being here since the dawn of time.

h She's been climbing mountains since she was a child.

i I've been dreaming about skydiving.

j How many dreams about skydiving have you been having?

18 Conversations Match the conversations to the pictures.

1 A: How have you been keeping?
B: Not too bad, but I don't get out much.

2 A: What have you been doing with yourself since we last met?
B: Oh well, I went skiing a couple of weeks ago.

3 A: Where have you been hiding recently?
B: What? Oh, er, nowhere. I've just been working quite hard, that's all.

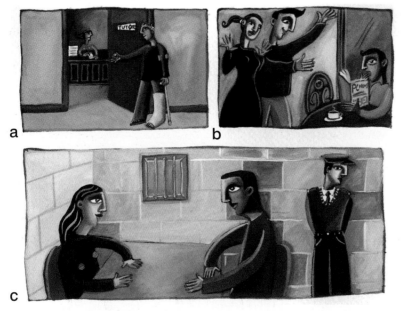

a

b

c

Choose one of the pictures a–c and continue the conversation. How many examples of the present perfect continuous can you include in the conversation? (You may want to use questions like the ones in the box below.)

Have you been getting enough sleep?
Have you been skiing since you got back?
Have you been seeing anyone special?
How have you been keeping up with your work?
How have you been getting on with your colleagues / fellow inmates?

Reading: looking danger in the face

19 Copy the table. Choose <u>one</u> of the three texts, read it and complete the appropriate column of your table about that person.

	Text 1	Text 2	Text 3
a Name of main character	Dustin Webster		
b Name of person in the photograph (if different)			
c Date and place of birth of main character			
d What the main character does			
e What is special about what he does			
f How the main character started			
g Achievements (if listed)			
h Any other interesting information			

20 Talk to students who read the other two texts and complete your table based on what they tell you.

Example: Text 1
STUDENT A: What's the main character's name?
STUDENT B: Dustin Webster.

American-born Dustin Webster has loved high diving ever since his parents took him to see high divers at an amusement park in San Diego when he was 11. He went backstage to ask the divers how they did it and six years later he joined their team. He has been high-diving ever since.

The kind of diving Dustin does is called cliff diving, and it's not like the diving you see in the Olympics. For a start the distance from the board to the water (about 25 metres) is much greater than that. And secondly, cliff divers like Dustin do triple and quadruple somersaults on the way down. This makes cliff diving highly skilled and extremely dangerous. Many of them suffer injury and, on occasions, death if they land in the water on their stomachs or their backs. 'From 25 metres up, you fall a bit like a grand piano,' Dustin says cheerfully. They have been known to break their legs if they land on a fish or a piece of seaweed.

When you watch cliff divers, you get a real sense of how absolutely terrifying it is. They stand on the edge of the board and look down, far far down, and then they launch themselves twisting into the air. No matter how many times you do it, Dustin and his colleagues say, you never lose the fear just before you jump.

So how come Colombian Orlando Duque, who has just beaten Dustin to become the latest cliff diving champion, looked so still and God-like as he stood above a seawater lake in Greece, arms outstretched, his long black hair falling down his back, protected by nothing except a small pair of red swimming trunks? That day, back in July, he looked more like the statue of Christ in Rio de Janeiro than a frail human being. And then he was gone, falling through the air, doing his famous back loop with four twists, incredibly graceful and frighteningly vulnerable. And it worked. When that day's competition was over, Duque had won the prize.

When world champion Francisco 'Pipin' Ferreras went to Baja California in 1996 to try and break the world freediving record he did not realise that he would meet the young woman who would soon become his wife. But that is what happened, for she had been doing a university thesis on freediving and he was the one person she wanted to talk to about it. Audrey Mestre, the woman doing the thesis, was born in France on August 11, 1974. Her grandfather and her mother were both spearfishers and, as a result, Audrey had been diving since she was a child. She won her first swimming race when she was two and a half years old and began scuba-diving when she was 13.

In 1990 she moved (with her family) to Mexico, and it was there that she started freediving – diving with no breathing apparatus, something that people who fish with spears have been doing for as long as there have been people living by the sea. But modern freedivers try to break world records all the time to see who can go deepest, and for how long, without any oxygen at all.

Pipin Ferreras is a world champion and pretty soon his new girlfriend (Audrey, soon to be his wife) was joining him in his record attempts. In 1997 she did a free dive of 80 metres and in 1998 she dived to 115 metres with her husband. Things really took off in May 2000, however, when off the coast of the Canary islands she broke the female freediving world record by reaching a depth of 125 metres and coming back in two minutes and three seconds. Only one year later, she reached 130 metres.

But freediving is a dangerous sport. On October 12, 2002, Audrey was in the Dominican Republic attempting to beat a record set by UK freediver Tanya Streeter. This time she went too far, there was an accident, and she died.

When carpenter Mark Houlding took his seven-year-old son Leo climbing up a 10,000 ft mountain in Morocco a few years ago, he probably didn't realise what he had started. But ever since then, Mark's little boy has been climbing higher and higher, and doing more and more dangerous things just for the fun of it.

People first started to hear of Leo Houlding when one day at the age of 16, he walked up to a highly dangerous cliff face in Wales and chose to climb it 'on sight' instead of planning it and doing a practice climb with ropes like most experienced climbers do. At one point he became stuck for more than half an hour, but he closed his eyes and felt for good holds with his hands. Then he lost his grip and thought 'this is it!' but he kept going and made it to the top.

With his crazy courage, youthful good looks and disrespectful attitude, Houlding is not popular with everyone in the careful world of climbing – the activity which is still his first love. But that has not stopped him having a go at other sports too. For example, he only tried snowboarding a few times before he took himself down one of the most dangerous mountain runs in Switzerland.

His special party trick, however, is called slack-lining, which is like tightrope walking except that the rope is much looser and, as a result, much more difficult to walk on – and therefore much more dangerous. He does this everywhere, on fences or even on rope barriers hundreds of feet above nothing.

'I don't want to die,' Leo says nonchalantly, 'but I'm not particularly afraid of it. I just want to make enough money as a climber so I can keep doing it. And for the last three years I've been travelling all over the world doing exactly that.' And it's true: he's climbed in Chile, India, Thailand, Switzerland and Britain to name just a few of the countries he gets to. Recently, for example, he's been climbing in and around Barcelona in Spain. And how did he spend his spare time when he was there? Looking down at the city from the very top of some of the biggest construction cranes in the world.

21 In pairs Discuss the following questions.

a Which of the three activities in Texts 1–3 would you most or least like to do? Why?

b Choose one of the three characters in the texts. What would you most like to ask them?

22 Vocabulary Look at these sentences from the texts. What parts of speech are the words in blue? What words or phrases can replace the words in blue without changing the meaning too much? The first one is done for you.

a Then they launch themselves twisting into the air.

verb – 'then they throw themselves'

b They have been known to break their legs if they land ... on a piece of seaweed.

c He looked more like the statue ... than a frail human being.

d And then he was gone ... incredibly graceful and frighteningly vulnerable.

e She had been doing a university thesis on freediving.

f She ... began scuba-diving when she was 13.

g Freediving [means] diving with no breathing apparatus.

h With his crazy courage ... and disrespectful attitude, Houlding is not popular with everyone.

i 'I don't want to die,' Leo says nonchalantly.

Language in chunks

23 Match the phrases in italics from the text (a–g) with their meanings (1–7).

a *break world records*
b *having a go at*
c *lost his grip*
d things *really took off*
e *this is it*
f *to name but a few*
g *went backstage*

1 a small number of a much larger list
2 started to become really successful
3 visited the area where the performers were relaxing / getting changed
4 I am going to fall / die
5 become the best a number of times
6 trying something for the first time
7 couldn't hold on to something

24 In pairs Ask your partner the following questions.

a What world record would you most like to break?
b What new activity would you like to have a go at?
c Have you ever lost your grip – either in actual fact or metaphorically?
d Has there ever been a time in your life when things really took off for you?
e Has there ever been a moment in your life when you thought 'this is it'?
f What people do you most admire (answer using the phrase *to name but a few*)?
g Have you ever been backstage in a theatre / concert hall? Describe it.

25 Noticing language How many examples of the present perfect continuous form can you find in the texts?

26 Memory Choose one of the people in the texts and write five comprehension questions about that person.

Close your book. Ask someone your questions. Try and answer someone else's questions. How good is your memory?

Functional language: asking for clarification / buying 'thinking time'

27 Listening Read the conversation. What is it the woman doesn't want to do? Find a suitable word for the gap.

WOMAN: I've been looking for you everywhere.
MAN: Sorry?
WOMAN: I've been trying to find you but I couldn't see you anywhere.
MAN: Well now you have found me! I haven't been hiding or anything. I've been around. Actually I've been ...
WOMAN: Look, it's not that I'm not interested or anything, but I need to talk about the ... umm ... about the .... tonight.
MAN: Yeah?
WOMAN: Yes. I'm not sure if I really want to go.
MAN: Why not?
WOMAN: Well because I'm not really in the what-do-you-call-it? ...

MAN: Mood?

WOMAN: Yes, that's it, I'm not in the mood.

MAN: Uh-huh?

WOMAN: And anyway there'll be lots of people from the office, and I see enough of them during the day. Do you know what I mean? I just don't want ...

MAN: Well yes, but they all really want you to go and there'll be lots of other people too. Anyway, I want to go.

))🎧 Listen to Track 20. Were you correct?

28 Copy and complete the table with the expressions in blue from the conversation in Activity 27.

If you:	Words and phrases
... can't think what something is called:	a
... want time to think as you are speaking because you don't know what to say next or because you don't want to say what you are going to have to say:	b
... want to check that someone understands or agrees with what you are saying:	c
... want to ask someone to repeat something that they have just said because you didn't hear or understand it:	d
... want to show that you're listening to what someone is saying and you want them to go on (two examples):	e
... want to say something / interrupt when someone else is talking:	f
... want to change the topic of the exchange or go back to an earlier subject:	g

29 Add the following to the table in Activity 28 (some words and phrases can be used more than once).

1 Could you repeat the question / that?
2 Er ...
3 I didn't quite catch that.
4 Mmm.
5 Pardon?
6 Right.
7 Sorry to interrupt, but ...
8 Well ...
9 what's-her-name / what's-his-name
10 thingamajig
11 Yes.
12 You know ...

30 What words or phrases from Activities 27–29 could you use in the following conversation? Choose a word or phrase for each letter (a–f).

A: Have you seen my dark glasses anywhere?
B: (a) ....
A: I can't find my glasses. Have you seen them?
B: Weren't you using them earlier on?
A: Well yes, (b) .... I was but I can't remember where I put them.
B: Honestly, you are hopeless. Sometimes I don't know what to do with you.
A: (c) ....
B: It's true. You're always forgetting things. Losing things. I mean only yesterday you couldn't find ...
A: (d) .... I do need to find my glasses.
B: It's really irritating, always having to look for things that you've lost. It gets me all irritated. (e) ....
A: Yes.
B: And that's not a good thing.
A: (f) .... It's not that serious, honestly.
B: Hey, wait a minute. Aren't those your glasses there?
A: Oh yes. Great. I'll be going then. Goodbye.
B: Bye.

● ● ● Pronunciation: intonation

31 Listen to Track 21. Is the man just showing that he is listening or does he want the woman to repeat what she has said – or say more? Write a full stop (.) or a question mark (?) after each of his words.

a	Yeah	e	Right
b	Sorry	f	Sorry
c	Uh-huh	g	Uh-huh
d	Yeah	h	Right

Did the man's voice go up or down in each case?

32 In pairs Student A reads the statements and Student B responds with one-word answers (*yeah, right, sorry, uh-huh*, etc.). Is Student B just listening or do they want Student A to say more or repeat?

Example: **a**

STUDENT A: You know I've been reading that book about skydiving.

STUDENT B: Sorry?

STUDENT A: You want me to repeat!

a You know I've been reading that book about skydiving.
b I've been looking for you everywhere.
c I've always wanted to see that singer in concert.
d I had a really fantastic time at Morag's party.
e I've just finished reading Sarah's new book.
f That film was really shocking.
g It was a beautiful day yesterday.
h I didn't enjoy that class.

Writing: email interview

33 Read the email interview with Emma Sanchez Moore and answer the questions.

a Would you like to meet her? Why? Why not?
b Are there any words you do not understand? Check them with a partner. If you still don't know what they mean, use your dictionary.

The email interview

Twenty-three-year-old Emma Sanchez Moore is a paraski champion. Paraskiing, whether on snow or on water, uses a small parachute to pull the skier along. Emma lives in Detroit with her family, but she spends a lot of her time paraskiing off beaches all over the world, especially in Mexico, her parents' native land. Both her brothers have won titles as barefoot skiers, but Emma still prefers the parachute.

What is your most vivid childhood memory?
When my Dad took me water-skiing for the first time in Acapulco. We were in Mexico for a holiday with my grandparents. All I was told was 'shut up and hold on!'.
Which living person would you most like to go on a fantasy date with?
Enrique Iglesias – because he's got the best voice, he's good-looking and he's like me, he lives in two cultures.
What three words best describe you?
Fit, funny, beautiful (only joking about the last one!).
What is your idea of perfect happiness?
Calm water and early morning sunshine, just before the skiing starts.
What is your greatest fear?
That I'll break something and not be able to ski anymore.
Who or what is the greatest love of your life?
My family, especially my two brothers Ryan and Oliver.
What is your greatest regret?
That I didn't work harder at school.
How do you relax?
I go clubbing with my friends.
How would you like to be remembered?
As someone who loved life.
What is the most important lesson life has taught you?
If something's worth doing, it's worth doing well.

34 Are the following phrases, sentences and questions more writing-like or speaking-like? How do you know?

a Fantastic, aren't they?
b I think they are fantastic.
c See you later.
d I was like 'fine' and he was like 'OK'.
e I said that it was fine and he replied that it was OK.
f I'm not going to put up with it any more.
g I'm not going to tolerate it any more.
h You're not from round here, are you?
i Do you come from this neighbourhood?
j You're a skydiver?
k Check out the new cafeteria! Awesome!
l It is worth investigating the new cafeteria.

Include two speaking-like phrases in a short conversation.

35 Answer the questions from the interview in Activity 33 about you. Compare your answers with a partner.

Example: My most vivid childhood memory is ...

36 **In pairs** Think of ten more questions you could send for an email interview (e.g. what makes them sad / happy, things they like / don't like, friendships, tastes in music, hopes for the future, etc.).

37 Send your questions to your classmates, or email your interview questions to a friend.

Review: grammar and functional language

38 Match the questions in the first list (a–j) with the list below (1–10). You could look at Activities 14–18 for help.

a Have you been reading my private diary?
b Have you been studying as hard as you ought to?
c Have you been taking money from my wallet?
d How have you been getting on with your new flatmate?
e What have you been eating since you last came to see me?
f Who have you been seeing recently?
g Why have they been following us for the last hour?
h Why have you been missing lessons recently?
i You look exhausted. What have you been doing?
j You've been falling asleep in class. Why is that?

1 Absolutely fine. She's really good company.
2 I don't know. Perhaps they think we'll lead them to the money.
3 I've been practising for the diving competition.
4 I've been working nights at the local hospital.
5 No one special. Just a friend. Honestly.
6 No, honestly I haven't. It just fell open when I picked it up.
7 No, of course I haven't. But I'd like a bit more pocket money every week.
8 Not really. I keep getting distracted.
9 The same as before. I haven't managed to cut down on chocolate, I'm afraid. I just can't do it.
10 Working out at the gym. I really gave myself a hard time.

Who asks the questions, do you think? Who answers them? What's the situation?

Example: a It could be brothers and sisters, or a teenager and a parent.

39 Think of activities for each of the following categories.

a something you haven't been doing recently (but should have been doing)
b something you've always done
c something you've been doing for the last few weeks
d something you've done a few times (but would like to do more often)
e something you've done, but wouldn't like to do again
f something you've never done

In pairs Tell your partner about the activities. Does your partner have similar things to say?

40 Rewrite the following conversation, trying to ask for clarification and 'buy time'. Include as many expressions from Activities 27–30 as you can.

A: I've been thinking of taking up water-skiing.
B: Have you?
A: Yes. It looks quite exciting.
B: Do you think you're strong enough?
A: Yes, of course, why not?
B: Well, you're not exactly fit, are you?
A: I'm not sure that's true. I walk to work every day, and I walk backwards and forwards to the water-cooler in the office at least three ...

Review: vocabulary

Word List

album   angling   apparatus
bee-keeper   binoculars
bird-watcher   disrespectful
flower arranger   frail   gloves
glue   goggles   golfer
helmet   hillwalker
magnifying glass   mask
model-maker   money
mountain-climber   net
nonchalantly   notebook
oxygen tank   potholer
rock-climber   rod
scuba-diver   skateboarder
skis   skydiver
snowboarder   stamp-collector
thesis   to launch yourself
torch   train-spotter   vase
vulnerable   water-skier
wetsuit

Word Plus

'It doesn't do much for me!' *
'it turns me on'
things really took off
'This is it!'
to be addicted to
to be keen on
to be mad about
to be not crazy about
to be not very interested in
to be not very keen on
to be obsessed by
to be really into
to break a world record
to get a kick out of
to go backstage
to have a go at
to lose your grip
'to name but a few'
to really enjoy

*Phrases in inverted commas are
conversational phrases.

41 Choose three of the occupations from the Word List that you would like to try. What three objects would be the most important for each of the occupations? Can you find the objects in the Word List?

Compare your answers with a partner.

Pronunciation

42 Listen to Track 22. How many sounds are there in the following words?

Example: glue: three (/g/, /l/ and /u:/)

a angling
b binoculars
c goggles
d notebook
e skateboarder
f thesis
g trainspotter

43 Find all the words in the Word List with three or more syllables (including compound nouns). Which is the stressed syllable in each case? Which words are always stressed on the first syllable?

Example: 'bee-keeper

Check your answers by listening to Track 23.

44 **Instant role-play** Choose two of the hobbies / activities. Two people, one for each hobby / activity, meet and have a conversation. Decide where they meet and what the topic of the conversation is. Role-play the conversation as quickly as possible.

45 **In pairs** Design a questionnaire to find out how people feel about either different sports or different hobbies. In your questionnaire, make sure you have a way of writing down how interested people are, using phrases from Word Plus.

Example:

How would you describe your interest in football?	Addicted to it	Crazy about it	Keen on it	Interested in it	Not interested in it

Use your questionnaire to ask other students about their interests.

Example: How would you describe your interest in football? Are you addicted to it? Crazy about it? ...

UNIT 5
Getting angry

→ the third conditional
→ being angry
→ wishes and regrets

Reading: what's anger all about?

1 **Discussion** How would you answer the following questions?

- What is anger?
- Why do people get angry?
- What's wrong with anger?
- What should you do if you start getting angry?

Now read the web page. Are the opinions there the same as yours?

THE ANGER PAGE

What is anger?

Anger has many sources. Often it is an emotion which is <u>secondary to some other emotion</u> that you are feeling – like fear, guilt or relief. So the parent who shouts at her kid who gets home late is using anger as a way of displacing fear. Sometimes it is the result of a sense of great unfairness – such as when someone is wrongly accused of a crime, or finds that their partner has not been telling them the truth, or feels a passionate sense of social injustice.

But anger may have other causes as well. We know that animals can be made more aggressive if the limbic parts of their brains are stimulated; thus overstimulation of the limbic (emotional) centre of the brain may override the neocortex (the reasoning part).

Changes in hormone levels seem to cause anger too, and inheritance plays a part as does our upbringing. The more we are raised in anger, the more anger we are likely to feel later in our lives.

Is anger bad for you?

Most researchers think that chronic anger leads to an increased risk of heart attack, but studies show that suppressing anger is bad for you too. Women who constantly suppress their anger, for example, show a higher mortality rate than those that don't. When partners suppress their anger, one study suggests, this is more damaging to the woman's health than the man's. So it seems that while frequent anger is bad for you (heart attacks, high blood pressure, suppression of the immune system), the suppression of anger is worse.

Some commentators suggest that using anger consciously is a good thing, provided it is not too extreme or out of control, but others are convinced that anger could be one of the main factors controlling our emotional and physical health.

Dealing with anger

Almost everyone agrees that dealing with anger is important so that we don't let it control us or make us say or do things we would later regret. We should be aware of our angry thoughts and try to challenge them. Perhaps when someone cuts us up at the traffic lights, we should worry about why they drive that way rather than get furious. We should try and relax, take a deep breath and decide whether we really want to go over the top! That way we can be angry only when we want to be.

<u>Are there anger types?</u>   <u>Differences between men and women</u>   <u>Controlling anger</u>

Home | About Us | Subjects A – Z | Contact Us | Behaviour modification classes | Search

2 Meaning check Find words and phrases in *The Anger Page* which tell you that the following statements are true. The first one is underlined for you.

a Anger is often a reaction to some other feeling.
b We often shout to get rid of other feelings.
c Anger may be the result of some particular brain activity.
d Family background may affect how angry we are.
e We think anger is bad for us.
f Controlling anger may be harmful.
g We should try to be in charge of our own anger.
h We should pause before we get angry.

3 Follow the links Work in groups of three.

STUDENT A: follow the first link (Are there anger types?) by looking at Activity Bank 3 on page 157.

STUDENT B: follow the second link (Differences between men and women) by looking at Activity Bank 8 on page 159.

STUDENT C: follow the third link (Controlling anger) by looking at Activity Bank 15 on page 163.

4 In groups of three Students A, B and C, discuss the links you have followed. What did they say? Do you agree with what you read there?

5 Comprehension check Complete the following tasks based on what you found out in Activity 4 (do not look back at the text).

In your own words,

a ... describe different anger personality types.
b ... explain how or if anger affects men and women differently.
c ... give advice on how to deal with anger.

Language in chunks

6 Complete the sentences with these phrases from the text in Activity 1 and the Activity Bank. You may have to change the phrases a little.

> build up over (a long) time (see Activity Bank 3)   cut somebody up
> feel trapped (see Activity Bank 3)   go over the top
> on the surface (see Activity Bank 15)   out of control
> shades of grey (see Activity Bank 3)   take a deep breath
> use your imagination (see Activity Bank 15)

a When we want people to think a bit more creatively, we often say '...................'.
b If something ...., it means it increases very gradually.
c If you ...., it is as if you are in a prison and can't get out.
d If someone is ...., it means it will be difficult to quieten them down or restrain them.
e If someone ...., it means that they behave in an exaggerated way which is not appropriate to the situation.
f If somebody ...., it means they drive right in front of you, often quite fast, and take your position.
g When you ...., you fill your lungs with air once – and perhaps it gives you time to think.
h Some people can look calm ...., but actually, inside, they're feeling very angry.
i If you see things in ...., it means you do not think they are completely simple.

7 Conversation writing Use at least three of the phrases in a conversation between two friends who are having (or have just had) an argument.

8 In pairs Copy and complete the table with ideas about what you can do when / if you meet someone who is angry.

Useful things to do when someone is angry	Things that are NOT useful to do when someone is angry
tell them to calm down	

Compare your table with another pair.

Grammar: the third conditional

9 Look at the following sentences. Which describes events:

a ... that are real?
b ... that may happen?
c ... that are hypothetical because they probably won't happen?

1 If you got angry with me, I'd get very upset.
2 If you get angry with me, I'll be very upset.
3 If you get angry all the time, people tend to get upset with you.

Look at 5A–5D in the Mini-grammar. Do you want to change your answers?

10 Answer the following questions.

- What do you do if people get angry with you?
- What will you do the next time your friend gets angry with you?
- What would you do if your friend got angry with you?

Write three similar *What ... if ...* questions for real, possible and hypothetical situations. Ask your partner.

11 Read the story and complete the tasks which follow it.

How Jesse got his arm back

Eight-year-old Jesse Arbogast was playing in the sea late one evening in July 2001 when a seven-foot bull shark attacked him and tore off his arm. Jesse's uncle leapt into the sea and dragged the boy to shore. Jesse's aunt gave the boy mouth-to-mouth resuscitation because he had stopped breathing. They called the emergency services and a helicopter flew Jesse to hospital. It was much quicker than a journey by road.

Jesse's uncle, Vance Flosenzier, ran back into the sea and found the shark that had attacked his nephew. He picked it up and threw it on to the beach. A ranger shot the fish, the shark's jaws relaxed and they were able to open them and reach down into its stomach and pull out the boy's arm.

At the hospital a plastic surgeon, Dr Ian Rogers, spent 11 hours re-attaching Jesse's arm. 'It was a complicated operation,' he said, 'but we were lucky. If they hadn't recovered the arm in time, we wouldn't have been able to do the operation at all.'

According to local park ranger Jack Tomosvic, shark attacks are not that common. 'Jesse was just unlucky,' he says, 'evening is the shark's feeding time. And Jesse wasn't in a lifeguard area. This would never have happened if he had been in a designated swimming area.'

When reporters asked Jesse's uncle how he had had the courage to fight a shark, he replied, 'I was mad and you do some strange things when you're mad.'

This is a true story.

a **In pairs** Ask and answer as many questions as you can about the story using *who* and *what*.

Example: STUDENT A: Who went swimming?
STUDENT B: Jesse.

b Look at the two *if* sentences spoken by Dr Rogers and Jack Tomosvic.

- Do they describe real or hypothetical situations in the past?
- How would you explain the grammar of the sentences to another student using these elements?

if	have + past participle	would	not

Compare your description with 5E in the Mini-grammar.

c Make as many similar *if* sentences about the story of Jesse Arbogast as you can.

Examples: If Jesse hadn't played in the sea, the shark wouldn't have attacked him.
Jesse would have died if his aunt hadn't given him mouth-to-mouth resuscitation.

12 A game of consequences Ask what people did yesterday – and then keep asking about what would have happened if they hadn't done it!

Example:
STUDENT A: What did you do yesterday?

STUDENT B: I got up at about 7 o'clock.

STUDENT A: What would have happened if you hadn't got up?

STUDENT B: I would have missed the bus.

STUDENT A: What would have happened if you had missed the bus?

STUDENT B: I would have got to work late.

STUDENT A: What would have happened if you had got to work late?

STUDENT B: etc.

13 Study **5E in the Mini-grammar** again. Now read the story. Who can make the most *if* sentences using different modals and different tenses in consequence clauses?

Jane passed all her school exams and so she got into university. It was there that she was introduced to Dave. He had just broken up with his girlfriend and was feeling sorry for himself, and so he was pleased to meet someone new. In the end they realised they were in love and so they got married.

Dave was taking a law degree and was all set to be a lawyer, but when Jane was accepted on a postgraduate course in Montreal they moved to Canada. Without that they would probably still be in England. Dave got a job as an actor on a radio programme, and now he is a well-known TV and radio personality. Jane works as a librarian. They have two children who are, of course, Canadian citizens.

They were thinking of returning to the UK next year, but Dave has just been given the main newsreader job on Channel 5, so it looks like they're going to stay.

Vocabulary: being angry

14 Look at the picture. Who:
a ... doesn't like someone?
b ... wants someone to be relaxed?
c ... finds someone's behaviour difficult to put up with?
d ... is / was surprised?
e ... describes the way someone is at the moment?
f ... got very angry?

15 Language research Use a dictionary to find out which of the words in the box mean (a) *angry*, (b) *fed up with*, (c) *to drive somebody crazy*, (d) *to get very angry*, (e) *to relax*, (f) *sulky*?

annoyed	to calm down
bad-tempered	to get on
cross	somebody's
furious	nerves
grouchy	to keep your cool
grumpy	to keep your head
hacked off	to lose it
(*informal*)	to lose your cool
irritable	to lose your
mad	temper
moody	to make somebody
sick and tired of	cross / angry

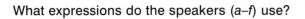

What expressions do the speakers (*a–f*) use?

16 Write four questions using language from Activities 14 and 15.

Examples: *When was the last time you lost your cool?*
When was the last time somebody got on your nerves?

Ask other people in the class.

Rules
- Answers may be true or false.
- Answers must not offend anyone else in the class.

17 Grammar What words follow the words and phrases from Activities 14 and 15? Copy the table and tick the appropriate boxes. The first one is done for you.

		about (something)	*at* (something / somebody)	*by* (something / somebody)	*of*	*with* (something / somebody)
to be / to get	angry	✓	✓			✓
	annoyed					
	cross					
	fed up					
	furious					
	hacked off					
	in a bad mood					
	mad					
	sick and tired					
to lose (your) temper						

18 Complete the following sentences.

a He got so fed up .... his brother that he lost his temper .... him.
b I wish she hadn't been in such a bad mood .... me.
c I only said it because I was so cross .... the things he had done.
d If I hadn't been so angry .... the situation I wouldn't have said what I did.
e He was sick and tired .... the way she talked to him.
f When he told her his news, she completely lost her temper .... him.
g I am annoyed .... her constant rudeness. She will have to leave my class.
h I'm sorry I got angry .... you.
i He was absolutely furious .... the decision we had taken.
j He got mad .... her, but she didn't notice.

Word choice: *argument, fight, quarrel* and *row*

19 Look at the Word Choice notes for *argument, fight, quarrel* and *row* on page 57 in the booklet.

20 Complete the gaps in the sentences with *argument, fight, quarrel* or *row*. You cannot use the same word in two consecutive sentences.

a Last night, Mr Leung and his boss had a blazing .... You could hear it from miles away!
b Normally, Mr Leung doesn't have .... with people. He's a very peaceful guy.
c His sister, however, often picks a .... with people who annoy her.
d She had a .... with someone across the street who was rude about her dog.
e Mr Leung got cross with her and they had a real ....
f But .... like that between brother and sister are rare.
g They do sometimes have silly .... about things like food and furniture.

Which three words can also be verbs? Which word has to change to be a verb?

21 Speaking Answer the questions about yourself. Then ask your partner. Do you have the same answers?

- What time would you like to get up in the morning?
- How do you usually feel in the morning?
- What's your 'low' time during the day?
- What's the best time of the day for you?
- What things make you annoyed or irritated during the day?
- What time do you usually go to bed?

Who are 'morning' people (= people who like to get up early and leap straight into action) in the class? Who are 'evening' people (who like to stay up very late and really come alive later on)?

Speaking: investigation role-play

22 The interview Read the situation for a role-play.

Last night, a car was stolen at 6pm from outside no. 23 Scholars' Lane. It was a red Jaguar, registration number Y253 YTF. The suspect is charged with the crime. If charged and found guilty, he may go to prison because he has been in trouble with the police before.

Two police officers are questioning the suspect in the interview room. Because the suspect is just under 18 years old, his parent is also present. And there is the suspect's lawyer there too.

In groups of five Choose one of the following roles: suspect, police officer 1, police officer 2, lawyer or suspect's parent.

SUSPECT: look at Activity Bank 4 on page 157.
POLICE OFFICER 1: look at Activity Bank 5 on page 158.
POLICE OFFICER 2: look at Activity Bank 9 on page 160.
LAWYER: look at Activity Bank 16 on page 164.
SUSPECT'S PARENT: look at Activity Bank 17 on page 164.

23 This is the start of the interview.

POLICE OFFICER 1: *All right everybody, I am switching on the tape recorder.*
This is an interview with [name of suspect]. My name is [name of police officer 1] and with me in the room is Police Officer [name of police officer 2], the suspect's lawyer [name of lawyer] and [name of parent], the suspect's parent. It is [time] on [day + date]. Now then, [name of suspect], let's start, shall we? Where were you last night?

The police officers have ten minutes to come to a conclusion about the guilt or innocence of the suspect.

Listening: keeping calm

24 How do you stop yourself from getting angry? Think of at least three ways.

Listen to Track 24. Are any of the ways that Dr Kepa Khan suggests similar to yours?

25 Copy and complete the table (in note form) with Dr Khan's anger management techniques.

One ... two ... three ... four ... five

Type of technique	Examples / What it means
a Relaxation	
b Cognitive restructuring	
c Silly humour	

26 In your own words, explain why Dr Kepa Khan gets angry and say what he does to control himself.

27 Listen to Track 24 again. Read the following tape extracts. Note the missing words and whether Jay Reno (R) or Dr Khan (K) said them. The first one is done for you.

a What's the ....._point of_..... this 'anger management'? R

b Umm, yes, well I .... , but anyway, the point of anger management ...

c You can't .... the causes of these feelings, you see, but with luck ...

d Well no, ... , it's not that simple.

e If you .... , it often helps.

f A lot .... that's going to do.

g .... boring.

h ... you understand why you're irritated but that .... isn't going to help.

i You're ....! Tell me you're ....

j I don't think so. It's all .... , isn't it.

k ... that would .... wouldn't it!

28 Based on what Dr Khan says, use these verbs to give advice about ways of managing anger.

visualise
breathe
repeat
picture
change

Example: *You can visualise a relaxing experience.*

Functional language: wishes and regrets

29 Look at the pictures. Guess what the people are thinking.

30 Wishes and regrets Based on the words of the four speakers, can you explain how we say that:

a ... we want something to change now or in the future?
b ... we regret something that happened / didn't happen?
c ... we regret something that we did or didn't do?
d ... it's a pity that a situation isn't different?

Listen to Track 25. Were you correct?

31 Use the following prompts to make sentences with *I wish* or *if only*. The first one is done for you.

What a pity that:
a ... I ever met you! *I wish I'd never met you!*
b ... I can't afford a new car.
c ... I can't understand the Welsh language.
d ... I don't like classical music like my friend does.
e ... I left my address book at home.
f ... I am in the doghouse.
g ... I went to their party.
h ... my parents keep asking me when I'm going to get a proper job.
i ... people keep swimming in unguarded areas.
j ... people won't stop criticising wolves.
k ... she keeps letting the cat out of the bag.
l ... she told me what she thought of me.
m ... the government won't do something about environmental pollution.

32 Choose one of the pictures (a–e). Write sentences about what the character (or shark) wishes about now and about the past.

Example: picture a

I wish I hadn't hit that policeman.

I wish I was at home.

33 Listen to Track 26. Which of the two words do you hear? The first one is done for you.

a <u>cash</u>   catch
b fuschia   future
c mashing   matching
d share   chair
e sheep   cheap
f shin   chin
g shoes   choose
h washing   watching
i wish   which

34 Which of the two sounds corresponds to the following spellings?

a *ch* in a few words, but not normally at the beginning unless they are foreign words (*machine, champagne*)
b *ch* in a lot of words (*chin, rich*)
c *sh* (*shop, wish, fashion*)
d *ture*, but not at the beginning of a word (*picture, future*)
e *tch* (*watch, kitchen*)
f *s* in some words (*sure, insurance*)
g *ci* + vowel at the end of many words (*musician, delicious*)
h *ti* + vowel at the end of many words (*education, intonation*)

Can you give more examples for each spelling?

Writing: designing leaflets

35 **In pairs** Look at the leaflet for *Aroma* on the next page and complete the tasks.

a Describe *Aroma* and what it does to your partner in your own words.
b Do any of the three courses interest you:

... a lot?
... a little?
... not much?
... not at all because they're all silly?

36 Look at the design for the leaflet.

a Do you think it is effective?
b What is the purpose of the front cover? Would you design a cover like that?
c Do you like the use of colour headings and 'bullet' points? Are they easy to read and notice?
d How important are the photographs on the back?
e How would you design a leaflet differently?

Aroma staff:

Sally Grace NAL, director

Justin Knocker, FSDE

Helena Kollect, CCE

Contact Aroma at:
The Aroma Centre
26 Carper Row Middleton Cleethorpe
Lancs LT6 5YW Tel: 01672 462057
Email: enquiries@arofengcol.com
Website: www.arofengcol.com

Using nature's gift to keep you calm

Courses in

AROMATHERAPY
- How different smells affect our mood
- Designing aroma zones
- Judging the best aromas on the market

FENG SHUI*
- The theory of Feng Shui explained
- Putting Feng Shui into practice at home
- Putting Feng Shui into practice at work

RELAXING COLOUR
- How colour affects our mood
- Colour combinations
- Designing rooms with colour in mind

*Feng Shui is the ancient Chinese science which tells people the best place to put furniture in a room or house for maximum comfort and success.

37 Choose one of the following and then copy and complete the table about it.

- an anger management centre (you can use the Audioscript for Track 24 for information about anger management)
- a centre offering tuition in different kinds of music (pop, rock, classical, techno, house, etc.)
- a new gym offering a variety of services
- a new cafeteria at school, college or work
- something else you would like to do if you had the money

38 Write the words for your leaflet based on your decisions in Activity 37.

Questions / Topics to be decided	Notes / Decisions
What kind of a place is it?	
The name of the place (think up something interesting)	
What services the place offers (and brief explanations of what these services are)	
Names of the staff	
An address, phone number, website, etc.	

39 Design your leaflet on a piece of A4 paper which will be folded in half, as in the following diagram.

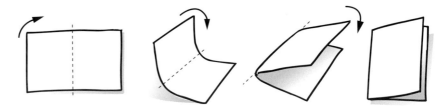

Review: grammar

40 Find pictures which answer the following questions about Zenta's bad luck / good luck story.

a What happened when Zenta switched off the alarm?
b Why did it take her a long time to get to work?
c What happened when she arrived at work very late?
d What happened when she told him that he was behaving badly?
e What did she do when she was sacked?
f What happened when she met the lawyer?
g What happened when she fell in love with the lawyer?

41 Zenta's day – and her life – could have turned out differently. Make *if* sentences about how things might not have been the same. You can look at Activities 9–13 for help.

Example: *If she hadn't switched off the alarm, she might not have gone back to sleep.*

42 Complete the following conversations. Say what the situation is in each case. Use your imagination.

a A: If only I'd brought my camera.
   B: Why?
   A: ....

b A: I wish I was just a tiny bit taller.
   B: What on earth for?
   A: ....

c A: I wish I hadn't called in sick at work today.
   B: Why? You <u>were</u> sick, weren't you?
   A: Yes, but ....

d A: If only I'd listened a bit more carefully!
   B: Why, what difference would that have made?
   A: ....

e A: I wish I'd watched that TV programme last night.
   B: Really? Why that one especially?
   A: ....

f A: If only you'd given me some warning!
   B: What difference would that have made?
   A: ....

Review: vocabulary

Word List

annoyed
bad-tempered
cross
furious
grouchy
grumpy
hacked off (informal)
irritable
mad
moody
sulky
to picture
to visualise

Word Plus

'Take it easy!' *
'Use your imagination.'
in a bad mood
on the surface
out of control
shades of grey
to be caught off balance
to be really fed up
to be sick and tired of
to build up over (a long) time
to calm down
to cut somebody up
to feel trapped
to get on somebody's nerves
to go over the top
to keep your cool
to keep your head
to lose it / your cool / your
  temper
to make somebody cross / angry
to take a deep breath

*Phrases in inverted commas are conversational phrases.

---

43 Where would you put words from the Word List and Word Plus on the following line?

not angry | -- | very angry

44 Listen to the speakers on Track 27. How would you describe their mood using words from the Word List? The first one is done for you.

a I don't agree with you.   *grumpy*
b Will you stop doing that?
c I don't want to go to the party.
d Why should I tidy my room?
e If I hear one more word from you, you'll be in real trouble.
f You are not going to get away with this.
g Oh why did you have to do that?
h No! No! No! No!

Apart from the words themselves, what tells you how they feel?

●●● Pronunciation

45 Write sentences using phrases from Word Plus. Say them aloud. Mark the stressed syllables and say where the main stress / stresses go.

Example: *On the 'surface, things seemed O'K, but ...*

46 **The last time** Choose a phrase from Word Plus and tell your partner about the last time you or somebody was in that situation. Use as many words and phrases from the Word List and Word Plus as possible.

Example: *I was really fed up last Monday, and this is why ...*

UNIT 6
Looking forward

→ future perfect and continuous
→ seeing and believing
→ speculating

Vocabulary: seeing and believing (multiple meanings in words and phrases)

1 Meanings Look at these groups of sentences. Are the meanings of *see* and *believe* (in blue below) exactly the same for each sentence in a group?

a 1 Looking up, he thought he saw something flash across the night sky.
2 He could see that she was unhappy, although he didn't know why.
3 Let's see if this works, shall we?
4 Did you see the match on television last night?

b 1 Now that you've explained it, I can see where I went wrong.
2 Now that I am a parent, I see things differently.
3 I can't see her being happy in that job, can you?
4 It's the same old story. I've seen it all before.

c 1 I'll be seeing her tomorrow.
2 I saw Jane yesterday. She was waiting for a bus.
3 He's seeing a patient at the moment.
4 They've been seeing a lot of each other recently.

d 1 You shouldn't believe everything you read in the papers.
2 Police believe that the attacker was male and about 30 years old.
3 It's hard to believe that the pyramids were constructed without any modern machinery.
4 Some people believe in reincarnation (having more than one life).

2 Choose three of the sentences in Activity 1 to match the pictures *a–c*.

3 a In pairs Choose one of the groups (*a–d*) in Activity 1 and find a different way of saying each sentence in the group using different words.

b Using a dictionary or any other source, what other words can you think of which have a number of different but related meanings?

4 Belief and disbelief Where do items *a–k* fit on this line?

complete |--|complete
disbelief   belief

a I accept what you say.
b I don't believe you.
c I think that's ludicrous. / That's totally out of the question.
d I'll give you the benefit of the doubt.
e I'll take it at face value.
f I'm rather cynical about your claims. / I'm not so sure about this.
g I'll take your word for it.
h I'm going to take that with a pinch of salt.
i I'm fairly sceptical about all this.
j I'll take it on trust.
k I doubt what you are saying.

How many phrases with *give* or *take* can you find in the list?

5 In groups Look at the following beliefs and predictions.

- By the year 2050, we'll be able to fly on our own.
- People with blue eyes are more intelligent than people with green eyes.
- Learning English is easy if you speak a European language as a first language.
- There is a world something like our earth somewhere in the solar system.
- Eating meat is bad for you.

Add two more (reasonable or crazy) of your own.

6 In pairs Student A offers a prediction. Student B uses one of the words or phrases from Activity 4 to comment on it.

Example: STUDENT A: By the year 2050, we'll be able to fly on our own.
STUDENT B: I'm going to take that prediction with a pinch of salt.

7 Word in phrases Read the explanations of the phrases *in italics*. Complete the sentences with *believe* or *see*. The first one is done for you.

Sentence	Meaning
a ......*Believe*.... *it or not*, they have agreed to get married.	I know it sounds ridiculous, but ...
b I *don't* .... *a word* of it!	It's just not possible.
c I just don't .... *eye to eye* with her.	She and I don't agree.
d It's difficult to .... *the point of* the film.	I don't understand why the film was made.
e Justice must be done, and must be .... *to be done*.	It must be clear that justice is taking place.
f Let's .... *how it goes*, shall we?	We'll try it and deal with any problems if and when they happen.
g *If you* .... *that, you'll* .... *anything.*	You can't possibly think that this is true.
h .... *you later.*	Goodbye.
i .... *from this distance*, the events of 1973 are difficult to understand.	When we consider something a long time after the event, ...
j *She* .... *herself* as the leader of the group.	She thought of herself as ...
k The cinema? *I don't* .... *why not.*	Yes, I agree with the idea.
l You're saying he's changed the way he behaves? *I'll* .... *that when I see it.*	I really don't think it is true unless I see it with my own eyes.
m The moment he finishes the course, you won't .... *him for dust.*	He will leave immediately.
n When they saw the spaceship, they could *scarcely* .... *their eyes.*	They were very surprised.
o You want your car fixed? I'll .... *what I can do.*	I will do my best.

Speaking and writing: spoken vs written phrases

8 Look at the phrases with *believe*, *see*, *take* and *give* in Activities 4 and 7 and answer the following questions.

a Is each phrase formal or informal?
b Which of the phrases are you more likely to hear in conversation rather than read in print?
c Which of the phrases sound more like written phrases?

9 Take any two of the phrases you chose in Activity 8 and write a short conversation which includes both of them.

Listening: the paranormal

10 **In pairs** The words on the right are all examples of 'paranormal' beliefs. Discuss the meaning of the words with a partner.

Which ones are connected with talking about the future?
Do you know any other ways of knowing what is in the future?

astrology   ESP   faith-healing
fortune-telling   ghosts   magic
palmistry   tarot cards   telepathy   UFOs

11 Look at the items in Activity 10. Give them a score from 1 (= 'I believe in this') to 3 (= 'I don't believe in this').

Compare your answers in groups and explain your answers. Are you a 'believer' in the paranormal or a 'sceptic'?

12 Now listen to Track 28. Who is the 'believer'? Who is the 'sceptic'? Why?

13 Listen to Track 28 again and match the beginnings of the sentences in the first column with the ends of the sentences in the second column. The first one is done for you.

a The man thinks that 6	1 ... without mystery life is very boring.
b Dr Hyman became a sceptic when	2 ... is too cynical.
c The man believes that if	3 ... he deliberately read someone's palm badly and they said it was accurate.
d The woman thinks that the man	4 ... the woman.
e When the woman calls the man 'Mr Clever', she is	5 ... we hear things often enough, we start to believe them.
f The woman thinks that	6 ... there is a rational explanation for everything. *a*
g The man likes	7 ... making fun of him in a friendly way.

Who do you agree with? The man or the woman?

14 Listen to Track 28 again and complete this summary of the conversation. The first one is done for you.

Two people are eating (**a**) ......*pizza*...... in a (**b**) .... They seem to have a friendly relationship. They start talking about the (**c**) .... and the man surprises the woman by (**d**) .... that he doesn't believe in any paranormal phenomena. His cynicism (**e**) .... when he heard an American professor talking about an (**f**) .... from his youth. Against the protests of the woman, the man suggests that he (**g**) .... write a zodiac description of her without (**h**) .... anything about astrology. He believes that there is always a (**i**) .... explanation for everything, but that people start to (**j**) .... things if they see or hear them often enough. The woman thinks that it is a pity that the man is so (**k**) .... since it makes his life less (**l**) .... The man admits that there is only one mystery he doesn't have the (**m**) .... to.

Do you think the woman will give the man some of her pizza?

15 Meaning check What does the man say about:

a ... crystal balls?
b ... tea leaves?
c ... 'Your stars' in the newspaper?
d ... people who have lived 'past lives'?
e ... people who see flying saucers?
f ... people's responses to suggestion?

16 Complete these utterances from Track 28 with one word for each gap.

a So you .... that stuff now?

b Oh come on, you're not saying all that is .... ?

c .... doing so far?

d There isn't any mystery ....

e How do you figure .... ?

f You wouldn't believe it, ... ?

g Well if there isn't any mystery in life, ... ?

h Well now, that ....

17 Group writing Read the man's pretend horoscope from the recording for Track 28.

You are a person who longs to be happy but sometimes you're sad. You like to shine in conversation but sometimes it's difficult for you. You sometimes don't get the love you think you need, but next week you should concentrate all your efforts on someone near to you.

Write your own short general star sign description like the man did. Show it to other students in the class. How well does it describe them?

Functional language: speculating

18 Listen to Track 29. Two friends are discussing a football game. Complete their conversation with the word or words that you hear. The first one is done for you.

4 - 4 - 2

STEVE: What (**a**) *do you think about* the big game on Saturday?

MELISSA: Well, it's (**b**) .... really. United have great forward players and City have a great defence.

STEVE: (**c**) .... , but United haven't lost a game for three months. What are (**d**) .... of City winning?

MELISSA: As (**e**) .... see, City need to sit back and wait for United to make a mistake and then take it from there.

STEVE: I see (**f**) .... , but United have scored ten goals in their last three games and City have only scored two. Any (**g**) .... how City might score a goal or two?

MELISSA: (**h**) .... , they're not great goalscorers, but you (**i**) .... They have a new striker who might score one.

STEVE: What (**j**) .... the score will be?

MELISSA: I (**k**) .... , but if (**l**) .... , City will surprise a lot of people.

STEVE: I'm (**m**) .... , but if they do, I'll buy you lunch.

MELISSA: All right. You're on.

19 Now copy the table and write the phrases in blue that you completed in Activity 18 in the correct column. The first one is done for you.

Asking for speculation	Speculating	Accepting / Rejecting speculation
What do you think about ...		

20 Now write these expressions under the appropriate heading from Activity 19.

a Do you think ... ?
b Not a chance!
c If you ask me ...
d It's hard to say for sure, but ...
e You may be right there.
f You must be joking!
g What do you reckon?
h Do you suppose ... ?
i I reckon ...
j I wouldn't be surprised if ...
k Do you have any idea about ... ?
l Is there any chance that ... ?
m Do you really think so?

21 In pairs Speculate about the following things in the future.

Example: a

STUDENT A: Do you think people will drive electric cars in the future?

STUDENT B: I wouldn't be surprised if that happened. People are already driving hybrid gas / electric cars.

STUDENT A: I'm not convinced. I think ...

a Will people drive electric cars?
b Will people live on the moon?
c Will computers do all the work?
d Will people learn everything using computers?
e Will there be no television?
f Will there be a cure for all major illnesses?
g Will new illnesses appear?
h Will human beings be able to live forever?
i Will people be able to travel in time?
j Will there be human clones?

22 In pairs Work with a partner and use at least three of the expressions you noted in Activities 19 and 20 to have conversations about these topics.

a your future
b the weather
c an important sports event
d your next English test

Speaking: interview and role-play

23 In groups Find out who:

- ... has been to a fortune-teller.
- ... has never been but would like to go to a fortune-teller.
- ... believes that fortune-tellers can say meaningful things about the future.
- ... would like to be a fortune-teller.

24 In groups Complete the following tasks.

a Think of six questions you could ask a fortune-teller. Make sure you have the right words to ask an English-speaking fortune-teller.
b Think of six predictions that fortune-tellers are likely to make.

25 Role-play Divide the class into fortune-tellers and customers.

a Each fortune-teller must decide what method they want to use (palm-reading, crystal ball, tea-leaves, etc.).
b Each customer must decide what questions they want to ask.

Customers visit as many fortune-tellers as they can. Who is the best fortune-teller?

Reading: what kind of future?

26 Make two predictions about the future under these headings, similar to the example.

Humankind and medicine	Humankind and the universe
By 2030, the common cold will have been cured.	

Now read the text *Wings, babies and the pollution of planets* on page 66. Are your predictions included in it?

27 Read the text again and match the titles *a–h* to the paragraphs *1–8*. The first one is done for you.

a Making it a place where we can live   7
b Operations at a distance
c Finding a new place to live
d Right *and* wrong about the future
e His predictions are based on fact
f Grow your own new body parts?
g Less than 100 years away
h A top doctor makes predictions

Wings, babies and the pollution of planets

Predicting the future has always been a risky business, but recent claims are almost literally unbelievable. Or are they?

Back in 1949, the scientist Johan von Neumann made a statement which was both extraordinarily wrong and profoundly correct. 'It would appear,' he wrote, ' that we have reached the limits of what it is possible to achieve with computer technology, although I should be careful with such statements, as they tend to sound pretty silly in five years.' How true! Looking into the future has always been a dangerous occupation.

William Futrell isn't afraid to make predictions, however. As one of America's top plastic surgeons, he foresees a time when people will be flying around using their own wings, men will be having babies, and when we lose a leg in an accident the hospital will just grow a new one for us – using our own DNA.

You can't dismiss Futrell's predictions as pure fantasy, not given the fact that he is one of the leading authorities in his field. He has trained at least 20 professors and directors of US medical institutions. 'What's changed,' he says, 'is that we're mapping the human genome, the code for all life. And we can now extract stem cells for this kind of reconstructive work from a person's adipose tissue' (that's fat, to you and me).

When people dismiss Futrell's ideas as fanciful, he points out how far we've come. At the hospital where he works, robots take X-rays and other medical supplies to and from the wards; in Florida, in 2001, a doctor operated on a patient by remote control for the first time. Using computers and the Internet, he removed the gall bladder of a woman in France, 3,500 miles away. These things were once unimaginable.

And now, perhaps, we'll be able to grow wings and replace any body parts which become old or damaged. 'Believe me,' Futrell says, 'wings are not a long way off.' And he means it.

But even if we learn how to cure our bodies and end up living for ever, there isn't anything we can do about the fact that one day, as the sun gets hotter, this earth will be an uncomfortable place to live. According to astronomical engineer Robert Zubrin, the earth will become extinct 'unless we bring earth life out with us into the universe'. And the only place to go is Mars – it has water, carbon dioxide and nitrogen. But at the moment it is too cold and dry for human habitation. We'd die within seconds of stepping onto its surface. So we'll just have to do something about it.

'The first step to making Mars habitable is to warm it up,' says NASA scientist Chris McKay. His plan is to drop off a pollution-making machine that will scoot around the surface of the planet spewing out greenhouse gasses, thus shortcutting the slow process of evolution. The next step is oxygen – and what better oxygen-makers have we got than trees?!

McKay predicts that we'll be living on Mars some time in the next 80 years. 'By that time,' he says, 'the planet will have its algae and bacteria, and we'll have planted forests of trees. It'll be just right for human habitation.' The only problem is that we won't all fit. Mars is only a tenth the size of earth.

28 Fact check Answer these questions based on the text.

a Why was von Neumann both right and wrong?

b What are the two developments that mean we could now potentially grow a new limb?

c What was so unusual about the gall bladder operation in 2001?

d Why would humans die on Mars?

e How could Mars be made habitable for humans?

f How soon could we live on Mars, according to McKay?

29 Find these words in the text and explain their meaning.

a foresees (paragraph 2)

b leading (paragraph 3)

c mapping (paragraph 3)

d reconstructive (paragraph 3)

e fanciful (paragraph 4)

f extinct (paragraph 6)

g shortcutting (paragraph 7)

Language in chunks

30 Look at how these phrases are used in the text and then use them in the sentences which follow. You may have to change them to make them fit.

> to tend to   to dismiss something as   a long way off
> to warm something up   to scoot around   to spew out   by that time

a I don't think we'll be living on the moon in the near future – I think that's still ....

b We need to .... these vegetables in the microwave before we can eat them.

c Mars might be habitable by the year 2100, but .... most of us won't be alive anymore.

d I can't believe you .... that idea .... foolish. I think it's a great idea.

e My mother just bought a new bicycle so that she can .... town to do her shopping.

f Most people .... think that doctors have to be present to perform an operation, but that's not necessarily true.

g The old car was .... clouds of smoke when I saw it at the side of the motorway.

31 Noticing language Here are five predictions from the text. How many different kinds of the *will* future are used? What do they mean?

a People will be flying around using their own wings.

b Men will be having babies.

c The earth will become extinct.

d We'll be living on Mars.

e By this time we'll have planted forests of trees.

32 Which of the predictions do you think will come true and which do you think are not going to happen?

33 Discussion Talk about these questions in groups.

Would you like to:
- ... live on Mars?
- ... have wings?
- ... have a remote operation?
- ... see men having babies?

Grammar: future perfect and future continuous

34 Read the following sentences. Which describe (1) something that (we guess) is happening now, (2) plans for the future which are fixed and decided, (3) something that is going to be completed in the future and (4) something that will be in progress at a particular moment in the future? The first one is done for you.

a By this time tomorrow, we'll have finished all our exams. *3*

b Don't bother to go to his house. He'll have gone to work by now.

c Don't go over to their house now. They'll be having dinner.

d I'll be leaving on Friday. I have my ticket.

e I'll have been working in this bank for 20 years in January.

f The garage says they'll have fixed the car by 6.

g This time next week, we'll be flying to Paris.

h Will you be coming to our party?

Look at 6A–6D in the Mini-grammar. Do you want to change your answers?

35 Invent answers for the following questions using the future continuous or the future perfect. You can use **6A–6D in the Mini-grammar** to help you.

a Do you know where Peter is at the moment?
b How long have you been studying English?
c Do you have anything fixed up for the weekend?
d Do you think they're having a good time on holiday?
e Are you an optimist or a pessimist about the future of the world?
f What are your hopes for the next ten years?

36 What, if any, is the difference between the following pairs of sentences? Can you think of a context for each one?

a 1 Will you stay the night at our place?
  2 Will you be staying the night at our place?

b 1 When will you finish that letter?
  2 When will you have finished the letter?

c 1 How long will you have worked at this school by the end of the year?
  2 How long will you have been working at this school by the end of the year?

d 1 They'll be putting the baby to bed at about 7pm.
  2 Let's not arrive just yet. They'll be putting the baby to bed.

e 1 We will have completed our research by October.
  2 We'll be completing our research in October.

37 Complete these conversations with an appropriate form of the future. If more than one answer is possible, explain why.

a HOTEL GUEST: I'm calling to tell you that we (**1.** arrive) .... late. We (**2.** be) .... there by 10pm.
   RECEPTIONIST: Well, I (**3.** go) .... home by then, but I (**4.** leave) .... a note for the person on duty.

b JANE: Wow! I can hardly believe it – we (**5.** come) .... to this restaurant for 14 years in August.
   DAVID: Is it that long? The food's great so I guess we (**6.** eat) .... here for the next 14 years, too.

c MAUD: (**7.** stay) .... you .... in tonight, dear? I think I (**8.** go) ....over to Judy's house for a couple of hours.
   HENRY: Yes, I (**9.** work) .... all night. I have a report to finish. But I think it's too early to go over. They (**10.** not have) .... dinner and they (**11.** not put) .... the children to bed.

●● ● Pronunciation: strong and weak forms in contracted sentences

38 Listen to these sentences on Track 30. Underline the stressed words and notice the pronunciation of *have*.

a I'll have been working here for five years.
b By next March we'll have been married for three years.
c Do you think they'll have finished by now?
d I'm sure she'll have arrived home by now.
e Soon we'll have been living in this town for 15 years.
f Yes, I think they'll have put the kids to bed by now.

Practise saying the sentences with the same stress and the same pronunciation of *have*.

39 In pairs Ask and answer these questions. Ask at least two more questions after each answer.

Example: a

A: What will you be doing at this time next year?

B: I'll have finished university and I'll be working.

A: Where will you be working?

B: ...

a What will you be doing at this time next year?
b How long will you have worked at your present job by the end of the year?
c Where will you be going on your next vacation?
d How long will you have been studying English by the end of this course?
e What will you be doing in five years' time?
f Name two things you will have finished by the end of this month.

Writing: planning compositions

40 What will life be like in the year 2050? Look at this student's notes on different aspects of the future. Use her notes to write her introductory paragraph about a day in her life in 2050.

Home
- living on Mars
- people. – live. forever
- scientists – discover a way for people to live forever

Technology
- a robot – bring me coffee and breakfast in bed
- talk to friends on earth / moon on X-ray communicator

Food
- food – dehydrated / in pills
- nothing will grow on Mars

Compare your paragraph with a partner's and then look at Activity Bank 18 on page 164.

41 Make notes about your own ideas about life in the year 2050 under the following headings.

Compare your ideas in groups.

- technology
- work
- transportation
- entertainment
- science and medicine
- school
- clothing
- problems

42 Use your ideas to write about a day in your life in the year 2050. Include the following information.

- general life circumstances
- getting up in the morning
- your daily routine
- the end of the day

Discussion Read each other's texts and decide which one you think is most likely to be a true picture of life in the year 2050.

Review: grammar and functional language

43 Put this conversation in order. The first one is done for you.

a You must be joking! Everyone listens to CDs.
b Thanks, but do you know what I heard the other day?
c Yes, but there'll be new technology by then.
d No. What?
e Wow! You have a great collection of CDs.   1
f And CDs will become like vinyl records are now – antiques!
g They reckon that by the year 2010, CDs won't be used much.
h Well yes, I suppose that's possible.

44 Read these predictions from Ray Kurzweil, an inventor, entrepreneur and futurist. Complete them, using a form for talking about the future. You can look at Activities 34–37 for help.

a In the year 2009, the majority of text (create – *passive*) .... by speech recognition.
b By the year 2020, computers (exceed) .... the memory capacity of the human brain and we (be able) .... to buy these computers for $1000.
c In the year 2020, we (have) .... relationships with automated personalities and we (use) .... computers as teachers and companions.
d In the year 2029, information (feed) .... from computers straight into the human brain along direct neural connections. By that year, computers (read) .... all the world's literature.
e The difference between humans and computers (become) .... unclear by 2029 and when machines tell us they are conscious, we (believe) .... them.
f In the year 2049, we (eat) .... food that has been created by molecular engineering and there (be) .... no need for agriculture.
g By the year 2099, computers and humans (join) .... completely.

45 **In pairs** Which of these predictions do you think will come true and which ones do you think will not come true? Ask for speculation, speculate and accept and reject speculation about these predictions.

Review: vocabulary

Word List

extinct
fanciful
leading
ludicrous
mapping
reconstructive
sceptical
shortcutting
to believe
to foresee
to tend to

Word Plus

'I could scarcely believe my eyes.' *
'I don't believe a word of it.'
'I don't see why not.'
'I'll see what I can do.'
'Let's see how it goes.'
'See you later.'
'Seen from this distance ...'
'believe it or not'
a long way off
by that time
not to see someone for dust
to accept what someone says
to be seen to be done
to dismiss something as
to give someone the benefit of
  the doubt
to have seen something all before
to scoot around
to see a game
to see a lot of someone
to see a patient / client, etc.
to see eye to eye with someone
to see someone
to see something being possible
to see the point of something
to see things differently
to see where you went wrong
to see yourself as something
to spew out
to step onto
to take somebody's word for
  something
to take something at face value
to take something on trust
to take something with a pinch of
  salt
to warm something up
totally out of the question

*Phrases in inverted commas are
conversational phrases.

46 Look at the phrases in Word Plus. Which do you think are the most useful? Choose five that you can learn as chunks of language and use regularly.

Pronunciation

47 Word stress Underline the stressed syllable in these words.

a extinct
b fanciful
c ludicrous
d sceptical
e reconstructive
f shortcutting

Now listen to Track 31 and check your answers.

48 Listen to these phrases on Track 32 and mark which syllables have the main stress.

a pinch of salt
b face value
c benefit of the doubt
d eye to eye
e take it on trust

49 Listen to these sentences on Track 33 and note the syllables that are stressed.

a That's totally out of the question.
b I could scarcely believe my eyes.
c I don't see why not.
d I'll see what I can do.
e Let's see how it goes.
f See you later.

50 Look back over the unit and use the words and phrases to talk about the future predictions that were made in the unit.

Example: STUDENT A: People living on Mars? I think it's totally out of the question.

STUDENT B: Really? I see it being possible in the future. When the machinery is better.

UNIT 7

Out of the blue

→ *needs doing | have something done*
→ colours
→ taking something to be fixed

Vocabulary: colours

1 **In pairs** Look at *Nataraja* by the British artist Bridget Riley. You have one minute.

a Now cover the picture with your hand. How many colours were in it? Make a list. (If you have any problem with the names of colours, look at Activity Bank 10 on page 160.)

b Look at the picture again. Did you remember all the colours?

c Do you like the painting? Why? Why not?

d Which room of your house would you put the painting in? Why?

2 **Language research** Using a dictionary or another source, join the following adjectives, used to describe colours, with a colour.

> brilliant dark faded bright
> pale dull light muddy

Which of your phrases describes (a) a strong colour, (b) a colour that is not strong, or (c) a colour that could be either strong or weak?

3 Describe things (objects, landscapes ...) you know or have seen, using as many words from Activity 2 as you can.

4 Match the following colour descriptions with the people's clothes.

> beige   coffee-coloured   cream   golden brown
> khaki   lime-green   mustard   scarlet

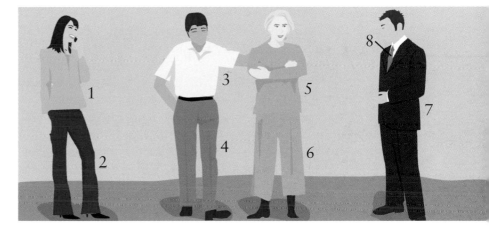

5 **In pairs** Ask your partner to describe the colour of some or all of the following.

- their bicycle, motorcycle or car
- a room in their house, and the things in it
- their favourite article of clothing
- the stationery they carry with them to class
- their bag or briefcase

6 **Colour meaning**

a What colour do people from your culture associate with the following emotions or events?

- anger
- cold
- cowardice
- death
- embarrassment
- fear
- jealousy
- purity
- sadness / depression

b Do you see colours in the same way?

Do other cultures associate colours in the same way?

c In your community:

- ... what colour do women traditionally get married in?
- ... what colour do people traditionally wear at funerals?
- ... are there any other colours for special occasions?

7 Metaphor Choose the correct colour for each gap (*a–o*). The first one is done for you.

black   blue   green   red   white   yellow

After an evening of painting the town (**a**) ....*red*.... (when we'd had a wonderful time going from club to club celebrating), I went round to my friend Matilda's house. The night was as (**b**) .... as ink, but I could see that the lights were on. Just as I got to the door, I heard the sound of raised voices and then the door opened and Henry (one of Matilda's colleagues) ran out of the house. In the light I could see that he was as (**c**) .... as a sheet. 'Henry,' I called when I caught up with him, 'what's the matter?' And he told me his story.

That morning, he had spoken to Matilda and they had realised that they were in love. I was (**d**) .... with envy. Matilda was absolutely beautiful. But that evening, while I was in town with the others, her father had come in just as they were kissing on the sofa. Matilda went bright (**e**) .... with embarrassment, and Henry jumped to his feet.

Matilda's father just saw (**f**) .... He started shouting. 'That's it,' he yelled, 'I've caught you (**g**) ....-handed!' and then pulled a pistol from his pocket. That's when Henry ran. 'You're (**h**) ....!' the older man shouted after him. 'Just a horrible little coward. Go away and never come back!'

By now the poor man was shivering, (**i**) .... with cold. I gave him my coat. 'The thing is,' he said unhappily, 'what am I going to do now?'

Henry walked around in a (**j**) .... mood for days because he thought he would never be able to see Matilda again. But then, out of the (**k**) .... , he got a call from her. It was a complete surprise. 'I'm sorry about my father,' she said, 'he's really not as (**l**) .... as he is painted. Everyone says he's cruel, but he isn't really. I know he screamed (**m**) .... murder at you, and I did try to talk to him about it. At first he just wouldn't listen to me. "You can go on till you're (**n**) .... in the face," he said, and I was about to give up when my mother persuaded him to let us see each other again. So now he's given us the (**o**) .... light. Do you want to come over this evening?'

'Will your father be at home?' Henry asked.

8 Complete the colour metaphors and then match them with their meanings. The first one is done for you.

a to be blue with ... *cold*
b to be in a black ...
c to be not as black as ...
d out of the ...
e to be ...
f to be as black ...
g to be as white ...
h to be green with ...
i to catch someone ...
j to give someone the ...
k to go (bright) ...
l to go on until you are ...
m to paint ...
n to scream / yell ...
o to see ...

1   to be better than people say
2   to be very dark
3   to be very gloomy
4   to be very jealous
5   to behave as if you are very afraid
6   to blush
7   to continue for some time without having any effect
8   to go out and behave exuberantly
9   to look very frightened
10 to look / feel very cold
11 to allow someone to do something
12 to shout very loudly for some time
13 to suddenly get very angry
14 to surprise someone in the middle of doing something wrong
15 with no warning

9 Storytelling Take one of the colour metaphors and use it as the title of a story about your life. Make notes about your story.

Use your notes to tell your story to the class. Include other colour metaphors too, if you can.

Reading: colour effect

10 Read the following sentences. They each summarise one of the paragraphs in the text *The pink police station*. What do you think each paragraph will say?

a Choose an appropriate colour for whatever you're doing
b Choosing room colours is important
c Colour and the nervous system
d Colour preferences reveal personality
e Good colour choices match eye colour

Read the text. Match the summaries with the correct paragraphs.

THE PINK POLICE STATION

If colour is energy, is blue right for the dining room?

1 Now here's a theory: you and I are energy. We are colour. When we're feeling fed up and run-down, this may mean that we have too much or too little colour in us. Each of us is inadvertently attracted to one colour more than others, and the reason for this is that colours have energy in them, and that is what draws us to them. Every colour affects our cell structures, sending very fine chemical vibrations on to our nervous system, which via the pituitary gland directs our body. For instance, blue light makes our cells expand but red light makes them contract. Each colour in the spectrum, in other words, has its own special effect on us and as we absorb its energy it travels via the nervous system to the part of the body that needs it. And so, as people look for alternatives to mainstream conventional medicine which they think is unsatisfactory and seek new ways of making themselves well, they – we – have turned to colour therapy as a new way of chilling out, a way of restoring our individual states of optimum well-being and restoring an appropriate physical and mental balance.

2 You think that sounds too extreme? Well, according to the Swiss psychologist Max Luscher, colour and personality are so closely linked that he developed a test to reveal character traits by the sequence in which a subject chooses colours. The test is now used by psychologists and governments across the world – and a version of it even appears on the Internet for anyone to use.

3 Top colour therapist Angela Wright agrees that colour elicits a strong psychological response – which is why the appearance of rooms in a house is so vital to its inhabitants' well-being. 'The biggest mistake interior designers make is not to take into account the personality of the client whose home they are decorating and the activity associated with a particular room', she says. For instance, if you painted your dining room blue, then, says Wright, 'you'd have very boring dinner parties because that colour is calming. As a result, everyone would be on their best behaviour.' One police force in southern Britain was so convinced by theories of colour that they painted their cells pink – a nurturing, romantic colour – to try and stop their temporary guests feeling aggressive.

4 According to fashion expert 'Annie', a columnist for Britain's *Observer* newspaper, certain colours suit people better than others, and so care should be taken when selecting clothes. There's nothing new about that of course. People with good dress sense have always worried about what to wear, and colours go in and out of fashion. But Annie goes further than this. She suggests that the best colours are those that complement or reflect the wearer's eye colour. If you have hazel eyes, for example, certain shades of green are just right. However, in what seems like a contradictory point of view, she is adamant that people should be allowed to wear whatever colours they feel good about, even if they are not appropriate: 'I know people who don't really suit red, for example,' she wrote in a recent column, 'yet derive enormous pleasure from wearing it, and who has the right to tell them otherwise?' Well no one has the right, but perhaps it would be kind!

5 So there it is. Colour counts, and it's important for all of us. If the kitchen needs repainting, or if you're thinking of having the living room done; if you feel like having your hair dyed or you just want to go out and spend money on clothes, work out what colour suits your personality and your looks best: learn which ones will affect your nervous system and how they will do this. Take colour seriously and it will improve your life – and make you feel good about it too.

11 Discussion Talk about the following questions.

- How do colours affect you psychologically?
- Would you be interested in taking the computer version of Max Luscher's colour test?
- Do you agree that a room's colour affects what happens there?
- How do you personally choose the colour of your clothes?
- Will you take the advice in the last paragraph?

12 Fact check Read the text on page 73 again and choose the best answer.

a The energy of a particular colour:
1 ... makes us feel fed up.
2 ... attracts us to the colour.
3 ... always expands our cells.

b People are attracted to colour therapy because:
1 ... they are disillusioned with their lives.
2 ... they've lost confidence in normal doctors.
3 ... their doctors say colour is good for them.

c Max Luscher's test:
1 ... is now only used by psychologists in Switzerland.
2 ... reveals the sequence in which governments use the Internet.
3 ... is designed to show what kind of a person you are.

d Interior designers make mistakes because they:
1 ... don't consider what kind of people they are designing for.
2 ... understand why they should paint dining rooms blue.
3 ... are convinced by the theory that pink calms people down.

e The best colours for clothes:
1 ... are hazel and green if your eyes are blue.
2 ... go with the colour of the wearer's eyes.
3 ... are shades of red that the wearer likes.

13 Vocabulary Which of the words in blue in the text on page 73 means the following?

a get
b gets something from someone
c look good with
d looking after, caring for
e ordinary
f relaxing completely
g small shaking movements
h the opposite of *expand*
i very sure
j without meaning to

Language in chunks

14 What do the following phrases from the text *The pink police station* mean?

a has its own special effect on us (paragraph 1)
b seek new ways of (paragraph 1)
c elicits a strong psychological response (paragraph 3)
d on their best behaviour (paragraph 3)
e has the right to (paragraph 4)

15 Re-write the following sentences using the phrases in blue.

a I don't like brilliant sunshine. *has a bad effect*
b Interior designers want to combine colours. *seeking new ways of*
c The colour red seems to make bulls react. *elicits a strong psychological response*
d When their grandmother comes to tea, the children are always good. *on their best behaviour*
e No one can order me about. I'm a free agent. *has the right to*

Speaking: making joint decisions

16 Look at the picture of the student common room and the items that can go in it.

In small groups You are going to live in student rooms and this is the common room (sitting room, TV room, etc.) that you share. Decide on the following.

a You can have any six of the items from the list. Which will you choose? ('Four chairs' or 'two armchairs' count as one item.)

b What colours will you choose for:
- ... the carpet?
- ... the curtains?
- ... the walls?
- ... the ceiling?

Explain the reasons for your decisions.

Example: I think we should have a brown carpet, because the coffee stains won't show.

17 Compare your decisions with other groups.

Listening: the new house

18 Listen to the conversation on Track 34 and answer the questions.

a Where are the speakers flying from?
b Where are they flying to?
c What's the weather going to be like on the journey?
d What do you know about Carol? Mark?
e How does Carol feel about getting home? Why?

19 Listen to Track 34 again. Copy and complete the table about the problems that Carol and her husband have with their house.

What part of the house?	What's the problem?	Who's going to fix it?
a		
b		
c		
d		
e		

20 Listen to Track 35. Answer the following questions.

a What colours are mentioned in the conversations between Bob and Carol? What are they for?
b Where is Bob when he calls the first time?
c What does Bob want Carol to decide about the first time he calls?
d Where is Bob when he calls for the second time?
e What does Bob want Carol to decide the second time he calls?
f What do you think Carol feels about returning home? Why?

Language in chunks

21 Look at the following sentences from Tracks 34 and 35 and complete the tasks.

a I'm not looking forward to getting home.
b We can't afford any more.
c I need you to make a decision.
d It depends on what light beige looks like.
e Looks like we're in for a bumpy ride.
f I'm glad we're out of it.
g For Heaven's sake, what is it this time?
h I haven't the slightest idea.

- Who says the sentences in the conversation?
- Explain what the phrases in blue mean as if you were explaining them to someone in a lower-level class.
- **In pairs** Use the sentences in two- or three-line exchanges.

Grammar: *needs doing*; *have something done*

22 Look at the pictures and say what needs to be done / what needs doing using the following verbs (you can use some of the verbs more than once).

change   clean   cut   fix   iron   mend   paint   repair   replace   respray

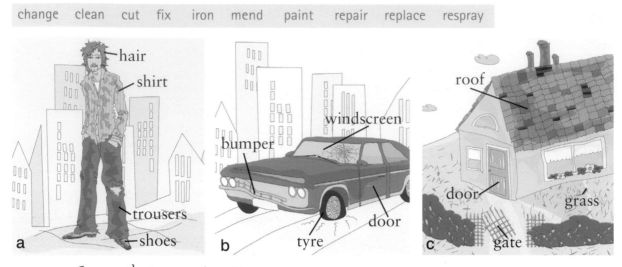

Example: *a The man's hair needs cutting.*

Look at 7A–B in the Mini-grammar. Do you want to change your answers?

Word Choice: *fix, mend, repair* and *service*

23 Look at the Word Choice notes for *fix*, *mend*, *repair* and *service* on page 57 in the booklet.

24 Note down the appropriate form of *fix*, *mend*, *repair* or *service* needed to complete these sentences.

   a The washing machine needs ... . It works, but it hasn't been looked at for two years.
   b You want me to ... your car, mate? I reckon I could do it sometime this afternoon, yeah.
   c In conclusion, I think we need to ... the damage to the building as soon as possible.
   d She's ... her dress at the moment. It got ripped when she climbed over the fence.
   e Your car should be ... every 10,000 miles.
   f When do you think the council will ... that hole in the road?
   g Why do you want to change things? You know that old saying, 'If it ain't broke, don't ... it.'
   h I wouldn't bother to have the radio ... . I'd just buy a new one. It's cheaper.
   i I'm taking my shoes to that shop on the corner. They need ... .

25 Read what Bruno is saying and complete the tasks which follow.

> I'm going to mend my shirt. Then I'm going to have my hair cut and dyed blond. Then I'm going to have my car serviced. And then I'm going to the theatre because we're having our new production designed by the famous artist Patricia Langley, and I have to meet her.

   a Which task is Bruno going to do himself? Which tasks is someone else going to do?
   b When do we include the name of the person who is going to do the task?
   c Where do we put adjectives which give details about the task?
   d What order do the following elements go in? Copy the diagram and complete it.

(optional) adjective   by somebody
done   have   something

     +   +   +   +

Look at 7C–D in the Mini-grammar. Do you want to change your answers?

26 Look at the people and say what they are going to have done.

Example: *a Ruth's going to have her dresses cleaned.*

27 Read **7D in the Mini-grammar** and then complete the sentences which follow with whichever is most appropriate, *get* or *have*. The first one is done for you.

a ... *Get* your teeth fixed – or they'll get worse.
b He didn't ... the tree cut down in time. It fell into the neighbour's garden.
c He ... his car resprayed a bright yellow. Now he wishes he hadn't bothered.
d I ... my leg operated on – that's why I can't play football at the moment.
e I think you should ... your brakes looked at. That bicycle is not safe.
f I'm going to ... my picture taken for a passport photograph.
g I'm going to ... this shirt dyed mauve. I think it'll go well with my suit.
h I'm never going to ... the heater repaired – I've rung the company at least 20 times.
i If you don't ... your thesis checked by your supervisor soon, you'll never be able to finish it.
j She ... her hair dyed pink yesterday.

28 Say what you would like to have done to some or all of the following.

• your house • your hair • your car
• your clothes • your bicycle • something else

Example: *I'd like to have the brakes on my bicycle fixed.*

29 Match the two columns to make sentences about Caroline's nightmare day.

a She got her mobile phone
b She got her parents' car
c She had her bag
d She had her coat
e She had her dinner
f She had her hat
g She had her photo

1 ... blown off in the wind.
2 ... confiscated by the history teacher.
3 ... eaten by the dog.
4 ... ripped by a passing cyclist.
5 ... stolen on the way to college.
6 ... taken before she was ready.
7 ... towed away by the police.

• Are the sentences describing something that Caroline organised or bad experiences that happened to her?
• Is the *have* construction the same as Activities 22–28? Are the meanings the same or different?
• Have any of these things (or something similar) ever happened to you? Tell your partner about it.

Functional language: taking something to be fixed

30 Listening Listen to Track 36. Which is the correct picture?

31 Listen to Track 36 again and answer the questions.

a What two problems is the car owner worried about?
b Who's going to look at the car?
c When will the car be ready, according to Mr Bolton?

32 Complete these sentences and questions from the conversation (one word per gap).

a MR BOLTON: Back .... a .... , Charlie.
b CLIENT: Well, there's .... coming from the ....
c CLIENT: Whenever I .... into fourth gear, it .... a .... click.
d MR BOLTON: Can you .... it .... us?
e CLIENT: When can I .... ?
f CLIENT: But you will .... it .... ?
g MR BOLTON: I'll try and .... it .... by 4 o'clock.
h MR BOLTON: How does .... ?
i CLIENT: I'll come .... 4 then.

33 Do sentences *a–r* below belong in the first or the second column? The first one is done for you.

What the customer might say

What the service provider might say
a, ...

a Can you leave it overnight?
b Could you have a look at the windscreen wipers?
c I can't get it to play CDs.
d I think I've got a flat tyre.
e I was wondering if you could fix my bike.
f I'll get it looked at.
g I'll have that seen to.
h I've brought my car to be serviced.
i It doesn't seem to want to play tapes.
j The brakes don't seem to be working.
k The radio doesn't work.
l There seems to be a noise coming from the engine.
m We don't seem to have a record of that.
n What seems to be the problem?
o What's the name?
p When do you need it by?
q When I turn it on, nothing happens.
r Whenever I try and record onto a minidisc, it just doesn't work.

● ● ● **Pronunciation** /s/, /z/ and /tʃ/

34 Look at the following words from the conversation on Track 36. Divide them into three columns, depending on the pronunciation of the letters in blue.

change   Charlie   checked   course
depends   noise   outside   perhaps
promises   said   suppose   switch   us

Check your answers by listening to Track 37.

35 Choose one of the three sounds. Who can think of the most words with the sound in 60 seconds?

36 Vocabulary Choose one of the following objects from the list.

- car
- bicycle
- stereo
- mobile phone
- watch
- printer
- laptop computer

In pairs Write about things that often / sometimes go wrong with these items.

37 Using language from Activities 32 and 33, make conversations in which Student A takes one of the items from Activity 36 to be fixed.

Writing: instructions

38 Discussion When you buy a new item of technology (cellphone, microwave oven, computer, digital watch, etc.):

- ... how easy is it to make it work?
- ... how easy is it to read the instructions that are given? Why?

39 Look at the pictures on page 79 and find an instruction that matches them.

Setting up your Sony notebook
1 *Unpacking your Sony notebook*
Unpack your Sony notebook and check the complete contents of the box. The letters A to H correspond to the letters on the cover flap image.
A) Main Unit   E) Rechargable battery pack
B) AC adapter   F) Sony Documentation pack
C) Power cord   G) Phone cable
D) Product Recovery CD-ROMS   H) Phone plug (country-specific)

2 *Inserting the battery pack*
Before inserting the battery pack, please turn off your computer.
Move the lock lever on the bottom of the computer to the UNLOCK

position. Align the grooves on the side of the battery with the tabs on the back of the computer, and slide the battery towards the computer until it clicks into place. Slide the lock lever into the LOCK position to secure the battery on the computer.
The battery pack supplied with your computer is not fully charged at the time of purchase.

3 *Attaching the power cord*
You may use either AC power or a battery pack as a power source. Plug the AC adapter cable into the DC connector of the computer. Plug the prongs into the AC outlet.

4 *Opening the notebook*
Lift the cover in the direction of the arrow.

5 *Starting the notebook*
Press the power button on the computer to turn on the power. The power indicator turns on.

For detailed information, refer to the printed documentation or have a look at the **VAIO Info Centre** installed in your hard disk drive.

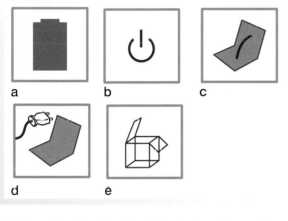

40 **Without looking back at the instructions above, can you re-create any of them, using the words and phrases in the boxes (and other words like auxiliary verbs, prepositions, etc.)?**

Verbs check insert lift plug press turn off unpack

Nouns AC adapter cable battery pack computer contents of the box cover DC In connector notebook power button

Now look back at the instructions. Were you right?

41 **Choose one of the following tasks and complete Tasks *a–c*.**

• recording a message on your telephone answering machine
• using a washing machine
• sending an email
• using a carwash
• something else that you choose

a Make a list of the words you need in your language and then find English equivalents.
b Make a list of the things that need to be done and put them in order.
c Write instructions.

Review: grammar and functional language

42 **Complete the conversation with one word for each gap. The first one is done for you.**

A: Good morning, sir. What can I (a) ....*do*.... for you?
B: Well, it's this watch of mine. It (b) .... seem to be working.
A: It probably (c) .... cleaning, sir.
B: Yes, I expect it (d) ....
A: Well, sir, can I have a look?
B: Yes, of (e) .... , sorry.
A: Hmm, now let's have a look. (f) ....
B: Interesting? Why?
A: How long have you had this (g) .... , sir?
B: About 62 years. Exactly 62 years, actually.
A: Fantastic. It's a real museum piece. But you (h) .... have brought it to me earlier, sir, if you don't mind me saying.
B: No, no, not at all. I was (i) .... to (j) .... it fixed about 20 years ago, I think, but then I (k) .... about it.
A: Forgot about it?
B: Yes, but I can't (l) .... why.
A: Ah, I see. But anyway it needs (m) ...., as I said, and I need to do a bit of (n) .... on the cogs and gears of the mechanism. Can you leave it with me for a (o) .... days?
B: Umm, well I ...
A: When do you (p) .... it back?
B: By Thursday next week at the (q) ....
A: That won't be a (r) .... , sir.
B: Good. Right then, now I'm going to have my hair (s) .... and then I'm going to the tailors – I'm (t) .... (u) to .... a new suit made for me, you see.
A: That sounds enjoyable.
B: Oh I don't know. But I'm (v) .... a new girlfriend out to dinner next week so I need to look smart, don't you think?
A: I suppose so, sir, yes.

Review: vocabulary

Word List

adamant	khaki
beige	light (+ colour)
bright (+ colour)	lime-green
brilliant (+ colour)	muddy (+ colour)
chilling out	mustard
coffee-coloured	nurturing
conventional	pale (+ colour)
cream	scarlet
dark (+ colour)	to complement
dull (+ colour)	to contract
faded (+ colour)	to derive
golden brown	vibrations
inadvertently	

Word Plus

'for Heaven's sake' *
'I haven't the slightest idea.'
as black as he is painted
as black as ink
as white as a sheet
blue with cold
can't afford
green with envy
in a black mood
it depends on what X is like
'out of the blue'
to be in for a bumpy ride
to be on your best behaviour
to be out of it
'to be yellow'
to catch someone red-handed
to elicit a strong psychological
  response
to give someone the green light
to go bright red
to go on until you are blue in
  the face
to have its own special effect on
  somebody
to have the right to
to look forward to
to make a decision
'to paint the town red'
'to scream blue murder'
'to see red'
to seek out new ways of doing
  something

*Phrases in inverted commas are
conversational phrases.

43 Find words or phrases in the Word List and Word Plus that make you feel warm, lukewarm (= neither hot nor cold) or cold. Explain why you feel like this about the words and phrases.

Example: *For me, 'beige' is a cold colour.*

Pronunciation

44 Copy and complete the table with as many words as you can from the Word List and Word Plus.

/eɪ/ – paid	/aɪ/ – fight

Check your answers by listening to Track 38.

Add more words of your own to the list.

45 Look at the phrases in Word Plus. How many words (apart from *to*) can you find with the schwa sound /ə/?

Example: *as black as he's painted*

a What kind of word or syllable is the schwa used for?
b Which syllables are stressed in the phrases you have chosen?

Check your answers by listening to Track 39.

46 **Fish bowl** Write the phrases from Word Plus on separate pieces of paper. Put the pieces of paper in a bowl.

In pairs, have conversations about one of the following topics.

- travelling by aeroplane
- favourite colours
- favourite songs or paintings
- favourite possession

The pairs must keep the conversation going.

At certain points, the student who is speaking takes a piece of paper from the bowl. They have to use the phrase on the piece of paper immediately as they continue the conversation.

UNIT 8
Food for thought

→ using articles
→ idioms (food and drink)
→ making a complaint

Reading: what we eat

1 In groups Look at these different pictures of food and discuss the questions below.

1 meat
2 fish

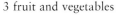

3 fruit and vegetables

4 sweets and desserts

5 fast food

6 vegetarian food

Which of these foods:

a ... are good for you?
b ... are bad for you?
c ... have you eaten?
d ... would you like to eat?
e ... would you not like to eat?
f ... are 'comfort food'?

2 Read the short extracts (*1–4*) from different websites and match the extract to the website (*a–d*) it came from.

a www.mercola.com
  the website of a medical doctor who specializes in nutrition and natural remedies

b www.monsantoafrica.com
  a company which produces genetically-modified (GM) crops

c www.greenpeace.org
  an organisation in favour of protecting the environment

d www.vegan.org
  a website dedicated to the arguments and health of people who don't use or eat animals

1 What is a vegan? A vegan (pronounced VEE-gun) is someone who avoids using or consuming animal products. While vegetarians avoid flesh foods, vegans also avoid dairy products and eggs, as well as fur, leather, wool, feathers and cosmetics or chemical products tested on animals.

Why vegan? Veganism, the natural extension of vegetarianism, is an integral component of a cruelty-free lifestyle. Living vegan provides numerous benefits to animals' lives, to the environment and to our own health – through a healthy diet and lifestyle.

The consumption of animal fats and proteins has been linked to heart disease, colon and lung cancer, osteoporosis, diabetes, kidney disease, hypertension, obesity and a number of other debilitating conditions. Cows' milk contains ideal amounts of fat and protein for young calves, but far too much for humans. And eggs are higher in cholesterol than any other food, making them a leading contributor to cardiovascular disease. The American Dietetic Association reports that vegetarian / vegan diets are associated with reduced risks for all of these conditions.

2 Genetic engineering of food is a risky process. Current understanding of genetics is extremely limited and scientists do not know the long-term effects of releasing these unpredictable foods into our environment and our diets. Yet, GE ingredients are freely entering our food without sufficient regulations and without the consent and knowledge of the consumer.

Although transnational companies and their political supporters want us to believe that this food is safe and thoroughly tested, growing awareness of the dangers from GE food has started a global wave of rejection by consumers, farmers and food companies in many of the world's largest food markets. Due to consumer pressure, supermarkets have taken GE food from their shelves, global food companies have removed GE ingredients from their products and leading pig and poultry producers have promised not to feed animals with GE feed.

3 Along with the saturated fat and cholesterol scares of the past several decades has come the notion that vegetarianism is a healthier dietary option for people. It seems as if every health expert and government health agency is urging people to eat fewer animal products and consume more vegetables, grains, fruits and legumes. Along with this advice have come assertions and studies supposedly proving that vegetarianism is healthier for people and that meat consumption causes sickness and death. Several medical authorities, however, have questioned these data, but their objections have been largely ignored.

Many of the vegetarian claims cannot be substantiated and some are simply false and dangerous. There are benefits to vegetarian diets for certain health conditions and some people function better on less fat and protein, but, as a practitioner who has dealt with several former vegans (total vegetarians), I know full well the dangerous effects of a diet devoid of healthful animal products.

4 What has come to be called 'biotechnology' and the genetic manipulation of agricultural products is nothing new.

Indeed, it may be one of the oldest human activities. For thousands of years, from the time human communities began to settle in one place, cultivate crops and farm the land, humans have manipulated the genetic nature of the crops and animals they raise. Crops have been bred to improve yields, enhance taste and extend the growing season.

Each of the 15 major crop plants, which provide 90 percent of the globe's food and energy intake, has been extensively manipulated and modified over the millennia by countless generations of farmers intent on producing crops in the most effective and efficient ways possible.

Today, biotechnology holds out promise for consumers seeking quality, safety and taste in their food choices; for farmers seeking new methods to improve their productivity and profitability; and for governments and non-governmental public advocates seeking to stave off global hunger, assure environmental quality, preserve bio-diversity and promote health and food safety.

3 **Fact check** Who believes these things: vegans, Greenpeace, Dr Mercola or Monsanto?

a Humans need to eat some animal products. *Dr Mercola*
b Humans do not have to eat meat.
c Genetically-modified food is bad for us.
d Genetic engineering could feed the world.
e Vegetarian diets can be more healthy than meat-based ones.
f Genetic engineering is not a new thing.
g We do not know what the effects of GM food on humans are.

4 Match the words from the extracts *1–4* with their synonym or definition (*1–11*).

a numerous (extract 1)   4
b risky (extract 2)
c consent (extract 2)
d urging (extract 3)
e objections (extract 3)
f substantiated (extract 3)
g cultivate (extract 4)
h yields (extract 4)
i enhance (extract 4)
j millennia (extract 4)
k advocates (extract 4)

1 grow
2 thousands of years
3 proved
4 many, lots of
5 dangerous
6 trying to persuade, strongly advising
7 productivity, harvests
8 permission, agreement
9 expressions of disapproval
10 supporters
11 improve

Language in chunks

5 **Complete the phrases *a–g* with as many of the words and phrases below as you can.**

condition   illness   sickness   disease   wave of rejection   hunger   terrorism   protest   destroying   winning   emotion   producing   protein   fat   animal products   vitamins   dying earlier   poverty   living longer

a a debilitating ...
b associated with ...
c global ...
d stave off ...
e intent on ...
f devoid of ...
g linked to ...

6 **Use one of the expressions you made in Activity 5 to complete these sentences as in the example.**

a The United Nations got together to try to do something about the number of poor people in the world in a conference on ...
global poverty.
b He ate a diet which was ... , because he knew of the dangers of fat to his health.
c Exercising every day has been ... . Experts say this can add five more years to your life.
d She was in a wheelchair, because of ... that she had had for 20 years.
e The football player was ... . This was his last chance before he retired from the game.
f She ate a chocolate bar to ... , as she would not be eating dinner for at least another two hours.
g Obesity has often been ... , probably because of all the illnesses that it can cause.

7 **Make other sentences using the expressions.**

8 Noticing language Look at these sentences from the four texts in Activity 2 and notice which nouns have a definite article, an indefinite article or no article.

a The consumption of animal fats and proteins has been linked to heart disease.
b Genetic engineering of food is a risky process.
c I know full well the dangerous effects of a diet devoid of animal products.
d The genetic manipulation of agricultural products is nothing new.

Find at least one more example from the texts of the use of the definite article, the indefinite article and no article before a noun.

9 In groups Answer these questions.

- What foods do you eat that are good for you?
- What foods do you eat that are bad for you?
- Do you approve of GM foods?
- What do you think about vegetarianism and veganism?
- How can we solve the problem of world hunger?

Vocabulary: food and drink (idioms)

10 Copy this nutritional pyramid and complete it with as many examples as you can think of.

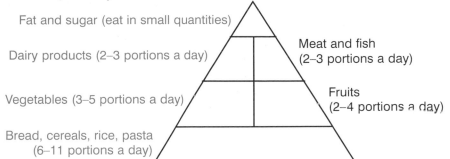

Fat and sugar (eat in small quantities)
Dairy products (2–3 portions a day)
Meat and fish (2–3 portions a day)
Vegetables (3–5 portions a day)
Fruits (2–4 portions a day)
Bread, cereals, rice, pasta (6–11 portions a day)

Compare your list with a partner.

11 Discussion Talk about the following questions.

a What does the pyramid suggest about the kind of foods we should eat?
b Does your average weekly food consumption look like this pyramid?
c How important is what you eat to you?

12 Food idioms Using a dictionary or any other source, complete the following idioms (in blue) by using words from the box. You will need to use some of the words more than once. You might have to change their form. The first one is done for you.

apple bacon beans bread cake cucumber egg
fruit cake hot cakes milk mustard pancake pie tea

a 'You want me to put up a picture? That's easy. It's a piece of ... cake.'
b I don't like him much, but I'm still nice to him – I know which side my ... is buttered.
c 'Don't think about the past because you can't change it. There's no point in crying over spilt ... .'
d I don't think we should give her the job. She's not good enough. She just can't cut the ... .
e I told a joke and absolutely nobody laughed. The joke fell as flat as a ... .
f 'If this plan goes wrong, you should have another one ready: don't put all your ... in one basket.'
g Mrs Allen's son is her favourite person. In fact he's the ... of her eye.
h My brother's crazy. He's as nutty as a ... .
i My friend helped me out of a really awkward and dangerous situation. He saved my ... .
j My sister is really happy at the moment, and fantastically energetic. I've never seen her so full of ... .
k Playing the piano? That's easy. In fact it's as easy as ... !
l She told me to do it, she encouraged me, even though I didn't want to. She ... me on.
m Some people like gardening, but I don't. It's just not my cup of ... .
n This new kitchen gadget is fantastic. It's the best thing since sliced ... .
o This year, the new iPods have been a fantastic success in the shops. They've been selling like ... .

p When she confronted him in front of all those people, his expression didn't change at all. He just stood there as cool as a ... .

q It was supposed to be a secret, but she couldn't help spilling the ... to her best friend.

r 'If you don't do your homework, you can't go to the concert. You can't have your ... and eat it too!'

13 Look at the idioms in Activity 12. Are any of them similar to idioms in your language? If not, how can you say these things idiomatically?

Speaking and writing: when words are used

Some words are much more common in spoken English than in written English – or vice versa.

14 Look at the dictionary entries from the *Longman Dictionary of Contemporary English*. Are the words used more in spoken or in written English, according to the dictionary makers? How do you know in each case?

fan·cy¹ S3 /'fænsi/ *v* fancied, fancying, fancies [T]
1 LIKE/WANT *BrE informal* to like or want something, or want to do something; ⊟ feel like: *Fancy a quick drink, Emma?* | **fancy doing sth** *Sorry, but I don't fancy going out tonight.*
2 SEXUAL ATTRACTION *BrE informal* to feel sexually attracted to someone: *All the girls fancied him.*
3 fancy yourself *BrE informal* to behave in a way that shows you think you are very attractive or clever: *That bloke on the dance floor really fancies himself.*
4 fancy yourself (as) sth *BrE* to believe, usually wrongly, that you have particular skills or are a particular type

favour² W3 *BrE*; **favor** *AmE v* [T]
1 PREFER to prefer someone or something to other things or people, especially when there are several to choose from: *Both countries seem to favour the agreement.* | *loose clothing of the type favoured in Arab countries* | **favour sb/sth over sb/sth** *Florida voters favored Bush over Gore by a very small margin.*
2 GIVE AN ADVANTAGE to treat someone much better than someone else, in a way that is not fair: *a tax cut that favours rich people* | **favour sb over sb** *a judicial system that favours men over women*
3 HELP to provide suitable conditions for something

fright·ened S2 /'fraɪtnd/ *adj* feeling afraid; ⊟ scared: *Don't be frightened. We're not going to hurt you.* | [+of] *I was frightened of being left by myself in the house.* | *Her father had an awful temper and she was always frightened of him.* | **frightened to do sth** *The boy was frightened to speak.* | **frightened that** *She's frightened that her ex-husband will find her.* | *To tell the truth, I was frightened to death* (=very frightened). | *a frightened horse* ⚠ Do not confuse **frightened**, which describes a feeling, and **frightening**, which describes something that makes you feel frightened: *a frightened child* | *a frightening experience*; → see box at FEAR¹

fre·quent¹ W3 /'fri:kwənt/ *adj* happening or doing something often; ⊟ infrequent: **more/less frequent** *Her headaches are becoming less frequent.* | *Trains rushed past at frequent intervals.* | *She was a frequent visitor to the house.*

Where can you see speaking-like language being used in writing in the modern world?

15 Look at your own dictionary. Find three words that are used more in spoken English than in written English, and three that are used more in written English than in spoken English.

Listening: where people like to eat

16 Look at these pictures. Which of these places would you like to eat at and why?

17 Which of these people would prefer to eat at the restaurants *a–e* in Activity 16, do you think?

Chris

Jed

Martin

Julia

Naomi

Listen to Track 40 and see if you were correct.

18 Listen again Who:

a ... thinks there are many factors to finding the perfect restaurant?

b ... doesn't like eating in expensive restaurants?

c ... thinks the people who serve at the restaurant are well-mannered?

d ... is well known in the restaurant where he goes?

e ... thinks that the experience of eating is as important as the food?

19 Make a table to show what each speaker says about (a) food, (b) service, (c) atmosphere and (d) price.

Compare your notes with a partner.

20 Imagine you are going to open a restaurant. Make notes about its food, design / theme and the price of food there.

Compare in groups. Decide who would have the best restaurant.

Functional language: making a complaint

21 Put the conversation in a restaurant in order. Start with line i.

a The beans are undercooked too.

b Well, first of all, it's cold and the fish has a strange taste.

c Yes, madam?

d Certainly.

e What seems to be the problem, madam?

f I'm sorry, but there's something wrong with my meal.

g Yes, please. Could I see the menu?

h Would you like to order something else?

i Excuse me.   1

j I'm sorry about that. I'll take it back to the kitchen.

Now listen to Track 41 and check your answer.

22 Read the following sentences which were heard in a restaurant. Put them into three groups. The first one is done for you.

Starting to make a complaint	a, ...
Reasons for the complaint	
Ways of dealing with a complaint	

a I'm sorry but, ...

b This fish tastes awful.

c I don't want to complain, but ...

d I'm very sorry. I'll take it back to the kitchen.

e This chicken is not what I asked for.

f Would you like to speak to the manager?

g I don't like this hamburger.

h I hate to complain, but ...

i I'm not happy with this salad.

j Would you like to order something else?

k I have a complaint to make.

l This chocolate cake looks stale.

m There doesn't seem to be anything wrong with it.

n I'm afraid there's something wrong here.

o I'm afraid there's nothing I can do about it.

p This salad is gritty.

q Excuse me, but I'd like to speak to the person in charge.

r This meat smells burnt.

23 In pairs Which adjectives in the box could you use to complain about foods a–h below?

undercooked	tough
overcooked	burnt	stale
greasy	raw	salty	awful
spicy	cold	bland	gritty

a soup   *bland, ...*

b salad

c chocolate cake

d steak

e fish

f hamburger

g doughnut

h chicken

24 Role-play Imagine you are the customer in each of these situations (a–c). Make a complaint in person or on the telephone to your partner, who is the service provider.

a You have been waiting to be served at a table in a restaurant for 30 minutes.

b You take some food back to the supermarket where you bought it because there is something wrong with it.

c You are overcharged at a restaurant for two sodas and two bottles of water that you did not order.

Speaking: restaurant jokes

25 There are a lot of jokes about restaurants. Do you have jokes like the one on the right in your culture?

26 In pairs Student A, turn to Activity Bank 6 on page 158. Student B, turn to Activity Bank 11 on page 160.

27 In pairs Can you explain the jokes? Which is the funniest joke? Compare with other groups. Do you know any funnier restaurant jokes? What's your favourite simple joke in your language? Can you translate it into English?

There's a fly in my soup!

Not so loud, madam! Everyone will want one.

Grammar: using articles

28 In pairs Look at these sentences and say why the definite article *the* is used or is not used before the nouns in blue.

a Breakfast is an important meal. The breakfast I had today consisted of cereal and toast.
b I find that I think a lot about food.
c She told him it was a ripe mango. The mango was soft to the touch and a deep orange colour.
d I love to cook vegetables.
e People are often happy to eat out in restaurants.
f You must read the recipe book that he wrote.
g We didn't see the restaurant that you recommended.
h Animal fat is very important in some diets.

Look at 8C in the Mini-grammar. Do you want to change any of your answers?

29 Complete this paragraph using *the* or no article. You can use 8C–D in the Mini-grammar to help you. Compare with your partner.

When you ask some people what their hobby is, they will often say (a) '.................... food'. There is no doubt that what to eat occupies a lot of (b) .... day for a lot of people. Nowadays, it's very hard to know if you are eating (c) .... healthy food. On (d) .... TV and in (e) .... newspapers and magazines, we read about different diets which are supposed to help (f) .... people to stay healthy. The problem is that (g) .... experts often contradict each other, so it's hard to know what to believe. Yesterday, I saw a show that said that we should only eat (h) .... raw foods, like (i) .... fruits and (j) .... vegetables. Then I watched a show where (k) .... presenter said that we should eat a diet free of (l) .... carbohydrates.

30 Look at these sentences and identify whether they use the definite article (the), the indefinite article (a, an) or no article before the noun in blue. Use 8A–8D in the Mini-grammar to help you to decide why the article is used or not used.

a Jackie has taken up the violin.
b Do you want an apple? The apples are from the market, you know.
c That's the craziest thing I've ever heard!
d She really loves popcorn.
e I'm sure I left a chocolate bar in the fridge.
f The cherries are 90 pence a pound.
g This lecture is about the potato and when it first arrived in Europe.
h We love making curries. You must come over for one some time.
i She looked at the chicken that the butcher was showing her.
j She eats very well – her mother is a nutritionist.
k The sun rises in the East and sets in the West.
l Goulash is a dish which was first made by the Hungarians.

31 Choose the best option (definite article, indefinite article, no article) to complete this paragraph. Use 8A–8D in the Mini-grammar to help you. The first one is done for you.

I've been (a) the / ⓐ vegan for about five years now. I was (b) the / a vegan for two years before that, but most of (c) the / vegetarians I've ever met end up becoming (d) the / vegans or going back to eating (e) the / meat. The reason I stopped eating (f) the / meat was that I didn't like how (g) the / people keep and kill (h) the / animals. It's not that I'm (i) the / an animal lover, but I have (j) a / lot of respect for (k) the / living things on this planet. I was (l) a / student at the time and now I'm (m) an / engineer and I have never regretted (n) the / a choice I made all those years ago.

32 Which of the following names do you know? Which need the definite article? Copy them out correctly. The first one is done for you.

Acapulco *no article*   Kremlin
Angkor Watt   Madagascar
Bermuda Triangle   Mississippi River
Buckingham Palace   Mount Vesuvius
Colorado   province of Buenos Aires
Eiffel Tower   Narita Airport
Grand Canyon   pyramid of Cheops
Golden Tower   state of Sonora
Harvard University   Statue of Liberty
Hilton Hotel   Taj Mahal
Igacu Falls   Temple of Heavenly Peace,
Krackow   Kyoto

Check you have understood by looking at 8C in the Mini-grammar.

Pronunciation: weak and strong *the*

33 Listen to these sentences on Track 42. How is *the* said?

a This is the best restaurant in the city.
b This is the restaurant to be seen in in this city.
c Could I have the Atlantic salmon please?
d Do you have the ..., the crabs that are in season?
e We went down to the self-service buffet.
f Would you like to help yourself to the ice-cream?

When do we use the two different pronunciations? Practise saying the sentences.

Writing: describing graphs and tables

34 Read the report about this table and identify these three parts of the report.

a conclusions which are based on the table
b description of what the table represents
c description of the information in the table

Table 1: *1,203 people in the UK were asked about GM foods.*

1	If you knew which food had GM ingredients and you could choose, which of these is your opinion?	
	I would never eat GM food.	42%
	I would prefer not to eat GM food.	51%
	I don't mind whether or not I eat GM food.	7%
	I would prefer to eat GM food.	0%
	I would always eat GM food.	0%

Report on Table 1
Part 1
This table shows the results of a survey carried out in the UK. 1,203 people were asked whether they would eat food which contained GM ingredients.
Part 2
The results show that 42% of the people asked would never eat GM food if they knew that it had GM ingredients while about half (51%) said that they would prefer not to eat GM food. 7% of the people surveyed said that they don't mind whether or not they eat GM food and no one said that they would prefer to eat GM food or would always eat GM food.
Part 3
This seems to show that people in the UK do not like GM food and do not want to eat it if they have a choice.

35 Now look at Table 2. Write a report on what the table shows, using the plan below.

Table 2: *Two hundred people were asked the following question by Australian High School students: 'In your opinion, are the dangers of genetic modification of plants more important than the possible advantages?'*

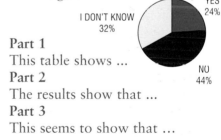

Part 1
This table shows ...
Part 2
The results show that ...
Part 3
This seems to show that ...

36 Choose a question to conduct a survey of your own. You can use one of the questions from this section or a different question connected with food.
Example: Do you eat foods that are bad for you?
never / sometimes / often

Make a table of the results like Table 1 or Table 2. Then write a short report of the results.

37 In pairs Check that your reports have the three parts that are needed and that they can be clearly understood by people who read them.

Review: grammar and functional language

38 Complete this conversation with the definite article (*the*), the indefinite article (*a / an*) or no article. The first one is done for you. You can look at Activities 29–34 for help.

CUSTOMER: Excuse me, but I'd like to speak to (**a**) ....the.... manager of this store.

SALES ASSISTANT: I'm afraid (**b**) .... manager is not here at the moment. Can I help you?

CUSTOMER: I want to make (**c**) .... complaint. I bought (**d**) .... box of (**e**) .... chocolates here last week and I tried one of (**f**) .... chocolates and it tasted stale.

SALES ASSISTANT: I'm afraid I can't do anything as we don't make (**g**) .... chocolates, we only sell them. It's not our responsibility to replace (**h**) .... goods that we sell in (**i**) .... good faith.

CUSTOMER: So, what can I do?

SALES ASSISTANT: You'll need to contact (**j**) .... manufacturers of (**k**) .... chocolates. They can refund your money or replace (**l**) .... chocolates.

CUSTOMER: How can I contact (**m**) .... manufacturers?

SALES ASSISTANT: They are based in (**n**) .... United States, but you can find (**o**) .... address in (**p**) .... United Kingdom, in (**q**) .... Scotland, on (**r**) .... side of (**s**) .... box.

CUSTOMER: Thanks for your help.

39 Match the complaint on the left with the response on the right. The first one is done for you.

a I'm sorry, but this steak is not what I asked for.   **3**

b I hate to complain, but this salad seems rather gritty.

c Excuse me, but I'd like to speak to someone in charge about this meal.

d This apple pie looks very stale.

e I have a complaint to make. This chicken is undercooked.

f Excuse me, but this chocolate mousse tastes awful.

g I don't want to complain, but these potatoes are burnt.

h I'm sorry to complain, but I don't think this fish is fresh.

1 Oh dear. Yes, it does smell a little strange. Would you like to order a different pudding?

2 What seems to be wrong with it? Desserts are our chef's speciality.

3 I'm very sorry about that. I'll bring you what you ordered immediately.

4 I'll take it back to the kitchen. Would you like it cooked more or would you prefer something else?

5 I'm afraid there's nothing I can do about that. All our lettuce is triple-washed.

6 I'm very sorry about that. Would you like to order a different vegetable?

7 That's impossible. It was caught today.

8 Certainly. I'll get the manager for you.

40 **In pairs** Look at this picture and imagine the conversation between this guest and the hotel manager, who has given the man the last available room in the hotel and wants the guest to stay at the hotel. Hotel rooms are hard to find in the city. You can look at Activities 21–25 for help.

Example: STUDENT A: I'd like to make a complaint about my room.

STUDENT B: How can I help you, sir / madam?

STUDENT A: The room is very dark and there is no bulb in the lamp.

STUDENT B: I'll send someone up to fix that immediately, sir / madam.

STUDENT A: Another thing is ...

Review: vocabulary

Word List

advocate	risky
awful	salty
bland	spicy
burnt	stale
consent	substantiated
greasy	to cultivate
gritty	to enhance
millennium	tough
numerous	undercooked
objection	urging
overcooked	yield
raw	

Word Plus

'(She) just can't cut the mustard.' *
a debilitating illness / condition
'a piece of cake'
'as cool as a cucumber'
'as flat as a pancake'
'as nutty as a fruit cake'
associated with living longer
devoid of emotion
global protest
intent on winning
'It's not my cup of tea.'
linked to poverty
'the apple of (her) eye'
'the best thing since sliced bread'
'to be selling like hot cakes'
'to cry over spilt milk'
'to have your cake and eat it'
'to know which side your bread
  is buttered'
'to put all your eggs in one
  basket'
'to spill the beans'
to stave off disease

*Phrases in inverted commas are
conversational phrases.

41 Look at the Word Plus list and answer the questions *a–d*.

   a Which is your favourite food expression and why?
   b Can you name something that is not your 'cup of tea'?
   c Who is the 'apple of your eye'?
   d Can you name something that is 'a piece of cake' for you?

●●● Pronunciation

42 Copy the table and put all the words in the Word List into the correct column according to the number of syllables they have. The first one is done for you.

One syllable	Two syllables	Three syllables	Four syllables	Five syllables
bland				

Now underline the stressed syllable in each word. Listen to Track 43 and check your answers.

43 **In teams** One team chooses Task A. The other team chooses Task B.

Task A: How many new words can you make from the letters of only the word *substantiated*? See who can make the most words.

Example: ant, bus

Task B: How many words can you make from the sounds of only the word *substantiated*?

Example: /ʃiː/ – she
        /eɪt/ – eight

Who has the most words after three minutes?

44 **In pairs** Talk about a time when:

   a ... you or someone you know 'put all your eggs in one basket'. Was it a good thing or a bad thing? What happened?
   b ... you or someone you know 'spilled the beans'. What happened? Did someone get into trouble? Did it help someone?

UNIT 9
First impressions

→ adjectives
→ physical description (connotation)
→ taking ourselves to be fixed

Listening: *Café Talk*

1 **In pairs** Discuss the following with your partner.

a When you meet a new person, what do you look at first?

- their hair
- their face (eyes, mouth, etc.)
- their build
- what they are wearing

b Which of the following will make you feel most positive about somebody?

- They are well groomed.
- They are well dressed.
- They have a good physique.
- They look interesting.
- They look like you.

Compare the answers with the rest of the class.

2 Look at this artist's impression from the programme *Café Talk*. Listen to Track 44 and answer the questions that follow.

The *Café Talk* cast. From left to right, Sally (Laura McHearty), Greenslade (Richard Whiles), Mitch (Andy Varshun) and Seb (Jason Cutting).

a Who does Sally like best, do you think: Greenslade, Mitch or Seb?
b Who sympathises with Greenslade's opinions: Mitch, Sally or Seb?
c Who is Raj Persaud?

3 Read the following summaries. Listen to Track 44 again. Say which one is correct.

a Greenslade has read an article which says that people like and are attracted to people they feel comfortable with, e.g. their friends and families. This is because they look at themselves in the mirror and love their pets. Sometimes they look like their pets too and go on to marry older men or women.

b Greenslade has read an article which says that people like and are attracted to people that look like their pets, e.g. their friends and families. This is because they see photographs of themselves and their pets. But some of them marry older people because they are very rich and have a lot of mirrors.

c Greenslade has read an article which says that people like and are attracted to people they feel comfortable with, e.g. their friends and families. This is because their face is the one they usually see in the mirror and in pictures. They are also used to their family's faces. All of this affects the choice of husband or wife, for example.

4 Who (Greenslade, Mitch, Sally or Seb) says each of these things?

a Their minds, of course.
b What are you talking about?
c Where do you get this stuff?
d Leave him alone, guys.
e It makes sense.
f This is just like so boring.
g Think about it.
h What is it with you, Mitch?
i You talk a lot of rubbish.
j OK, that's enough.
k That's my business.

Explain why they use these phrases in each case.

5 Listen to Track 45. What exactly do the phrases mean, and what attitude are the speakers conveying?

a Yeah, right.
b No really ...
c I read, Seb, OK?
d Says who?
e God!
f Well, sorry.
g You said.
h Pity.
i You do.

How could you tell what the speakers' attitudes were?

6 Say the phrases in exactly the same way as the speakers, using the same stress and intonation.

7 Acting out Read through the Audioscript for Track 44.

a Think about which words are stressed in each line.
b Think of how the phrases from Activities 4 and 5 are said on the recording.
c In groups, practise the conversation – or part of the conversation.
d Act out the conversation – or part of the conversation – for the class.

Vocabulary: physical description (connotation)

8 Copy and complete the table with the adjectives. Some may go in more than one column. Consult a dictionary if necessary. One is done for you.

appealing   bright   curly   dark   deep-set   fine   generous   kind   large   long
mean   pointed   protruding   receding   shiny   small   snub   soft   square
straight   strong   thick   thinning   turned up   wavy   weak   wide   wiry

Chin	Eyes	Hair	Mouth	Nose
	appealing			

What does someone's hair look like if they have:

a ... a crew cut?
b ... a bald patch?
c ... highlights?
d ... a perm?
e ... extensions?

9 Describe the following people using words from Activity 8.

Example: The person in Picture 'a' has a long nose, a wide, generous mouth and a strong chin.

10 Connotation Which of the following words have a positive meaning, which are neutral and which have negative overtones? Consult a dictionary if necessary.

a **thin:** emaciated lean puny skinny slender slight slim underweight

b **not thin:** chubby flabby muscular obese overweight plump pudgy stout voluptuous well-built

c **looks and appearance:** a bit of a mess attractive beautiful cute (US) elegant good-looking gorgeous handsome hideous plain pretty scruffy smart ugly untidy well-dressed

11 Intensifying and qualifying expressions Copy and complete the table with the phrases in blue.

> a little overweight   a little plump   absolutely gorgeous
> extremely beautiful   fantastically muscular   incredibly ugly
> kind of bald   kind of skinny   rather attractive   rather ugly

Phrases designed to make things not quite so strong

Phrases designed to emphasise an extreme quality

Make more combinations of phrase + description like the ones in the blue box above.

12 Describe the following characters in (a) a more positive and (b) a more negative way.

Gandalf

Amélie

Rocky

Bridget

Example: a Amélie is kind of slender.
b Amélie is rather skinny.

13 Describe someone (not in the class) who the other students should know. Can they guess who you are talking about?

Reading: hair

14 Read the two descriptions and match them with the photographs.

Emma is 26 years old. After school, she trained to be a hairdresser and worked for some time in a hairdressing salon. She re-trained some years ago as a secretary and is now an executive secretary at a large law firm.

Stephanie is 27 years old. She has a degree in English literature from the University of Warwick (UK). She has worked for a bank and is now the human resources (personnel) manager for a large educational publisher.

a

b

Compare your choice with the class. How many people matched Photograph a with Emma and how many with Stephanie? What are the reasons for your choice?

15 Do you agree with the following statements?

a There are more natural blondes than dyed blonde women in the world.

b Everyone thinks blondes are more attractive than, say, brunettes.

c It is an advantage for women to be blonde.

Read the text on page 93. Does the article have the same opinion as you?

THE NEW BLONDE BOMBSHELL

Do blondes have more fun? Women certainly assume so, for while only one in six is a natural blonde, almost half of all women lighten their hair in some way or another.

Peroxide was discovered in 1818. Two centuries on, most blondes get a little help from the bottle. Last year they spent over £100 million on hair dye – and that doesn't include what they pay at the hairdressers to help to emulate blonde role models such as Britney Spears, Sharon Stone and Gwyneth Paltrow.

In fact many of these golden-haired icons are not natural blondes either. Even Marilyn Monroe started out as a freckle-faced brunette with medium skin tone. She wore pale make-up and dyed her hair platinum. So what is the mystery magnet that draws women to becoming blonde? It must be strong, because even today across all races – not just white westerners – when people are asked to rate others for 'attractiveness', they usually opt for those with lighter hair and skin. You only have to check out the TV commercials around the world to see how important the image of the blonde has become.

Until recently, being blonde or brunette was reckoned to be merely a matter of fashion. But something much deeper is driving our reactions to hair colour. In fact, it turns out, being blonde, whether natural or 'fake', may not do women any good at all.

All blondes, but are they *real* blondes?

16 In groups of three Why do you think being blonde may be a disadvantage for some women? To find out:

STUDENT A: turn to Activity Bank 7 on page 158.
STUDENT B: turn to Activity Bank 12 on page 161.
STUDENT C: turn to Activity Bank 19 on page 164.

17 In groups of three Copy and complete the table in note form with opinions from the texts. Don't look back at the texts.

Advantages of being a blonde woman	Disadvantages of being a blonde woman
Reasons:	Reasons:

18 Vocabulary Complete the sentences with the following work-related words. You can find the words in the texts and the writing section of this unit.

applicant	appointed	CV	equally qualified
PA	reject	salary	

a If you apply for a job, you are a job _____ .
b When you apply for a job, you generally send information about yourself, called a curriculum vitae or _____ for short.
c Two people who have studied the same thing are _____ .
d If the interviewers don't give you the job, they _____ you.
e If you are the successful candidate for the job, you are _____ .
f The amount of money you get paid per month is called your _____ .
g The manager's chief aide is his/her personal assistant (often a higher-status job than a secretary). This is often shortened to _____ .

Language in chunks

19 Read the extracts from the texts on page 93 and in the Activity Bank. Replace the phrases in blue with words or phrases which mean almost the same.

a Most blondes get a little help from bottles of hair dye.
b While being blonde may boost your social life, it can also damage your career prospects. (page 158)
c It seems hardly credible that such changeable features as hair colour could so influence recruitment decisions. (page 158)
d The picture for me didn't play a major part. (page 161)
e I made a studious attempt to ignore the appearance of the applicants. (page 161)
f Under close questioning, they revealed that the ... stereotype had ... affected their judgement. (page 161)

20 Choose one of the blue phrases from Activity 19 and use it in an anecdote or a story.

21 **Noticing language** Look at all the texts (*The new blonde bombshell* and Activity Bank) and find as many examples as you can of adjectives where two words are joined together.

Example: *golden-haired*

Grammar: adjectives and adjective order

22 Look at these sentences and answer the questions a–c.

- He had always wanted to be a tall, muscular, attractive man.
- She was tall, slim, and incredibly beautiful.
- He was wearing a yellow and green tie.
- She had always wanted to work in one of those tall concrete and glass buildings.
- Her boss was a silly old man.
- For the first two weeks, they got on very well.
- The last ten minutes of the interview went terribly slowly for the nervous, unprepared, blonde woman.
- I want you to be quiet for the next three minutes. That's all.

a When do we use *and* between adjectives and when don't we use *and*?
b When do we use commas between adjectives and when don't we use commas?
c When we use *first*, *next* and *last* with numbers, what's the correct order?

Look at 9A in the Mini-grammar. Do you want to change your answers?

23 Re-write the following incorrect sentences.

a He had dark and thinning hair.
b They are coming to stay for the two next days.
c He looked handsome, elegant, rich. *
d He behaved like a silly, young and fool.
e She painted a happy voluptuous successful woman.

*In literary use, it is possible to miss out *and* when more than one adjective is used after a verb.

24 **Two–word adjectives** Read the text and complete the tasks which follow.

He was a well-off, good-looking, two-faced, red-haired TV presenter with a time-consuming job who married a world-famous, self-centred, big-headed singer after they had met in an air-conditioned duty-free shop at the airport.

At first things went well. It looked as if it would be a long-standing relationship. He was easy-going and she said she was warm-hearted. They bought a big house in a built-up area and installed bullet-proof windows. She stopped singing and took a part-time job. She had to wear a shocking-pink uniform and so she quit. When he asked her why, she said she only wore hand-made clothes, not badly designed coats. It was the first of many all-out rows.

a Describe the two people in your own words. Would you like to meet them? Why? Why not?
b How many different two-word adjectives can you find in the text? How many different kinds are there? You can use **9B in the Mini-grammar** to help you.

25 Make new adjectives by joining adjectives in the left-hand column with the words in the right-hand column. Say what they could describe.

absent	grey		
auburn	high		
bad	long	haired	
brown	narrow	minded	
curly	red	price	
cut	short	— sighted	
dark	straight	skinned	
fair	well	tempered	
good	white		
	hard		

Example: absent-minded – an absent-minded professor

● Word Choice: *seem, appear* and *look*

● **26** Look at the Word Choice notes for *seem, appear* and *look* on page 58 in the booklet.

● **27** Complete the sentences with the appropriate forms of *seem, appear* or *look*. The first one is done for you.

  a The president ...*appeared*.. to be happy with the arrangement, Mr Ambassador.
  b She .... to have had her hair dyed blonde.
  c She .... fantastic!
  d Your reaction .... to be kind of exaggerated, don't you think?
  e They .... as if they are enjoying themselves.
  f Ladies and gentlemen, the patient .... to be sleeping, but actually she is fully conscious.
  g I should be careful. He .... as if he's pretty angry.
  h What .... to be the problem?
  i I .... to have made a mistake. I apologise, sir.

28 Adjective order Read the following phrases and complete the task which follows.

  a a large knitted square Mexican blanket
  b a big new seat
  c a big-hearted curly-haired Spanish hunting dog
  d a black German car
  e a rectangular pink tablecloth
  f big appealing bright-blue eyes
  g gorgeous blonde hair

Copy the diagram and complete it by putting the following adjective types in the correct order, based on the phrases a–g.

- colour or origin
- opinion / judgement or size
- origin or material
- material or purpose
- shape / description or colour
- size or shape / description

   +   +   +   +   +   + noun

Are you right? Check you have understood with **9B–9C in the Mini-grammar.**

29 In pairs Ask your partner to list ten things he or she has in his / her room. Ask for descriptions and write the adjectives your hear. Give the adjectives and the nouns to another pair. Can they put them in the right order?

Example: STUDENT A: Describe your guitar.

      STUDENT B: It's an old Spanish guitar. My uncle gave it to me when he stopped playing.

guitar
Spanish
old

Functional language: taking ourselves to be fixed

30 Listen to Track 46 and choose the correct picture.

Now listen to Track 47. Were you correct?

31 Listen to Track 47 again and answer the following questions.

a When was Mr Boddington last here?
b What is he offered, and what does he get?
c What does he think of his appearance?
d What does he want to happen to his appearance?

32 Look at how we can keep appointments to 'have ourselves fixed'.

KEEPING AN APPPOINTMENT TO HAVE OURSELVES FIXED

a We can say why we have come like this:
I've got an appointment with Doctor Smith at 10 o'clock.

b The receptionist or professional might tell us what to do like this:
Would you like to } { *take a seat?*
If you'll just } { *go through?*
If you'd like to } { *come into my office?*

c The professional can ask us what we want like this:
How can I help you?
What can I do for you?
What brings you here?
Why have you come to see me?

d We can explain what we want like this:
I'd like a haircut, please.
I was thinking of having my nose straightened.
I was wondering if you could { *do anything about ...*
{ *give me advice about ...*
I've got a bit of a toothache.

e The professional can make suggestions like this:
I recommend having a bit off the top and keeping the hair just above the ears.
I would suggest that you take a few days off work.
I think you'd better take some aspirin.
I'm going to give you a prescription for some ...
I think we could do something about your nose, yes.

Make new sentences by replacing the blue words with words of your own.

Example: I would suggest a fringe, madam.
         I was thinking of having my hair really short.

33 Choose one of the following places.

a the hairdresser's
b the dentist's
c the doctor's

Think of why you are going there. You can look at Activity Bank 13 on page 161 for words that you might want to use.

34 Role-play Students who have chosen the same place in Activity 33 go to their appointment at the hairdresser's, dentist's or doctor's and wait their turn. Other students are receptionists, hairdressers, dentists or doctors.

Writing: curriculum vitae

35 Look quickly at the following document. What is it for?

CURRICULUM VITAE

Name:	Neil Todd
Date of birth:	30 / 10 / 85
Address:	26 Kingston Drive, Camelthorpe, Cornwall CT54 7RF

Schools / Colleges attended:
1996 – 2003   Parkridge Community College
1990 – 1996   Camelthorpe Primary School

Exams: 2003   'A' levels in History, Maths,
English Literature (waiting for the results)
2001   GCSEs
History (Grade B)
Geography (Grade A)
Maths (Grade A*)
Biology (Grade A)
Spanish (Grade B)
Music (Grade C)
English (Grade A)
Art (Grade A*)
Physics (Grade C)
Chemistry (Grade B)

Employment record (including holiday jobs):
2002 November – present:
part-time work at GAP clothing store
2002 March – September:
Saturday working at Sainsbury's supermarket
2001 July and August:
part-time working at McDonald's

Hobbies and interests:
I like listening to music and going out to clubs. I play the guitar. I'm keen on football (I go to Camelthorpe's matches when they play at home).

Anything else you wish to say to support your application:
My experience at the GAP clothing store means I know a lot about shops, so I would be just right for the job at the Speedo Sports Store.

I am trying to get a job for six months so that I can then travel to Latin America before I start University next year.

References:

Mary Fischer	Paul Pritchard
Manager	Headteacher
GAP	Parkridge Community College
23 High Street	34 Park Street
Camelthorpe	Camelthorpe
CT54 6SG	CT54 5SG

36 **In pairs** Compare people's CVs.

STUDENT B: look at the CV for Nigel Thomas in Activity Bank 14 on page 162.

STUDENT A: find out as many similarities as you can between Neil Todd and Student B's Nigel Thomas.

Example: When was Nigel Thomas born? (one similarity)

37 Answer the following questions.

a What jobs are Neil and Nigel applying for?
b What are the main headings that people put on their CVs? Which one does Nigel include which Neil leaves out? Why?
c What order do the dates go in?
d How important is it to put down some hobbies / interests, do you think?

38 Using the same headings as Neil and Nigel's CVs, write:

- ... your own curriculum vitae.
OR
- ... the curriculum vitae of a fictional person you have dreamed up.

Make sure you include:

- ... at least two jobs (even if they were / are only temporary or part-time).
- ... something about your interests.

Speaking: the interview

39 a Which of the following topics are appropriate for a job interview?

1 why the applicant wants the job
2 whether the applicant has a girlfriend / boyfriend or is married
3 how the applicant got on in their last job
4 what the applicant's favourite colour is
5 what the applicant does in their spare time
6 why the applicant thinks that he or she is right for this job
7 what time the applicant has dinner

b How would you ask the questions you have selected as appropriate?

Are there any other questions you would like to ask?

40 In groups Choose one of the following advertisements.

Train big cats in Las Vegas!

Appear in world-famous circus performances!

Big cats are lions, tigers, cheetahs, etc.

(No experience necessary: we supply on-the-job experience-based training.)

• Fabulous pay
• Fabulous conditions
• An exciting star-studded life

The successful candidate will be:

• energetic
• decisive
• ready for anything
• fit and healthy
• good-humoured
• ambitious

Don't wait! Apply now

Have you ever wanted to write for a popular magazine?

Well now's your chance!

We are looking for someone to write a weekly column in our magazine on any topic they want.

• Excellent pay
• You become well known
• You have influence and people everywhere read your opinions.
  It's a fantastic opportunity

We provide:
• training
• editorial help
• entertainment allowance (you get a sum of money to spend on going out)

You provide:
• ideas
• imagination
• opinion
• enthusiasm

Volunteers wanted for new TV show

Supreme Challenge ™ will take 15 ordinary members of the public and put them in difficult physical circumstances (on mountains, in the jungle, at sea, etc.).

The winner gets $5m!!!

We are looking for volunteers who are:

brave • cheerful • **fit** • **sociable** • good in a crowd • competitive

a Give yourself a new name and a fictional CV which would be appropriate for the job. Write down the main points.
b Think of the qualities and experiences that would make the interviewers like you.
c Think of the questions the interviewers are going to ask you and make a note of some good answers.

41 In groups Two or more students are interviewers. Two or more students are the applicants.

APPLICANTS: give the interviewers your name.
INTERVIEWERS: welcome the applicants and make them feel comfortable.

Role-play the interviews. Everyone votes on who should get the job (you cannot vote for yourself).

Example:

'INTERVIEWER': Good morning, Miss Clarkson, do please take a seat.

'APPLICANT': Thank you.

'INTERVIEWER': I hope you didn't have any trouble finding us.

'APPLICANT': No, it was easy, thank you ...

Review: grammar and functional language

42 Describe the following pictures using as many adjectives as you can in your sentence without making the sentence ridiculous. Pay attention to the order of the adjectives. You can look at Activities 22–25 and 28 for help.

Example: **a**

> This is an old, brown, Spanish ...

Made in Thailand

What Sweden does best!

43 How many questions? Describe an object using some adjectives, but don't say what it is, and don't use adjectives that are too obvious. The other students ask questions. You can answer only 'yes' or 'no'. How many questions do they need to find the answer?

Example: STUDENT A: It's an expensive silver-coloured flat Japanese thing.
STUDENT B: Is it a personal organiser?
STUDENT A: No, it isn't.
STUDENT C: Is it a minidisc player?
STUDENT A: No, it isn't that.
STUDENT D: Is it a computer?
STUDENT A: Yes, but ...
STUDENT B: Is it a laptop computer?
STUDENT A: Yes.

44 Complete this conversation with appropriate words (one for each gap). The first one is done for you. You can look at Activity 32 for help.

RECEPTIONIST: Good afternoon, sir, how can I (a) **help** you?
FARNABY: I'd like to (b) .... the doctor.
RECEPTIONIST: Do you have an (c) .... ?
FARNABY: Well no, but I just thought ...
RECEPTIONIST: Well you're in (d) .... I think we can fit you in.
FARNABY: Oh good. Thank you.
RECEPTIONIST: Can I take your (e) .... ?
FARNABY: Certainly. It's Farnaby, Giles Farnaby.
RECEPTIONIST: All right, Mr Farnaby, if you'd just (f) .... to take a seat. Oh no, wait a minute, that won't be necessary. You can go (g) .... right now.
FARNABY: Thank you.
DOCTOR: Come in, Mr Farnaby. Now (h) .... can I help you?
FARNABY: I just (i) .... to get something off my chest.
DOCTOR: Your chest?
FARNABY: Yes, (j) .... see, because ...
DOCTOR: If you'd just (k) .... to take off your shirt.
FARNABY: (l) .... ?
DOCTOR: Your shirt. Take off your shirt and (m) .... up on the bed. Then I can (n) .... you.
FARNABY: But I don't (o) .... to be examined.
DOCTOR: Why not? Your chest. You said (p) .... about your chest.
FARNABY: I said I wanted to get something off my (q) .... , you know ... tell you about something that's worrying me. Like getting the weight of this secret off my chest. You are a psychiatrist, (r) .... you?
DOCTOR: Oh I (s) ....
FARNABY: What?
DOCTOR: You want my brother, Angus McGloughlin. Mad as anything. He's (t) .... door. I'm sorry the receptionist didn't tell you.

Review: vocabulary

appealing	plump
applicant	pointed
appointed	pretty
attractive	protruding
bald patch	pudgy
beautiful	puny
bright	receding
chubby	salary
crew cut	scruffy
curly	shiny
cute (US)	skinny
CV	slender
dark	slight
deep-set	slim
elegant	small
emaciated	smart
extensions	snub
fine	soft
flabby	square
generous	stout
good-looking	straight
gorgeous	strong
handsome	thick
hideous	thinning
highlights	to reject
kind	turned up
large	ugly
lean	underweight
long	untidy
mean	voluptuous
muscular	wavy
obese	weak
overweight	well-built
PA	well-dressed
perm	wide
plain	

a bit of a mess
equally qualified
to damage your career prospects
to get a little help from
to make a studious attempt
to play a major part
to seem hardly credible
under close questioning

45 If you could only keep five words from the Word List, what would they be? Why? If you had to throw away five words from the Word List, which would they be? Why?

Example: I'd like to keep 'beautiful' because I like beautiful things.

 ● ● Pronunciation

46 Copy and complete the table with as many individual words as you can from the Word List and Word Plus. (Note: one of the sounds does not appear in the lists.)

/ʃ/ – <u>sh</u>ip	/ʒ/ – plea<u>s</u>ure	/tʃ/ – <u>ch</u>ur<u>ch</u>	/dʒ/ – <u>j</u>u<u>dge</u>

Check your answers by listening to Track 48. Can you add more words to your table?

47 Odd one out Which is the odd one out in the following?

a attractive   extensions   protruding   underweight   voluptuous
b appealing   deep-set   lean   receding   square
c bright   shiny   slight   thick   untidy

Check your answers by listening to Track 49.

48 Casting directors In pairs, think of a story you both know well – a film you have seen recently, for example, or your favourite TV show, or your favourite book. Imagine that you have been given money to make a new version of the story.

• Make a list of the main characters in the story.
• For each character, say what they should look like and what kind of character they should have.

Show your lists to other pairs. Has any one chosen the same story as you?

Reading: *The Storm*

1 Predicting The words in the box come from the text you are about to read. What do you think the text is going to be about (look at the title of this section too)?

boxes of pasta	candlelight
carpet	editors
espresso machine	floating
flower beds	frogs	reel of film
roads	shadows	water

Read the text on pages 101–102. Were you right?

2 Read the text again and put the following events in the correct order. Number 1 is done for you.

a Eleanor went downstairs.
b Eleanor's sons and another man played cards.
c Francis thought pasta was the answer.
d Francis arrived home.
e Francis pushed the car.
f Francis put some music on.
g It stopped raining.
h Larry and Dean collected boxes of pasta.
i People from the office came back to the house because they hadn't been able to get home.
j Sofia caught some frogs.
k The music started again.
l Water began to get into the house. **1**

Note: *Cannes* is a place in France where they hold an annual film festival. *La Bohème* is an opera.

Eleanor Coppola is the wife of the film director Francis Ford Coppola, and mother of Sofia Coppola who is also a film director. Many years ago, Eleanor went with Francis and their children Sofia, Roman and Giancarlo (Gio) to the Philippines where Francis was making one of his most famous films, *Apocalypse Now*. Eleanor wrote a diary of those days called *Notes*. The following extract describes an evening at the house they were renting.

The Storm

The storm got more exciting. Water started coming in the rooms downstairs. In some places the carpet looked like it was floating because there was a layer of water between it and the floor. The kids thought it looked like a water bed and were jumping on it. Pretty soon, the water was about six inches deep and it started out the bedroom door into the other rooms. Several people arrived from the office because the roads were so flooded they couldn't get home. It had taken them two hours just to get to our house. We were all in the kitchen opening bottles of Italian wine when someone realized that the boxes of pasta were sitting downstairs in the water. Larry and Dean took off their shoes and waded across the room, and started carrying the cartons upstairs. Francis finally arrived. He had been stuck at some flooded intersection for the past hour and a half. He had gotten out to push the car and was completely soaked. The editors had been at the house all day, preparing a reel of film for a screening at Cannes. They decided it was hopeless to try to make it home. So we began counting how many there were for dinner. There were 14, and the little half-eaten roast left over from lunch was about enough for four. Francis decided to make pasta.

Sofia put on her raincoat and was running around in the backyard. One section was under water and the frogs that usually hop around on the lawn there were all swimming. Sofia was chasing them and actually catching one now and then. The dirt from the flower beds was streaming into the swimming pool. Francis turned on *La Bohème* full volume. Marc, Roman and Gio were playing a noisy game of poker. The thunder and rain were so loud we were all shouting at each other. Finally, we did have a terrific dinner. ▶▶

As we got to the dessert the electricity went off. We had bananas flambé by candlelight. After dinner, Francis and I were sitting on the couch looking toward the table. There were three candles and a group of people at each end of the long oval table. Francis was talking about how fabulous our eyes are that they can compensate for the low level of light and see perfectly clearly. You could never shoot in that amount of light. It was really beautiful. Francis was marvelling at how the people at the table were so perfectly staged. Now and then, someone would get up and go to the kitchen, crossing behind or in front of the light. Each person was so perfectly placed, leaning a little forward or a little back, catching the light, making shadows on the wall behind and silhouettes in front. He said you could never get it as good if you staged it. After a while we went to bed. I guess the rain stopped for a bit and everybody decided to try to go home. They started out, they got to the main road and had to turn back.

The electricity came on at about four in the morning, and *La Bohème* started up, loud. The espresso machine began steaming, all the lights went on, and I went downstairs to shut things off. People were sleeping all over the place.

3 Did Eleanor enjoy the evening? How do you know?

Tell your partner about a meal with your family or friends that you have really enjoyed.

4 Vocabulary Match these definitions to the words in blue in the text on pages 101–102.

a a loud noise in the sky   *thunder*
b a piece of meat that has been cooked in an oven
c a place where roads cross each other
d arranged as if in a theatre performance
e covered with water
f flowing quickly and in large amounts
g very wet
h walked slowly through water
i wonderful

5 Fact check Why:

a ... were the kids jumping on the carpet?
b ... did people arrive from the office?
c ... did Larry and Dean take off their shoes?
d ... was Francis very wet?
e ... did they cook pasta?
f ... was the swimming pool dirty?
g ... was everyone shouting at each other?
h ... did they eat by candlelight?
i ... are eyes better than cameras?
j ... did Eleanor get up in the middle of the night?

Language in chunks

6 Find the following phrases in the text *The Storm*.

a two examples of *looked like*
b a phrase which means *to succeed in getting back home*
c to turn on something full volume
d a phrase which means *from time to time*
e an activity that took place by candlelight
f something that can compensate for something

7 Use the phrases in blue and the two phrases you've found in sentences of your own. You may need to adapt them.

8 Varieties of English What words or grammar tell you that the following sentences are written in American English?

a It started out the bedroom door into the other rooms.
b Someone realized that the boxes of pasta were sitting downstairs.
c He had gotten out to push the car.
d Sofia ... was running around in the backyard.
e I guess the rain stopped for a bit.

How would you change each sentence for a different language variety (e.g. British English)?

9 Noticing grammar Read the text again and find verbs written in the past. How many different types of past tense can you find?

10 Speaking Without looking at the book, tell the story of Eleanor's evening in your own words.

Speaking: consensus-reaching and role-play

11 Dinner party First, select the guests.

a Individually, write down the names of two people, living or dead, real or fictional, who you would most like to invite for dinner.

b In groups of five, compare your lists and agree on a final list of five guests (five of the original suggestions will have to be eliminated).

12 Now, organise the dinner itself.

a Agree on a seating plan and decide what you will serve the guests.

b Copy and complete the table.

> **Good topics for discussion**
> the weather, ...

> **Topics we should try to avoid**
> the war, ...

13 Role-play Join together with another group and either role-play their guests or ask them to role-play your guests for part of your dinner party.

Grammar: narrative (past simple, past perfect simple, past continuous, past perfect continuous)

14 a Match the words and phrases in the box with the days of the week.

> arguing with her colleagues   attending a long meeting
> partying till late the night before   driving too fast
> visiting her parents   watching sport on TV
> working out in the gym

MARTHA'S WEEK

MONDAY
physically exhausted

TUESDAY
mentally exhausted

WEDNESDAY
upset

THURSDAY
well-fed

FRIDAY
stopped by the police

SATURDAY
relaxed

SUNDAY
headache

b With a partner, make up questions and answers about Martha's week. You can use **10B** and **10D** in the **Mini-grammar** to help you.

Example: STUDENT A: Why was Martha exhausted on Monday evening?

STUDENT B: Because she had been working out in the gym.

15 Choose the best alternative in blue in the following story.

As he (**a**) walked / had walked out of the building where he worked, Simon was exhausted. He (**b**) worked / was working / had worked / had been working since 7 in the morning and he (**c**) was only finishing / had only finished / had only been finishing a few minutes before. Before (**d**) he had got / had been getting / got into the car, he (**e**) called / was calling his wife on his mobile phone and (**f**) asked / was asking her if he should get anything on the way home. She said she (**g**) went / was going / had gone to the supermarket that morning before she (**h**) drove / was driving to the TV studio to be interviewed about her new book. He asked her about the interview. She said that she (**i**) talked / was talking / had talked / had been talking about her book when a studio light fell from the ceiling and (**j**) nearly killed / was nearly killing / had nearly been killing her. 'I (**k**) was / had been really frightened,' she said, 'but I (**l**) continued / was continuing with the interview and gradually I (**m**) felt / was feeling OK. Still, it's great to be home. And no, we don't need anything.'

Twenty minutes later, Simon had his own lucky escape. He (**n**) drove / was driving / had been driving along the ring road when he (**o**) was noticing / noticed something strange about the lorry in front of him. Two minutes later, a large wooden plank (**p**) fell off / was falling off / had fallen off the back of the lorry. Luckily, however, Simon (**q**) braked / was braking / had braked a few minutes before when he (**r**) saw / was seeing / had seen / had been seeing a movement on the truck and so the plank (**s**) was just missing / had just missed / just missed him.

The next morning, Simon (**t**) woke up / was waking up suddenly. He (**u**) had / was having / had had / had been having a terrible nightmare. It was all about studio lights and wooden planks. He (**v**) looked / was looking / had looked / had been looking over at his wife. She (**w**) was / was being / had been still asleep. He realised how lucky he (**x**) was / had been.

Look at 10A–10D in the Mini-grammar. Do you want to change your answers?

16 Join the sentences together using all the verbs. You can look at 10E in the Mini-grammar to help you. The first one is done for you.

a Mary woke up. Mary got out of bed. Mary looked out of the window. Mary saw the tiger.
Mary woke up, got out of bed, looked out of the window and saw the tiger.

b Sally was sitting at her desk. Sally was talking on the telephone. Sally was drawing pictures on her notepad.

c They had been there all day. They had been studying the pictures. They had been deciding what to do with them.

d He took the ball from a player on the opposing team. He ran past a defender. He shot the ball into the back of the net.

e She was writing a letter. She was listening to music. She was eating a biscuit. She was drinking a cup of tea.

f They had been at the dinner table for an hour. They had been laughing. They had been enjoying each other's company. They had been talking about their holiday.

17 Look at the following pictures. Say what is happening in each one.

18 In groups Complete the following tasks.

a Think of a story which links all of the pictures *a–d* from Activity 17. You may have to change the order of events. Use as many simple and continuous tenses as you can.

b Compare your story with the other groups. Have they interpreted the pictures in the same way?

Vocabulary: weather words

19 Language research Copy the table. Complete the *Least severe /
Most severe* column with words and phrases from the box.

> blazing sun   blizzard   breeze   downpour   gale   heavy shower
> heavy snowfall   light breeze   light shower   light snowfall
> strong breeze   strong sunshine   strong wind   sunshine
> torrential rain

	Least severe <-------------> Most severe	Associated verbs
rain	light shower, heavy shower, ...	
snow		
sun		
wind		

Put the following verbs in the right-hand column of your table.

> blow   drizzle   fall   howl   pour
> roar   scorch   settle   shine   whistle

20 Choose the correct verb for each gap.

a A light snow   *fell*   in the night.
b The rain was .... down the neck of my raincoat.
c A strong wind was .... from the south-west.
d The hurricane was nearly upon us. The wind was .... in my
ears and I could hear nothing.
e It was .... Light rain fell continuously from a very dark
sky.
f The wind was .... through the holes in the roof.
g The sun was .... through the afternoon clouds.
h The snow began to .... on the ground after two hours of
heavy snowfall.
i She could see the blazing sun .... the earth and small cracks
began to open.
j The wind was .... like a wolf as the storm began.

**21 Read the following description of weather in Tikan (Guatemala).
What is *thunder*? What is *lightning*?**

The weather is completely predictable. In the summer – that's from
January to May or June – we have bright sunshine every day. The
only thing that stops that is the occasional cyclone. Then in the
winter we have a rainy season – that's sunny mornings and then
torrential rain (even thunder and lightning) in the afternoon, from
two until six or seven.

a How different is this weather from the weather where you live?
b What is your favourite kind of weather? What is your least
favourite kind of weather?

22 a Metaphor How many words
or phrases based on weather
can you find in the text? What
do they mean?

Mary had a very sunny disposition
and she was extremely generous.
She constantly showered all her
friends with presents. But when she
appeared in the crowded room
dressed in the latest clothes she had
designed, people started to giggle
and soon gales of laughter were
echoing around the room. Pretty
soon she was blazing with anger.
'You have no right to laugh at me!'
she thundered, and she stormed out
of the room.

At first, everyone there was
thunderstruck – shocked and silent.
But then someone started to clap,
very slowly, and then they all joined
in, faster and faster until the
ballroom was full of thunderous
applause – though exactly what they
were applauding was not quite clear.

The incident caused a storm of
protest in the fashion world, but
Mary's designs were a huge success.

22 b What's the worst weather
you've ever been in? Write
two sentences about it using
words from Activities 19–22a.
Read your sentences to the
class.

Listening: *Stormy Weather*

23 Read the mini web biography and answer the questions which follow.

Billie Holiday (called 'Lady Day' by her admirer and colleague, saxophonist Lester Young) was one of the most famous jazz singers of the 20th century. Although she had a small voice – she could not sing either very high or very low – her 'behind-the-beat' phrasing, where she hung back from singing strictly in time, has been copied by many singers ever since. But what makes her special is the emotional intensity of her singing. When we listen to her performance she really seems to be living the words that she is singing.

Billie Holiday was born in Baltimore, USA in 1915 and started singing in clubs in Harlem, New York, when she was only 16 years old. Her finest period was between 1935 and 1942 when she made many recordings, often with Lester Young playing saxophone, including her most famous song, *Strange Fruit*, about a black victim of a lynching. She toured with the best jazz orchestras of the time, including the famous Count Basie orchestra.

Billie Holiday died aged 44 in New York in 1959.

Who:

a   ... called Billie Holiday 'Lady Day'?
b   ... didn't have a very big voice?
c   ... copied Billie's singing style?
d   ... started a career at a very young age?
e   ... seems to live the words of the songs?
f   ... often played saxophone in Billie's recordings?
g   ... had his own orchestra?
h   ... was the subject of the song *Strange Fruit*?

24 Listen to Track 50. Answer the following questions.

a   What is Monica Marcello's job?
b   What kind of jazz does she like?
c   Why does she like jazz?
d   What's special about Billie Holiday, in Monica's opinion?
e   Who was Harold Arlen?
f   What's the song about?

25 In pairs Discuss the song. Did you enjoy it? Have you heard it before? Are you tempted to buy it?

Tell the class about your discussions.

26 Complete the song lyrics with one word for each blank. Some lines are repeated.

Don't know why there's no (a) .... up in the (b) ....
Stormy weather
Since my (c) .... and I ain't (d) ....,
Keeps rainin' all the time.

Life is bare, (e) .... and mis'ry (f) ....
Stormy weather
Just can't get my poor self (g) ....,
I'm (h) .... all the time, the time
So weary all the time.

When he went (i) .... the blues walked in and (j) .... me
If he stays (k) .... old rockin' chair will get me.

All I do is (l) .... the lord above will let me (m) .... in the (n) .... once more.

Can't go on, ev'ry thing I had is (o) ....
Stormy weather
Since my (p) .... and I ain't (q) ....,
Keeps rainin' all the time
Keeps rainin' all the time.

Check your answers with the Audioscript for Track 50.

27 Vocabulary What do you understand by the words and expressions in blue from the radio programme and the song lyrics?

a   not everyone's taste
b   as a kid
c   It just sort of started then.
d   She doesn't even have much of a range.
e   the way she puts over a lyric
f   It gets to me every time.
g   the blues walked in and met me
h   old rockin' chair will get me

Speaking and writing: shortening things

28 Look at the extracts from the studio conversation and the lyrics for *Stormy Weather* and answer the questions which follow.

Any favourite kind of jazz?
Not everyone's taste.
Don't know why ...
Keeps rainin' all the time
Gloom and mis'ry all the time

Just can't get my poor self together
Old rockin' chair will get me
Can't go on
Ev'rything I had ...

a Find examples where sentences have been shortened so that certain words such as pronouns and verbs have been omitted. Why does this happen in conversation and in song lyrics?

b Find examples where an apostrophe (') is used. What are the reasons for the apostrophe?

29 Look quickly at the Audioscript for Tracks 1–50. What kind of shortening can you find?

30 **In pairs** Role-play a radio programme in which the presenter asks you questions about the following.

- your life
- your favourite sports, hobbies, etc.
- your favourite songs and why you like them so much.

Functional language: conversational gambits

31 Complete the dialogue with one of the following phrases.

- I don't want to interrupt, but
- On another topic altogether,
- Wait a minute, I'd just like to say ...
- Yes, and what's more ...
- Yes, and one shouldn't forget

MARION: I really worry about global warming, you know. We're having a lot more storms these days.
KURT: Yes ...
KARL: **(a)** .... you can't rely on the weather at all these days.
KURT: But ...
MARION: **(b)** .... that this has all happened only in the last 60 or 70 years.
KURT: But I think ...
MARION: **(c)** ...., have you seen the latest opinion poll?
KURT: **(d)** ....
WAITER: Excuse me, **(e)** .... do any of you own a Volkswagen Passat?
MARION: Yes, why?
KURT: But!.....

Now listen to Track 51 to check your answers.

32 Copy and complete the table with the following phrases.

(Yes, and) on top of that
(Yes, and) what's more
(Yes, but) looking at it from another angle / viewpoint
And as if that wasn't enough
And that's not all
By the way, talking of ...
Could I just ask a question / say something?
Excuse me
Furthermore
Hey hold on / hang on a minute
I don't want to interrupt, but
If I could just get a word in edgeways
If I might just make a point / come in here
In addition
Incidentally, on the subject of ...
Moreover
Moving swiftly on
On another matter / topic altogether
One shouldn't forget
Wait a minute
We should remember
Yes, but on the other hand
Yes, but there again

Reinforcing what's being said	
Balancing what's being said	
Changing the subject	
Interrupting	

Which of the phrases are likely to be (a) more formal, (b) neutral, or (c) less formal?

33 In groups Write 'reinforcement', 'balancing', 'changing the subject' or 'interrupting' on many separate pieces of paper. Put the pieces of paper in a pile, face down, in the middle of the group. Individually, write sentences giving your opinion on some or all of the following topics.

- the weather
- restaurants
- keeping a diary
- people with blonde hair
- the kind of food we eat
- the paranormal (fortune-telling, etc.)
- a topic of your choice

A student in the group says their sentence. Another student picks up one of the pieces of paper and reinforces, balances, etc., depending on what's written there.

Example: STUDENT A: I think the weather's getting worse.

STUDENT B: *picks up a piece of paper with 'reinforcement' on it*

Yes, I agree, and it's making planning very difficult.

⬤⬤⬤ Pronunciation: intonation

34 Listen to the conversations *a–h* on Track 52. Is the man going to do what the woman asks or not? How do you know?

Example: a Yes.

He sounds ...

35 Reply to the people on Track 52 using the same intonation and tone of voice as the man did in activity 34. Then you'll hear if you were right.

a Well ...
b I'd rather not ...
c That depends on what it is.
d Why should I?
e I'd rather not.
f Well, I would really ...
g Why should I?
h I'd rather not.

Now listen to Track 53. Did the speakers reply in the same way as you?

Writing: diaries

36 Discuss the following questions with a partner.

a What different reasons are there for people to write diaries?
b What do people put in their diaries?
c Have you ever written a diary?
d Whose diary (anyone living or dead) would you most like to read?

37 Read these diary entries. Which of the following (*a–d*) describes them best, do you think (answer at the bottom of page 109)?

The diary entries are written by:
a ... a bicycle thief who lives in Oxford.
b ... a fictional character (who wants to be a writer), and the diary entries are meant to be funny.
c ... a Polish tourist, who is on holiday and goes sightseeing.
d ... a male model with a fear of dogs, who wants to find work in Oxford.

Monday April 15th
I was ten minutes late for work this morning. The exhaust pipe fell off the bus. Mr Brown was entirely unsympathetic. He said, 'You should get yourself a bicycle, Mole.' I pointed out that I have had three bicycles stolen in 18 months. I can no longer afford to supply the criminals of Oxford with ecologically sound transport. Brown snapped, 'Then *walk*, Mole. Get up earlier and *walk*.'

Friday May 24th
A house on my way to work has acquired an American pit bull terrier. On the surface, it seems to be a friendly dog. All it does is stand and grin through the fence. But in future I will take a different route to work. I cannot risk facial disfigurement. I would like the photograph on the back of my book to show my face as it is today, not terribly scarred. I know plastic surgeons can work miracles, but from now on I am taking no chances.

Saturday May 25th
Oxford is full of sightseers riding on the top deck of the tourist buses and walking along the streets looking upwards. It is extremely annoying to us residents to be asked the way by foreigners every five minutes. Perhaps it is petty of me, but I quite enjoy sending them in the wrong direction.

38 Choose one of the dates and answer the questions about it.

Monday April 15th
a Who is Mr Brown?
b What is the diary writer's surname?
c Why doesn't the writer use a bicycle?
d Is the writer's comment about Oxford criminals serious, sarcastic or funny?

Friday May 24th
a Why has the diary writer changed his route from his house to his work?
b What is the animal like?
c What does the writer fear?
d What is the connection between the following: disfigurement, scar, plastic surgery?

Saturday May 25th
a Where does the diary writer live?
b What do the tourists do?
c What does the writer enjoy doing?
d Do you sympathise with his criticisms of foreigners?

39 **Diary writing** Complete one of the following tasks.

a List four things you did yesterday and write them as a diary entry.
b Write a diary entry for yesterday in which you put four things that you would really like to have happened, but which did not actually happen.
c Choose a famous character (living or dead). Write a diary entry which they might have written.

The diary entries are from *Adrian Mole: the Wilderness Years* by Sue Townsend, the humorous diary of a fictional character who always has bad luck and has peculiar opinions about everything (and who dreams of being a famous writer).

Review: grammar and functional language

40 Read the English teacher's story and underline all the past tense verbs. How many different kinds are there? Can you find examples of sentences and clauses with one subject but more than one verb? You can look at Activities 14–18 for help.

A student once told me this story. He said he was walking along a street in Moscow thinking about nothing in particular and smoking a cigarette. It was the middle of winter. There was snow underfoot and on the rooftops above him there were huge blocks of ice. That's what he said anyway, and I had no reason to disbelieve him.

Anyway, this student's problem was that he was a heavy smoker. He had tried to give up many times and each time, he said, giving up had not been hard, but it had been impossible preventing himself from starting again. So right there, on the pavement of a Moscow street with tall buildings all around him, he finished his cigarette and that would have been that, except that he instantly thought that he would like to have another one. So he took off his gloves, reached into his jacket pocket, got a packet of Marlboros and pulled out a cigarette. Next, as you would expect, he reached for the lighter he had bought himself the day before and then, right there in the street, in the cold, he stopped to light his cigarette, and another man who had been walking just behind him passed him as he went on down the pavement.

At that moment, a large block of ice detached itself from a roof above them and came crashing down into the street. It hit the man who had just passed my student, killing him instantly. If my student hadn't stopped to light a cigarette ... 'Which just goes to show,' he said to the other students in my class as he told his story, 'that smoking is good for you.' He swore that it was a true story and that he hadn't made it up.

Cover the story with your hand and re-tell it from memory.

41 **In pairs** Student A chooses one of the situations *a–f* and asks for help.

Student B answers and uses stress and intonation to mean the opposite of what is said. You can look at Activities 34–35 for help.

Example: a
STUDENT A: *Could you help me to move a table in the garden?*
STUDENT B *(sounding doubtful): Sure.*

You would like someone to:
a ... help you to move a table in the garden.
b ... help you push your car which has just broken down.
c ... talk to someone you know to find out what they really think of you.
d ... give you some advice about how to succeed in your work or your studies.
e ... post a letter for you when they go to the shops.
f ... take a parcel for a friend or family member in their suitcase on their flight to the place where your friend or family member lives.

Review: vocabulary

blazing sun	sunshine
blizzard	thunder
breeze	thunderstruck
downpour	to blow
equivalent	to drizzle
fabulous	to fall
flooded	to howl
gale	to pour
heavy shower	to roar
heavy snowfall	to roast
intersection	to scorch
light breeze	to settle
light shower	to shine
light snowfall	to stream (into)
soaked	to thunder
staged	to whistle
strong breeze	torrential rain
strong sunshine	waded
strong wind	

a storm of protest
a sunny disposition
by candlelight
gales of laughter
it crossed (my) mind
now and then
thunderous applause
to blaze with anger
to compensate for something
to know for sure
to look like
to make it home
to shower people with presents / gifts
to storm out of
to turn something on full volume

42 Choose your favourite kind of weather from the Word List. Why do you like that weather? What do you do in weather like that? Choose your least favourite kind of weather. Why don't you like that weather? What do you do in weather like that?

What is your favourite phrase from Word Plus? Tell the other students about your words and phrases.

Pronunciation

43 Put words from the Word List in groups depending on the vowel sound of their stressed syllable. Each word in a group must share the same sound. Do not include *fabulous* or *strong*.

Example: *The words 'blizzard', 'drizzle', 'equivalent', 'wind' and 'whistle' all include the vowel sound /ɪ/ as part of their stressed syllable.*

Listen to the speakers on Track 54. Have you made the same groups?

44 Find words in the Word List and Word Plus which have the following sound clusters. The first one is done for you.

a	b	c	d
/bl/	/br/	/dr	/fl/
blazing, …			
e	f	g	h
/kr/	/kʃ/	/str/	/pr/

Check your answers by listening to Track 55. Which do you find difficult to pronounce?

45 **In groups** Using phrases from the two lists, tell a story about being in a particular weather situation. Don't say what the weather was like when you tell your story. The other students have to guess.

Example: STUDENT A: *Well, he had quite a sunny disposition, but that night, when we were watching television, the lights went out and we ended up having to rely on candlelight. He blazed with anger for some reason.*
STUDENT B: *It was a storm?*
STUDENT A: *Yes.*
STUDENT C: *With thunder and lightning? …*

→ phrasal verbs
→ fame and notoriety
→ checking and confirming

Reading: reality TV

1 Complete these descriptions of TV shows with a word or phrase from the box.

eliminated   deal with   reveal   criticised   humiliated   betraying

8 pm Pop Idol
See ten young singers sing and be
(**a**) … and encouraged by a group of
professional judges. Then we get to
vote and one person will be (**b**) …
from the show. Who will be the last
singer left?

9 pm Survivor
First episode of a new series. Sixteen
people are put on a remote island and
have to (**c**) … the difficulties of living
on an island. One by one, they vote
each other off the island, often (**d**) …
their friends, until one person is left.
The one person left wins one million
dollars.

11 pm Blind Date
Anything can happen on Blind Date.
Watch two strangers go on a date with
each other. Who will (**e**) … a lot of
personal details about themselves?
Who will be (**f**) …?

2 In groups If you were planning a reality TV show like the ones above,

 a … what area of life would you choose (e.g. the army, school teaching,
   nursing, hairdressing)?
 b … what would the 'contestants' have to do?
 c … how would you choose the winner?

3 Read the text on page 112 quickly. Copy and complete the table with the four types
of reality TV show mentioned. Give one example of each one.

	a	b	c	d
Type of show	shows that go into someone's home			
Example				

Look at the TV shows in Activity 1. Which type are they all? Write them in your table too.

Why on earth do they do it?

In 1968 Andy Warhol said, 'In the future, everybody will be world-famous for 15 minutes.' He was referring to the commercialisation of all aspects of our lives. With the growth of reality TV, his prediction seems to be coming true.

Reality TV shows are becoming more and more popular in Britain, the USA and other parts of the world. You may not understand why, but the ratings for these shows are high and they are relatively cheap to produce as the makers of the shows don't have to pay actors – they often star ordinary people eager for fame and who will jump at any chance to achieve it. We'll tell you why later, but first, let's look at the different types of show that come under the heading of 'reality TV'.

Firstly, there are shows that go into someone's home and life and follow them around – *The Osbournes* is a typical example. The people on these shows are often famous and unusual in some way. This isn't always the case, of course, and sometimes the cameras may follow an ordinary doctor around or look at an everyday family as they deal with their problems. We get to look at other people's lives and compare them with our own.

Next, there are reality shows manufactured for TV, where the producers of the show put people into some kind of unusual situation and see how they react. In *Joe Millionaire*, 20 women were flown to a castle in France where they had the chance to meet Evan Marriott, who they were told was a multi-millionaire. In fact, Evan was a construction worker. In *The Real World*, seven young strangers are put together in a house for four months and cameras follow them around; the audience gets to observe how they get along with each other as they gradually open up about who they are. By now, we're all familiar with shows like this.

Then, what about those reality shows about real life where the people who come on seem to have no limits about revealing all – about their private lives and anyone else's! *The Jerry Springer Show* is famous for its controversial subject matter and guests on the show often get into physical fights with each other. Then, there are real-life courtroom TV shows such as *Judge Judy* where people dispute a legal claim before millions of viewers. It seems that people on these shows will give very intimate details away and have no qualms about betraying their friends and family. Where do they find these people?

Last but not least, my own personal favourite, dating shows like *Elimidate* or *Blind Date*. On *Elimidate*, one person (either male or female) goes out on a date with four people of the opposite sex and one by one eliminates them until they finally choose the one person they would like to go on a 'real' date with. People criticise and humiliate each other (and themselves in the process) to 'win the competition'.

So, can someone tell me why these shows are so popular? Why do we love to see people doing desperate things for their '15 minutes of fame'? Is it that we see ourselves in these ordinary people? Or is it the opposite? Do we like to be reassured that we are normal and it's everyone else that's crazy? And anyway, do the people on these shows really act like this when the cameras are not following them around?

Well, maybe they're not crazy, nor are they even trying to act naturally. Do you remember the days when people appeared on TV because they were famous? Well, times have changed and now appearing on TV is a good way to *become* famous. Many people are using their appearances on a reality TV show as a step into show business, hoping that their careers will take off once they have been seen by millions of people. Think about it – do you know any 'celebrities' who started their career on a reality TV show? People who appear on reality TV are hoping for a bit more than the 15 minutes promised by Andy Warhol!

See you next week.

4 **Fact check** Read Julie Marsfield's article again. *True* or *False*?

a Andy Warhol's quotation is about reality TV.
b Huge numbers of people watch reality TV.
c Reality TV shows are usually expensive to make.
d Ordinary people often want to be on reality TV.
e Producers sometimes lie to people who go on the shows.
f People never talk about their personal lives.
g People on dating shows are always nice to each other.
h Most people probably act 'unnaturally' on reality shows.
i After appearing on a reality TV show, some people become famous.

5 Explain the meaning of the following words as they appear in the text.

a commercialisation (paragraph 1)
b ratings (paragraph 2)
c star (paragraph 2)
d eager (paragraph 2)
e manufactured (paragraph 4)
f controversial (paragraph 5)
g desperate (paragraph 7)
h appearances (paragraph 8)

Language in chunks

6 Look at how these phrases are used in the text and then use them in the sentences which follow. You may have to change them a little to make them fit.

> with the growth of   jump at the chance   to reveal all   no limits as to
> no qualms about   one by one   to be reassured

a I don't want .... My private life should be private.
b He .... of being on the show. At last he was going to be famous.
c She has .... going by herself. She loves travelling alone.
d Do you have .... what you will do for money? How could you take that job?
e Jake's parents were worried about leaving him, but they .... by the fact that Lois was an experienced babysitter.
f .... the sales of DVD players, there are fewer VCRs being sold.
g They went into the room .... and sat down at their desks.

Use the phrases in sentences of your own.

7 **Noticing language** Find the following verbs in the text.

> get along with   give away   look at   take off

What do the verbs mean? Can you find other multi-word verbs in the text?

How are multi-word, or 'phrasal' verbs, different from other verbs in the text?

8 **Discussion** Copy and complete the table about yourself.

	Agree	Disagree
I would never appear on a reality TV show.		
I would like to be famous.		
People should not become famous just because they have been on TV; they should have done something important first.		
If you want to be famous, you should be prepared to sacrifice your privacy.		

Check your answers with a partner and ask them at least two questions about each one of their answers.

Example: STUDENT A: I would never appear on a reality TV show.
STUDENT B: Why not?
STUDENT A: I'm a private person and I don't want everyone to know my business and ...

Tell the class what your partner said.

Vocabulary: fame and notoriety

9 Related words Look at the words associated with fame.

> celebrity eminence fame infamy legend
> notoriety renown star stardom superstar

Which of them can you make into (a) adjectives and (b) verbs? What changes (if anything) in each case?

10 Complete the following sentences with words (nouns or adjectives) from either Activity 9 or the box below.

> well-known eye name VIP headlines

a Shortly after winning Pop Idol, she *achieved* .... by spending all her winnings at expensive stores all over London.

b You don't have to do anything much to be a .... You just have to be seen in the right places at the right time.

c Everyone knows this actress. She's a *household* ....

d *At the height of his* ...., he was known by almost everyone in the world.

e The problem about being famous is that you are always *in the public* ....

f He's having a fantastic career right now. You see him everywhere and *his* .... *is on everybody's lips.*

g As a result of her arrest, her name really *hit the* ....

h She made her .... as a gossip columnist on a national newspaper.

i To be a real ...., you have to be a film star, famous fashion designer or world leader. Or something else. But anyone can be quite .... in their own country just by being on television.

j To be *world-* .... , you need to be on every TV station on the planet!

11 Connotation Look at these sentences. Which of the words and expressions are <u>neutral</u> ways to talk about fame and which imply being famous in a <u>negative</u> way?

a He became *world-famous* after a number one hit single in 2003.

b They *achieved notoriety* for robbing five banks in a year.

c Stephen Hawking is an *eminent* scientist, known for his work on black holes.

d She's a *celebrated* author, who has had several bestsellers.

e Tonight the *renowned* journalist, Greg Pallast, will be appearing and presenting his new book.

f The *legendary* guitarist, Jimi Hendrix, died at a very young age. His music is still played widely.

g Tonight we welcome a pianist *of great renown*, Judy Marston.

h The *well-known* actress has appeared in three movies this year.

i She is known as an *infamous* liar and cheat in the world of sport.

j He rose to a position of *eminence* among followers of that faith.

k The singer *rose to stardom* in the 1980s, selling millions of records that were played everywhere.

12 How many people do you know about in the following categories?

a ... a classical musician? c ... a sportsperson?

b ... a pop star? d ... an army general?

Describe the people you have chosen using words from Activities 9–11.

13 Look at these pictures of people who are or were famous in the 20th and 21st centuries.

- Which ones do you know about?
- Why are they or why were they famous?
- What is your opinion of them?

a 'If people don't get ... , it's a nice feeling.' *Bono, U2*

b 'Heartthrobs are ... .' *Brad Pitt*

c 'It has its ... and it has its ... .' *Marilyn Monroe*

d 'The world needs ... and it's better they be harmless men like me than ... like Hitler.'
Albert Einstein

e 'I cannot drink, smoke or go to the karaoke. I must present a good ... .' *Jackie Chan*

f 'I'm always trying to escape from the ... of expectation.'
Shakira

g 'It doesn't exactly feel like a shock, but it's all new to me and I'm ... .' *Eminem*

h 'I won't let all the money and glory ... .'
Ronaldo

i 'I don't think I realized that the cost of fame is that it's ... on every moment of your life.'
Julia Roberts

14 Complete what the characters in Activity 13 once said about fame, using one of the following words or expressions for each gap.

> a dime a dozen   compensations   drawbacks
> go to my head   heroes   image   in your face
> open season   pressure   taking it as it comes
> villains

Grammar: phrasal verbs

15 Phrasal verbs – Types 1 and 2 Match the verbs in italics in sentences *a–h* with their meaning below (*1–8*).

a The plane *took off* from Paris at half past three.
b A beautiful old building was *pulled down* to make room for the new motorway.
c He was *turned down* for the job of manager, but at least they gave him a pay rise.
d For two days the water heater was not working properly, and then it *blew up*.
e My plans didn't *work out*, so I've decided to leave the city and live in the country.
f I believed in you, but you *let* me *down*.
g She *put off* solving the problem until later.
h The couple had a lot of problems so they decided to *break up*.

1 demolish
2 disappoint
3 explode
4 leave the ground
5 postpone
6 refuse
7 separate
8 succeed

Read 11A–11C in the Mini-grammar and say whether the verbs in italics are Type 1 or Type 2.

16 Read the story and match the phrasal verbs (in blue in the text) to the meanings *1–8* at the top of page 116.

This is a story told by Edward de Bono, the famous professor.

A film producer owes his old business partner a lot of money over a movie project that failed. One day, the man comes by to collect his money. He has worked out a plan to get his money and he also wants to ruin the producer. He tells the producer that he will place a white stone and a black stone in a bag. The producer agrees that if his daughter chooses the white stone from the bag the debt will be cancelled, but if she picks the black stone out, the man will get his house and land. The daughter sees that the man puts two black stones in the bag to trick the producer. The producer has brought his daughter up to be a fast thinker, so she does not speak up at this moment. Instead, she takes a stone from the bag and immediately drops it on the ground where there are many other stones – both black and white. The stone gets lost. She then points out that the stone that is left in the bag must be the opposite color of the one she chose. The man cannot admit that he was taking the producer in, so he has to agree to write off the debt.

a	come by	....	1 cancel
b	work out	....	2 devise, invent
c	pick out	....	3 explain, show
d	bring up	....	4 fool, deceive
e	speak up	....	5 raise, educate
f	point out	....	6 say something
g	take in	....	7 choose
h	write off	....	8 arrive

Are they Type 1 or Type 2 verbs?

Cover and practise telling the story from page 115 to your partner. Each time you use a phrasal verb, your partner writes down a synonym. Your partner now tells the story, replacing the synonyms with the original phrasal verbs.

17 Complete these sentences with one of the phrasal verbs from Activity 16 in the correct form.

a Sometimes my friend .... to help me with my homework.   *comes by*

b I want you to help me .... a new textbook .... for my maths class.

c Her parents .... her .... to be very independent.

d To get what you want, you have to .... You can't stay silent.

e She had no money. She needed to .... a way to make more money.

f The magician .... the little children .... They didn't realise it was a trick.

g The car was so badly damaged that they decided to .... it .... , claim the insurance, and get a new one.

h The teacher .... that there was a mistake in the book.

18 **Phrasal verbs – Types 3 and 4** Copy and complete the table with words from the sentences below. Use **11D and 11E in the Mini-grammar** to help you.

Type 3	
Type 4	

a If you want to be famous, you have to *put up with* losing your privacy.

b He was *looking for* his glasses and found them on the sofa.

c She had *fallen for* him the moment she saw him and they married within a year.

d Charlie Sheen and his brother Emilio Estevez *take after* their father, Martin Sheen. They are also actors.

e Stars often don't have time to *look after* their children themselves. They need someone to help them.

f Are you *looking forward to* the next Julia Roberts movie? I can't wait.

19 Match the verbs in italics in Activity 18 with their meanings.

a	put up with	1	search, try to find
b	look for	2	fall in love with
c	fall for	3	want something to happen soon
d	take after		
e	look after	4	tolerate
f	look forward to	5	resemble, look like
		6	care for

20 Read each conversation. Choose the correct form of one of the verbs in the box to fill the gaps.

> check up on   come across   get along with
> look down on   look into   pay back   run into

Jane and Don

JANE: You'll never guess who I (a) ...*ran into*... this morning?

DON: Who?

JANE: Martha Westley, my old school friend. I (b) .... her so well when we were teenagers. Well, at the beginning anyway.

DON: And now?

JANE: I don't know. She really seemed to be (c) .... me, you know, disrespecting me.

DON: Why is she doing that?

JANE: I think she's (d) .... me .... because I stopped being her friend when we were about 14.

Harry and the detective

HARRY: I need someone to (e) .... my lawyer. I think he's stealing my mother's money.

DETECTIVE: I'll (f) .... it right away, sir. What makes you think he's stealing from her?

HARRY: I was helping my mother manage her accounts and I (g) .... some cheques to him that my mother says she didn't sign.

DETECTIVE: OK, sir. I'll start right away.

21 Complete these sentences about yourself.

a At work / school, I'm not prepared to put up with ....

b I'm looking forward to ....

c In my family, people say I take after ....

Compare answers with a partner and explain what you've written.

22 **Team game** Using a dictionary, find as many phrasal verbs as you can. Write down their definitions.

a Team A reads the definitions to Team B.

b Team B gets one point if they say the correct phrasal verb and one point if they make a sentence using the phrasal verb correctly.

c Now Team B reads a definition to Team A.

Functional language: checking and confirming

23 Listen to Track 56. Complete the conversation with words or phrases that you hear there.

JOHNNY: OK. Let's do that one again.
CARRIE: When's the gig? Friday, (a) .... ?   2
JOHNNY: No, I keep telling you, it's on Thursday.
CARRIE: Oh, that's right. (b) .... we only have ten days?
JOHNNY: That's right. We really have to practise hard.
DAVE: And it starts at 7, (c) .... ?
JOHNNY: No, it starts at 8.
DAVE: Oh yeah. I remember now.
KATIE: And we're playing for an hour, (d) .... ?
JOHNNY: No, we're playing for 30 minutes.

KATIE: And we're doing ten songs, (e) .... ?
JOHNNY: No. We're doing six songs. I've told you all this three times.
DAVE: So, (f) .... make us famous?
JOHNNY: Listen. Rock bands are a dime a dozen. Fame takes hard work.
CARRIE: He's right. Come on, guys – let's take it from the top.

24 Read the information below and decide whether the words and phrases you chose for the conversation in Activity 23 are examples of:

1 a tag question (e.g. *It's at 7, isn't it?*)
2 a checking question to get confirmation (e.g. *She's a great actress wouldn't you say?*)
3 a question to find out information (e.g. *Do you mean we have to leave early?*).

The first one is done for you.

25 Using the descriptions from Activity 24, say whether these sentences are examples of question types *1, 2* or *3*. The first one is done for you.

a They're famous, huh?   2
b They have a lot of fans, don't they?
c She's a good actress, wouldn't you say?
d Does the show start at 7?
e He never practises, does he?
f He's great, don't you think?
g Do you mean to say that we have to be there at 6?
h It's at 7, isn't it?
i Does that mean we have to practise tomorrow?
j They're celebrities, aren't they?
k It's on Friday, right?

26 Use checking questions to ask your partner their views about the following things.

a Reading about famous people is fun.
b Jennifer Lopez is a great singer.
c Tom Cruise was good in his last movie.
d Pele was the greatest soccer player of all time.
e Jackie Chan grew up in Hong Kong.
f Neither Mexico nor the USA have ever won the World Cup.
g The new term begins in September.
h You need to get 80% to pass this English test.
i All famous people are talented.

Example: STUDENT A: **Reading about famous people is fun, don't you think?**
STUDENT B: **Sure. They have extraordinary lives, don't they?**

27 In pairs Look at Activity Bank 21 on page 165.

a Student A, ask B checking questions without looking back at the Activity Bank.
b Now change round. Student A can look at Activity Bank 21. Student B cannot, and so asks checking questions.

Example: STUDENT A: **The flight's at 8 o'clock, right?**
STUDENT B: **No, it's at 6 o'clock.**
STUDENT A: **Does that mean you have to be at the airport at 4 o'clock?**

●●● Pronunciation: intonation in tag questions

28 Listen to these sentences on Track 57. Draw the arrow ⟋ or ⟍ according to the intonation you hear. The first one is done for you.

    a That was a great game, wasn't it?
    b You're coming to the party, aren't you?
    c Brad Pitt lives here, doesn't he?
    d She hasn't made a record in two years, has she?
    e They were on TV last night, weren't they?
    f You hadn't asked her about going on a trip, had you?
    g They didn't want to eat in that restaurant, did they?

Are the speakers asking because they want confirmation of something they know or because they probably don't know the answer?

29 Say the sentences using the same intonation as the speakers on Track 57.

30 Complete the sentences with the appropriate tag question and practise using the appropriate intonation.

    a The flight is at 2 o'clock, ... ?   – That's right.
    b He isn't coming, ... ?   – No, he isn't.
    c They live here, ... ?   – Uh-huh.
    d John and Maria don't like concerts, ... ?   – No.
    e You've been to Paris, ... ?   – Yes, I have.
    f They haven't eaten their dinner, ... ?   – No, they haven't.

Now listen to Track 58 and check your answers.

●●

Listening: Diana's story

31 Look at the picture of Diana. Guess as you much as you can about who she is, where she's from, what she does, etc.

32 Read the following questions about Diana.

    a Where is Diana from?
    b What happened when she was 13?
    c How did she try to get accommodation when she went to Mumbai (then called Bombay)?
    d What time was it on Diana's watch when she knocked on the lady's door?
    e Why do you think the lady said 'Come inside'?
    f What lesson does Diana draw from this experience in her life?

Now listen to Track 59. Answer the questions.

33 Diana went on to become quite famous. She won something. What do you think she won?

Listen to Track 60. Were you right?

34 Copy the table and make notes as you listen to Track 60 again.

What Diana was afraid of and why
The number of people watching the second competition
How she felt when she won her second big competition
What she did with the thing she won
What happened immediately after she won

35 Vocabulary Answer the questions about the words and phrases in blue. They are words and phrases that Diana uses.

a What is a bedsit?
b What does it mean if we say that our hair is standing on end? Does Diana use the same expression? Why?
c If you give something your all, do you make a lot of effort or a little?
d If to trip means to fall over because something got in the way of your foot, what does trip over your words mean?
e When your mind goes blank, is it easy to decide what to say?
f If you feel euphoria, are you fantastically happy or terribly sad?
g Is a regular person an important person (like a movie star), or are they ordinary, like everyone else?
h What does a chaperone do?
i What is a cockpit and who usually sits there?

36 Listen to Tracks 59 and 60 again and follow the interview in the Audioscript. Then close your books and, in your own words, tell the story of one of the following events.

a the evening Diana found accommodation in Mumbai
b the time Diana won her big competition

37 Discussion In groups, give your opinions about these questions.

a What do you think about contests like the one Diana took part in?
b Would you like to meet someone who has won what Diana did? What would you say to them?

Speaking: decision-making (making a star)

38 In pairs Read this information about these singers and groups. Their musical / dancing ability has been rated from ***** (excellent) to * (bad).

Which ones would you listen to and why?

Name: The Brainstormers
Ages: 18–25
Image: rebellious, non-conformist
Musical ability: *****
Dancing ability: **
Type of music: rock

Name: Caitlin Curbey
Age: 22
Image: lively, sweet
Musical ability: ***
Dancing ability: *****
Type of music: pop music

Name: Ben Lomax
Age: 34
Image: deep, spiritual
Musical ability: *****
Type of music: intelligent ballads

Name: Star
Ages: 16
Image: clean, sweet
Musical ability: *****
Dancing ability: **
Type of music: pop

Name: LoneMan
Age: 23
Image: tough
Musical ability: ****
Dancing ability: ***
Type of music: rap / hip-hop

Name: Crystal
Ages: 28–30
Image: country, simple girls
Musical ability: *****
Type of music: country

39 Group work Imagine you are record producers. You can give a recording contract to one of these six acts. Decide who you are going to give the recording contract to and why.

Points to consider:
• age (of artist and listeners / buyers)
• market (what is 'hot' at the moment)
• musical ability
• things you would like to change

Compare your decision with other groups. Give reasons for your decision.

Writing: researching for writing

40 Where do you usually get information when you need to write? Put *often* (o), *sometimes* (s), *rarely* (r) or *never* (n) in the brackets.

the Internet	[ ]	textbooks	[ ]
the library	[ ]	asking other people	[ ]
encyclopaedias	[ ]	magazines	[ ]
a dictionary	[ ]	talking to an expert	[ ]
a grammar book	[ ]	other sources	[ ]

Compare with a partner. Which resource is the most valuable for you? Which one is the least useful?

41 Read this biography of Jackie Chan.

Jackie Chan was born in Hong Kong in 1954. His real name is Chan Kong Sang. His parents were very poor – his father worked as a cook and his mother worked as a housekeeper in the French Embassy. Jackie hated school and left after primary school.

When he was 7, Jackie's parents enrolled him in the China Drama Academy and he often performed in public. Jackie Chan learned how to perform stunts at the academy, which he left when he was 17 to take up a career as a professional stuntman, appearing in Bruce Lee movies. Jackie's early career as an actor was not very successful and it was not until he added comedy to his action movies that he became very popular. Jackie Chan broke into Hollywood in the 1990s and is the biggest Hollywood movie star from Hong Kong. Today, Jackie Chan is famous all over the world with such movies as *Rush Hour 1, 2* and *3*, and *Around the World in 80 Days*.

Write information from the text in note form about the following:

a [ ] date of birth
b [ ] his early career
c [ ] how famous he is
d [ ] what he learned in his studies (after school)
e [ ] what he thought of school
f [ ] what his position is today
g [ ] what made him famous
h [ ] where he studied after school
i [1] where he was born
j [ ] where he went to school
k [ ] who his parents were

In what order is the information presented in the text? Write 1–11 in the brackets. The first one is done for you. Why are things in this order?

Word Choice: *at the moment, at present, at this moment in time, at this time, currently, these days, today*

42 Look at the Word Choice notes on page 58 in the booklet.

43 Complete the sentences with *at the moment, at present, at this moment in time, at this time, currently, these days, today*. You can often use more than one phrase.

a .... I'm not practising as much as I used to.
b .... we – that is the government – are looking at new ways of funding the film industry.
c .... she is one of the most famous people on the planet.
d He's directing a film in Vietnam ....
e '..................... I would like to turn to foreign policy,' said the American President.
f They're .... unavailable.
g .... we are at a crossroads for mankind.
h .... I have nothing to add to my previous statement.
i .... I'm not planning any new movies or other project.

44 Now match the information about Shakira (Shakira Mebarak Ripoll) with the headings *a–k* in Activity 41.

– February 2, 1977
– started writing songs at 8 years old; signed a recording contract in 1990
– famous worldwide; best-selling records in English, Spanish and Portuguese
– developed her own style of music, combining her Latin and Arab influences with modern rock music
– Barranquilla, Colombia
– Colombian mother, Lebanese father

Now write a short biography of Shakira using the same information sequence as that in the text about Jackie Chan in Activity 41.

45 In groups Who is your favourite celebrity? What do you know about them already?
Discuss your celebrity with your group.

a Find out as much as you can about your celebrity using any or all of the resources mentioned in Activity 40.
b Write a short biography of your celebrity.

Review: grammar and functional language

46 Use the correct form of the phrasal verbs in the box to complete the sentences *a–h*. You can look at Activities 15–20 to help you.

> turn down   pick out   put up with   fall for   break up
> look forward to   take after   look for   bring up

a If you want to be famous, you have to .... losing your privacy.

b Sometimes people go on reality shows .... fame.

c Film stars often .... people because of their physical appearance and their relationships don't last long. They can .... within a year or two of meeting.

d People often .... their parents if they're in show business and become actors or musicians too.

e The children of famous people are often .... by other people because their parents are so busy and consequently the children don't have a normal childhood.

f If you're an actor, you have to accept that you will sometimes be .... for roles that you want. You have to be tough and accept rejection.

g People who are .... the latest record from their favourite singer will pay a lot of money to get it.

h Famous actors are very special and talented because they have been .... from the crowd and they stand out in some way.

Do you think these statements are true? Discuss them in groups and give examples of people you know.

47 What are the drawbacks and compensations of being famous? Copy and complete the table.

Drawbacks

Compensations

Now check your answers with a partner. Ask questions to check. You can look at Activities 23–27 to help you.

Example: STUDENT A: *Losing your privacy is a drawback, don't you think?*

STUDENT B: *Yes, but having a lot of money is a compensation, isn't it?*

Review: vocabulary

appearances	legend
celebrity	manufactured
chaperone	notoriety
cockpit	ratings
commercialisation	renown
controversial	star
desperate	stardom
disputes	superstar
drawbacks	to betray
eager	to criticise
eliminated	to deal with
eminence	to humiliate
euphoria	to open up
fame	to reveal
heroes	villains
image	world-famous
infamy	

'a dime a dozen' *
a (household) name
a regular person
at the height of (your) powers
in the public eye
'in your face'
'it goes to my head'
no limits as to
no qualms about
one by one
open season
to achieve notoriety
to be reassured
to give something your all
to have your name on everybody's lips
to hit the headlines
to jump at the chance
to make your name
to reveal all
to rise to fame
to stand on end
to take something as it comes
to trip over your words
with the growth of
(your) mind goes blank

*Phrases in inverted commas are conversational phrases.

Word Plus 2 (phrasal verbs)

blow up	pick out
break up	point out
bring up	pull down
check up on	put off
come across	put up with
come by	run into
fall for	speak up
get along with	take after
let somebody	take in
down	take off
look after	turn somebody
look down on	down
look for	work out
look forward to	write off
look into	
pay back	

48 If you were famous, which of the words in the Word List and Word Plus on page 121 would you like people to use about you? Imagine you are appearing on a TV show and write how you would like to be introduced. In groups, practise introducing each other using the introduction that you wrote.

Example: 'Tonight on the show, we have the guitarist who has hit the headlines and has become a legend in the music world. Ladies and gentlemen, please welcome ... (person's name).'

● ● ● Pronunciation

49 a Copy and complete the table with as many words as you can from the Word List and Word Plus 1 and 2.

/ʊ/ – pull	/uː/ – dispute

Add more words of your own to the list.

b Nonsense stress game Say the phrases from Word Plus 1 on page 121 using the nonsense syllable *der*, but get the stress right. Can the other students guess which phrase (or phrases) it can be?

Example: STUDENT A: *der DER der DER*

STUDENT B: *Your mind goes blank!*

50 Find a word from the Word List and Word Plus 1 and 2 to complete this dialogue. The first one is done for you.

MATT: Did you see *Pop Idol* last night?

CARMEN: Yes, I love that show. Those singers! I don't know how they (**a**) ....put..up..with..... the pressure.

MATT: Yeah, they're good, but good singers are (**b**) .... It's hard to get noticed. They have to have something special to sing in front of millions of people.

CARMEN: Yes, there's one singer who has a really cool (**c**) .... He always looks good and wears the latest clothes and has the latest haircut. He seems really calm and relaxed, he's just a (**d**) ....

MATT: Did you watch *Blind Date* after *Pop Idol*? That's always funny. Last night this one girl just (**e**) .... the guy all the time – she told him everything that was wrong with him. I felt so sorry for him. She was really (**f**) .... , she just wouldn't leave him alone. The guy didn't (**g**) .... at all – he hardly said a word about himself.

CARMEN: No, I don't watch that show. I hate the way they're always (**h**) .... the trust of the other person. They talk about really personal stuff that should be a secret between the couple. I watched *The Osbournes*, though. That show fascinates me. They will (**i**) .... any secret they have. There's nothing we don't know about them.

MATT: Yes, I think fame (**j**) .... They think they're so important and interesting. I'm not a fan of that show. I was watching *Survivor* on the other channel to see who would be (**k**) .... this week. You never know, there are always unexpected things that happen on that show. Wow! Listen to us, we watch too much TV, don't we?

Writing and writers

→ relative clauses
→ writing, books and authors
→ agreeing and disagreeing

Vocabulary: writing, books and authors

1 **In pairs** Read about these authors and complete the texts with the words in the box.

| background | plot | characters | prize-winning | prolific | adapted | best-selling | acclaimed | twists |

Stephen King has written more than 30 books since 1971, proof that he is a (**a**) .... author. His work deals mostly with horror and the supernatural.

John Grisham is a lawyer from Mississippi, who has penned more than 15 (**b**) .... novels, which have sold millions around the world. He's famous for (**c**) .... in his stories that leave the reader guessing until the last page.

Zadie Smith writes about the richness and diversity of multicultural, multi-ethnic Britain in her (**d**) .... first book *White Teeth*, which won the Whitbread Award for a First Novel. She was born in London in 1975.

Amy Tan, born to Chinese parents, grew up in California. She writes about the problems of combining her Chinese (**e**) .... with her American reality and lifestyle.

Alice Walker is a highly (**f**) .... and respected author whose novels deal with the rights of women and African-Americans.

Nick Hornby is a London-based author who describes simply, intelligently and hilariously everyday (**g**) .... and their lives.

Danielle Steel has authored around 60 books; most are romance novels. Over 20 of her books have been (**h**) .... for TV movies.

Isabel Allende is a Chilean writer who is known as a great storyteller – she has a gift for finding a good (**i**) .... and making it interesting.

2 Find as many similarities as you can between the writers. Put them into different groups. Some writers may go in more than one group (e.g. Stephen King is American, a man, a thriller writer, etc.).

List the writers in order of preference. Who would you like to read? Compare your list with a partner.

3 Read this text about writing a book and getting it published, and discuss these questions.

  a Would you like to write a book? Why? Why not?
  b What kind of book would you write if you were a writer?

Becoming an author is no easy option when it comes to making a career move. First, there is the actual process of penning your first book. Whether you're interested in factual writing or fiction, be it an autobiography, a novel, a travel book, or even poetry, it will involve doing research of some kind before and as you write. Once you have the basic outline written and notes made (and that involves coming up with a good plot or story and devising all its twists and turns), you'll need to work on a draft of your first version. All this may take you longer than you think, especially if you have a full-time job at the same time.

Let's say you do have a completed manuscript: if you're a first-time writer, there follows the process of trying to find a publisher. You may have to read a few rejection letters and even consider self-publishing. If your work is to be published, next comes the whole editing process which may totally change your original work, but a good editor will help you to improve your descriptions and characters as well as the language used for the narrative and the overall structure of the work. Are you interested?

4 **Word building** Find as many words as you can from Activities 1–3 that can fit into this map of words associated with writing.

  Add more words to the word map.

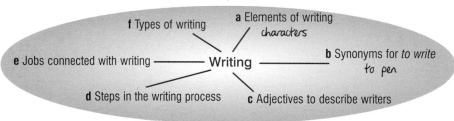

- **f** Types of writing
- **a** Elements of writing — *characters*
- **e** Jobs connected with writing — **Writing** — **b** Synonyms for *to write* — *to pen*
- **d** Steps in the writing process
- **c** Adjectives to describe writers

5 **Same word, different grammar** Look at these sentences and notice how the words are used.

- He published the results of his *research* on Shakespeare. (noun)
- She knew she would need to *research* the topic further before starting her book. (verb)

Complete the following sentences with verbs made from nouns which are used in Activity 3.

  a The latest computer programme was .... by a young teenager from Cambridge, UK.
  b The written portrait of the president was .... by a close aide in the president's office.
  c When she came to our office, she .... her plans for the new company.
  d My advice is to .... your letter, show it your friends and then edit it before you send it. Otherwise you might regret it.
  e He .... the piece of paper in his hands so that in the end it was a crumpled mess.
  f There is no doubt that some people are .... to bring down the government.

Note: The words in (a) and (b) are only used as verbs in formal settings.

6 Using a dictionary, find words that can be both nouns and verbs. Do they have the same or different meanings?

  a Write sentences using the words as either nouns or verbs. Who can write the most correct sentences in the time?
  b Read your sentences to another pair. Tell them the word. They have to say whether it is a noun or a verb.

Reading: the blurb

7 How do you choose what to read? Which of these apply to you?

  a My friends suggest ideas.
  b I look at headlines or captions.
  c I look at the pictures.
  d I flick through the book or magazine.
  e I read the blurb (the short piece of information) on the back of a book.
  f My teacher assigns a book, newspaper article or magazine for a class.
  g I read book reviews.
  h I belong to a book club.
  i I have a subscription to a newspaper / magazine.

Discuss the results with the whole class.

8 Look at the back cover from an extremely popular book. How is this 'blurb' constructed? What is being written about in the sections *a–d*? (page 125)

Hugh Grant and Nicholas Hoult in *About a Boy*

a **From the acclaimed author of *High Fidelity* and *Fever Pitch* comes a great new novel about being a boy and becoming a man.**

b **ABOUT A BOY**

Will is 36 and doesn't want children. He's selfish and self-centred and doesn't mind admitting it. Will thinks of himself as an island like Ibiza and he just wants to be left alone in his world without any responsibilities from the mainland. Thanks to his dad writing a song which is known all over the world, he has a great income and will never need to work a day in his life and he leads a life he loves. The last thing on his mind is settling down or getting married or doing anything as uncool as having a family. He just wants to live blissfully by himself in his cool apartment in London, where he has massive speakers and an awe-inspiring music collection. Is that too much to ask?

Marcus is 12 and he knows he's weird. He has a strange habit of singing for no reason – sometimes in the middle of maths class. This, unfortunately, makes him a figure of fun to the whole school. Marcus blames it all on his mother, who makes him listen to Joni Mitchell instead of Nirvana and read books instead of playing on his Gameboy. He loves his mum, but she is kind of different from everyone else's mum. She won't let him eat fast food or drink soda and she wears strange clothes – and makes Marcus wear them too.

Then Marcus meets Will and he recognises from a mile off that Will is cool. Marcus needs someone who knows what kind of trainers he should wear and who Kurt Cobain is. And Marcus's mother needs a husband. It all seems so perfect to Marcus ...

c NICK HORNBY was born in 1957 and studied at Cambridge University. He is a former teacher and now lives and works in North London. He is the author of several novels and is also the pop music critic for The New Yorker magazine.

d *"In his third novel, Hornby delivers another guaranteed bestseller – brilliant!"*

Books Today Magazine

"Hornby is one of the funniest contemporary writers ... Will is a character every man struggling to face up to his responsibilities will relate to."

The Sunday Review

9 Fact Check Who:

a ... wrote a very famous song?
b ... wears unusual clothes?
c ... doesn't want to have children?
d ... tends to sing out loud?
e ... makes her son do things that are not cool?
f ... writes about pop music for a famous magazine?
g ... has a very large collection of music?
h ... wants someone to help him to be more cool?

10 In groups Does this sound like your kind of book? Why? Why not?

11 Vocabulary Find these words in the text and explain what they mean.

a mainland
b uncool
c blissfully
d massive
e trainers
f former
g delivers
h guaranteed
i struggling

Language in chunks

12 Match these expressions from the text with a definition (1–7).

a to not mind admitting something
b to settle down
c awe-inspiring
d figure of fun
e from a mile off
f to face up to
g to relate to

1 to accept
2 to start living a stable, secure life
3 to be proud of, to not be ashamed of
4 easily, without difficulty
5 someone that people laugh at
6 to identify with, to understand
7 amazing, incredible

13 Now use the expressions in Activity 12 in the sentences below. You may have to change them a little to make them fit.

a My daughter liked to go to parties all the time, but now she has _____ and is married with two children.
b He finally had _____ the fact that he was 30 years old and needed to get a job and earn some money.

c Janet could tell .... that this man did not want to have any responsibilities.

d She was sick of being a .... Why did no one take her seriously?

e The view from the top of the mountain was .... It was absolutely beautiful.

f She found the characters in the novel very difficult to .... as they lived in a different country and in a different time.

g It was his 50th birthday and he .... He knew he looked good for his age and he had made a great life for himself.

14 **Noticing language** Look at these relative clauses from the blurb of *About a Boy*.

... a song which is known all over the world ... (section b, paragraph 1)
... his cool apartment in London, where he has massive speakers ... (section b, paragraph 1)
... his mother, who makes him listen to Joni Mitchell ... (section b, paragraph 2)

Why are the three different relative pronouns (in blue) used?

Find other examples of relative clauses in the text. Identify exactly what or who the relative pronoun refers to.

15 Choose *Paula* (on the left) or *The Green Mile*. Read the blurb about 'your' book, but do not read the other blurb.

With *Paula*, Allende has written a powerful autobiography whose acceptation of the magical and spiritual worlds will remind readers of her first book, *The House of the Spirits*.

Paula is a vivid memoir that captures the reader like a suspense novel. When the daughter of Isabel Allende, Paula, falls into a coma, the author begins telling the story of her family for her unconscious daughter. In the development of the story, there appear before us bizarre ancestors, we hear both delightful and bitter childhood memories, incredible anecdotes from her young years, the most intimate secrets passed along in whispers. In the background, Chile is ever present as we read about the turbulent history of the nation and her family's years of exile.

"Beautiful and moving ... it has everything and everything is marvellous."
Los Angeles Times Book Review

"Fascinating ... in a rich, impeccable prose, she shares with us her most intimate sentiments."
Washington Post Book World

Born in Peru, Isabel Allende was raised in Chile. She worked as a journalist for many years and only began writing fiction in 1981.

Now, for the first time, all six exciting parts of *The Green Mile* come together in one volume to let you enjoy Stephen King's gripping masterpiece.

At Cold Mountain Penitentiary, along the lonely stretch of cells known as the Green Mile, killers like the psychopathic 'Billy the Kid' Wharton and Eduard Delacroix await execution. Here guards as decent as Paul Edgecombe and as sadistic as Percy Wetmore watch over them. But good or evil, innocent or guilty, none have ever seen anything like the new prisoner, John Coffey. Is Coffey a devil in human form? Or is he a far, far different kind of being?

The truth emerges in shock waves in a way that will truly blow your mind.

"King surpasses our expectations, leaves us spellbound and hungry for the next twist of plot." Boston Globe

"King's best in years ... A prison novel that's as haunting and touching as it is just plain haunted."
Entertainment Weekly

STEPHEN KING, the world's best-selling novelist, lives with his wife in Bangor, Maine.

a **In pairs** With a partner who read the same blurb as you, close your book and prepare an oral summary in your own words of the plot, the author and what people think of the book.

b **In groups** Work with another pair who read the blurb of the other book. Listen to their oral summary and then write your version of their blurb.

c Compare your written summary with the actual blurb of the book. What are the similarities and differences?

Listening: books and films

16 Discussion List books that have been made into films. If you have seen a film of a book that you know (e.g. one of the Harry Potter stories), say which you prefer (book or film) and why.

17 Read this plot description from the novel *White Teeth* by Zadie Smith and answer the questions *a–h*.

Archie (Archibald) Jones, a British man, and Samad Iqbal, originally from Bangladesh, have been friends since they were soldiers together in the British Army in World War II. They both live and work in London where Archie is married to a Jamaican woman named Clara with whom he has one nine year-old daughter, Irie, while Samad is married to Alsana and has twin boys, Millat and Magid, who are also nine. Samad, who works as a waiter, has decided that Britain in 1984 is an unhealthy place to bring up his sons and is planning to send Magid to his family in Bangladesh in order to offer him a better education and upbringing. He has not told anyone except Archie about his plan; Magid does not know that his father is going to send him away. Archie has agreed to drive Samad and the child to the airport so that Magid can be put on the plane at 3 am.

Who:

a ... served in the British Army?
b ... is married to Archie?
c ... is Irie?
d ... is Samad married to?
e ... are Millat and Magid?
f ... has family in Bangladesh?
g ... is going to go and live in Bangladesh?
h ... is going to drive to the airport?

18 Read the following scenes from a film treatment of *White Teeth*. What, in your opinion, is the relationship between Millat and Magid? Between Archie and Samad?

SCENE 25
Outside an Indian restaurant, Archie Jones is dressed in a long coat and is standing in front of his car. Samad Iqbal leaves the restaurant and approaches Archie, with his hand out to shake Archie's hand.
SAMAD
I won't forget this, Archibald.
ARCHIE
That's what friends are for, Sam, but I have to tell you something. I had to bring Millat and Irie too.
SAMAD
Why did you bring them?
ARCHIE
They all woke up when I went to get Magid.

SCENE 26
Interior of Archie's car. The three children are in the back seat, asleep, and wake up as the adults get in.
MILLAT
Hey Daddy! Where are we going, Daddy? To a secret disco party?
MAGID
Are we really? Where are we going?
IRIE
I want to go home. *(starts to cry)*

SCENE 27
Close-up on Samad's face. There are tears coming down his face. He looks straight ahead as he speaks.
SAMAD
We're going on a trip to an airport. To Heathrow.
IRIE, MILLAT, MAGID
Wow! Really?
SAMAD
And then Magid is going on a trip with Auntie Zinat.

SCENE 28
We see the three children in the back seat again.
MILLAT
Will he come back?
MAGID
Is it far? Will I be back in time for school on Monday? Only I've got to see what happens with my science experiment in photosynthesis – I put one plant in the cupboard and one plant in the sunlight and I have to see what happened.
MILLAT
Shut up about your stupid plants!
MAGID
Will I be back for school, Daddy?

SCENE 29
Close-up of Samad's face again as he struggles to answer his son.
SAMAD
You'll be in a school on Monday, Magid, I promise.

19 In groups For each scene explain where the camera has to be positioned.

20 Listen to the same incident from the original book on Track 61. Find:

a ... one scene that has been completely changed by the scriptwriter.
b ... some dialogue that has been changed by the scriptwriter.
c ... some dialogue that has been added by the scriptwriter.
d ... some dialogue that has been omitted by the scriptwriter.

Which version do you prefer? Why? Would you like to read the book? Would you like to see a TV or film adaptation of this book?

21 Fact check Listen to Track 61 again and say whether the following statements are true or false.

a The three children are warm.
b The twins are excited to see their father.
c Samad hugs his son tightly.
d Millat doesn't want Magid to come back.
e Samad wants to remember this car ride.
f Archie is worried that they will not get to the airport on time.
g Magid will be able to see his science experiment on Monday.

22 Pairs and groups Read the text of Track 61 in the Audioscript. Find words you don't completely understand.

a Compare your list with a partner. Agree on the five words you would most like to know the meaning of.
b Compare your list with another pair. Agree on a new list of three words.
c Look for the words in a dictionary.
d Tell the class what your words were and what they mean. Did any of the other pairs choose the same words?

Speaking: telling a story

23 Look at the pictures of Mary, her children Jake and Rachael and her husband.

a Put the pictures in order to tell a story.
b Think about how you would tell the story to a friend. You can make notes, but don't write the whole story down.

24 Pairwork Compare your versions of the story. Prepare a new version of the story that you are both happy with. Close your book and practise telling your story without looking at the pictures or your notes.

25 Tell your story to the whole class. Whose story is best?

Grammar: relative clauses

26 Read the sentences. Identify the relative clauses. Which are the relative pronouns / adverbs? The first one is done for you.

   a The meal that we ate at that restaurant was delicious.

     that we ate at that restaurant

   b The place where we went on holiday was very hot.

   c I didn't like the water that I drank from the tap.

   d Are you talking about the woman who lives next door?

   e He's the man whose children were at the gym.

   f I remember a time when I was very tired and couldn't sleep.

Look at 12A and 12B in the Mini-grammar. Do you want to change your answers?

27 Say whether the relative pronouns in Activity 26 are subjects or objects of the verb in the relative clause. You can use **12A–12C in the Mini-grammar** to help you.

   Example: *a that = object*

28 Combine these two ideas using relative clauses. Leave out the relative pronoun or adverb if possible. The first one is done for you.

   a The child was at the party and he was asleep.

     The child who was at the party was asleep.

   b I made this pie and it has a lot of calories.

     The pie ...

   c My mother grew up in a city and the prime minister was born in the city.

     My mother ...

   d There used to be no computers. My aunt remembers this time.

     My aunt ...

   e They are the parents of that child. They are very athletic.

     That is the child ...

   f Did you see that place? I used to live there.

     Did you see the place ... ?

29 Complete these definitions in your own words. Remember to use relative clauses.

   a A city is a place where ...

   b A great restaurant is a place ...

   c A healthy person is someone ...

   d A great party is one ...

   e A good book is one ...

   f A library is a place ...

   g The USA is a country ...

   h The weekend is a time ...

Compare and explain your answers to a partner. Do you have similar or different definitions?

30 Read these sentences and answer the questions below.

   a I walked her to her room, which was downstairs, and told her to get some more rest.

   b The bedroom which was downstairs was the coldest of all the bedrooms.

Look at the relative clauses in blue. Which one:

• ... is essential to the meaning of the sentence? (defining relative clause)

• ... provides extra information and could be omitted? (non-defining relative clause)

Look at 12A–12C in the Mini-grammar to help you.

31 Complete these relative clauses with appropriate pronouns.

   a The house .... I lived as a child was very big.

   b This is the man .... told me he saw a ghost.

   c Her dog, ... lay in the corner, looked at me the whole time.

   d My grandmother, ... is 92, is having a birthday party next week.

Are they defining or non-defining relative clauses?

32 Listen to Track 62. Which sentence (*a* or *b*) does the speaker use? How do you know?

a My sister, who lives in Sydney, never complains about the heat.
b My sister who lives in Sydney never complains about the heat.

What is the difference in meaning between the sentences?

33 Now listen to Track 63. Put commas where necessary.

a The house where I grew up is supposed to be haunted.
b The houses where many people still live are over 200 years old.
c His children who sometimes played by the river said they heard noises.
d Her daughter who plays the piano once saw a ghost.
e People who say they have seen a ghost often just imagined it.
f Professor Macpherson who is an investigator of strange phenomena has never actually seen a ghost.
g The ghost in our house which most of us have seen only appears about twice a year.

Are the relative clauses defining or non-defining?

34 Say the sentences like the speakers on Track 63.

35 Connect the sentences in this paragraph using defining and non-defining relative clauses.

Example: *My family, which is unusually large for a modern family, is very international.*

My family is very international. It is an unusually large family for a modern family. One of my brothers is an architect. He lives in Brazil. One of my sisters lives in Argentina. She is a singer. My parents are French. They live in Mexico. My aunts and uncles have houses all over Europe. They move house a lot. My grandparents are both in their nineties. They live in France. I once saw a ghost in our house. It is in Paris.

36 Write a paragraph about your family, using defining and non-defining relative clauses. Read the paragraph you wrote with the appropriate pauses and intonation.

Functional language: agreeing and disagreeing

37 Listen to Track 64. Match these four books with a summary (*a–h*). There is only one correct summary per book.

- *Reaching the Top*
- *Where the Flowers Grow*
- *Watching Time Go By*
- *Crying Over Spilt Milk*

a succeeding in the business world
b a biography of a famous person
c a children's novel
d a novel about human relationships
e how to be a better gardener
f a true story about climbing a mountain
g using humour to improve your life
h a book about movie stars

38 Listen to Track 64 again. Who liked which book? Copy and complete the table with ticks (✓) if they liked the book or crosses (✗) if they didn't.

	Reaching the Top	Where the Flowers Grow
Rachel	a	b
Garry	c	d
Marsha	e	f
Chris	g	h

	Watching Time Go By	Crying Over Spilt Milk
Rachel	i	j
Garry	k	l
Marsha	m	n
Chris	o	p

39 Match the start of phrases *a–i* with the appropriate endings *1–9*.

a I agree up to a
b Absolutely,
c I couldn't
d I couldn't agree
e I see what
f I'm with Marsha
g I'm going to have
h Nonsense! I have to
i Well, I disagree with both

1 point with Rachel on this one.
2 agree more with Marsha.
3 disagree with Garry here.
4 less with Garry.
5 Marsha and Chris.
6 on this one.
7 to disagree with everyone here …
8 you're all saying, but …
9 Chris!

40 Listen to Track 64 again. Which of your phrases go in the gaps *a–i*?

PRESENTER: Marsha Macdonald?

a MARSHA: .... For me it was a marvellous book, truly amazing. I loved it.

PRESENTER: Chris Rogers?

b CHRIS: .... it's just not my kind of book, but it's quite good at what it tries to do, I suppose.

PRESENTER: Marsha?

c MARSHA: .... I think this book is very interesting.

d RACHEL: It's such a clever and novel idea, using a garden growing as a symbol for a relationship and its development. .... I think this is a beautiful piece of fiction.

e CHRIS: .... – a particularly dull account of an interesting life.

f RACHEL: ....

PRESENTER: Garry?

g GARRY: .... There were a few new insights into Monroe's life.

h RACHEL: .... ! A very funny book ...

i MARSHA: .... and say that I found it very childish in dealing with very serious topics. Not my kind of book.

Are the expressions you have used for gaps *a–i* demonstrating strong agreement (*SA*), strong disagreement (*SD*), mild agreement (*MA*) or mild disagreement (*MD*)?

Example: a *SD*

41 Now decide whether the expressions *a–v* indicate strong or mild agreement, strong or mild disagreement. The first one is done for you.

a But don't you think that ...   *MD*
b Exactly!
c Fair enough, but on the other hand, ...
d I agree to a certain extent, but ...
e I couldn't agree more.
f I guess so.
g I know that's true.
h I suppose so.
i I'm afraid I just can't agree ...
j I'm not so sure.
k I'm sorry, I can't accept that.
l Rubbish!
m That's exactly what I think.
n That's not true.
o That's so right / You're so right.
p Yes, and on top of that ...
q Yes, but there's something else.
r Yes, I think that's right.
s You must be joking!
t You're surely not suggesting that ...
u You're telling me!
v I take your point, but what about ... ?

Now replace the expressions in Activity 40 with different expressions from Activity 41 so that the meaning stays the same.

Example: a MARSHA: I'm afraid I just can't agree with Garry.

42 The agreement / disagreement chain Write three sentences giving your opinion about one of the following topics.

a the money paid to actors / sportsmen and women
b whether reading novels is a good thing or a bad thing
c what you think of the fashion industry
d the effect of television violence on young viewers

Read your sentences to the class. Another student agrees or disagrees with what you said and gives their opinion. A third student agrees or disagrees, then adds an opinion. Now it's the turn of a fourth student ... No student can use agreement / disagreement language that has been used already.

Example: STUDENT A: I think footballers are paid too much money.

STUDENT B: You're so right. They earn more in one game than most people earn in a year.

STUDENT C: Rubbish. That's a myth. And anyway, they give a lot of pleasure so why ...

43 Group role-play Make a list of movies, books or TV shows that you have all seen or read. Make notes about your opinions of each one.

Role-play a TV or radio show like the one on Track 64. One of you is the presenter and the other four are critics / guests. Give your opinions about the movie, show or book. Use expressions from Activities 40 and 41 to agree and disagree with each other. You can discuss the following topics.

- acting
- characters
- descriptions
- dialogue
- filming / scenery
- plot
- special effects

Writing: book reports

44 Read the first parts of these two book reports and decide whether you would like to read the book or not and why.

Gandhi: A Life by Yogesh Chadha is a book about the life of Mahatma Gandhi. It starts off with information about his life, such as where he came from and how he became a lawyer and then goes on to tell the incredible story of how this unusual man became one of the most influential men of the 20ᵗʰ century.

Carrie is a book by Stephen King about a young high school girl who has dangerous 'special' powers. At school everyone thinks she is weird, so she decides to use her powers to get revenge.

What other information would you like to have seen to help you decide?

45 Look at these questions that you can use to help you to write a book report.

Are there any other questions that you think are important?

What's the name of the book?
Who's the author?
Where and when does the story take place?
Who are the main characters?
What are the main events? / What is the plot of the book?
Would you recommend this book to someone else? Why or why not?

Copy and complete the table with information about the last book that you read. Add your own questions to the table and answer them too.

46 Writing Use the answers to the questions to write a report on the book. Share your report with a partner.

Review: grammar and functional language

47 Punctuate the following sentences with full stops, commas, question marks and capital letters where necessary. You can look at Activities 26–35 to help you.

a have you ever read the book i gave you

b have you seen the movie michael moore made about the american president

c i just can't relate to people who don't like turkish food

d i read my favourite book which was given to me by my sister-in-law in just one day

e in 1961 when i wasn't even born things were so different

f my aunt who just had her 90ᵗʰ birthday remembers a time when there were hardly any cars on the road

g she often travels to mexico where she once lived to see her friends

h the manuscript which can be seen at the british museum from january 2ⁿᵈ until april 30ᵗʰ is valued at about £350,000.

i when did you first meet mr graham whose house is up for sale

j when i was at school writing compositions which is easy for some people was very difficult for me

k written by a first-time author this book which has already sold one million copies is to be made into a film

48 Write definitions for the following, using relative clauses.

a A good movie is ...
b A terrible restaurant is ...
c Good friends are ...
d A typical movie for young people is ...
e A good place to take someone in this town is ...
f The best thing to read when you're on holiday is ...

49 Read the conversation and then agree or disagree, using the words given in appropriate phrases. The first one is done for you.

HEATHER: I think footballers are paid far too much money.

MAUREEN: (**a**. agree: *right*) You're so right . They earn more money in one game than most people earn in a year.

JED: (**b**. disagree: *true*) .... And anyway their careers are only very short.

RUTH: (**c**. agree: *with Jed*) .... Footballers deserve everything they get.

MAUREEN: (**d**. disagree: *joking*) .... Just because they can kick a ball they become millionaires.

RUTH: (**e.** agree: *point*) .... , but what about the pleasure they give to everyone?

MAUREEN: (**f.** disagree: *sorry / accept*) .... There are lots of people who don't like football at all.

JED: Well they're crazy then!

MAUREEN: (**g.** disagree: *suggest*) .... people who don't like football are mad, are you?

JED: Yes.

MAUREEN: (**h.** disagree: *disagree*) .... That's like saying that all people who like classical music are snobs.

JED: (**i.** agree: *more*) ....

Review: vocabulary

Word List

acclaimed	pen
adapted	plot
author	poetry
autobiography	prize-winning
background	prolific
basic outline	publisher
best-selling	rejection letters
blissfully	research
characters	self-publishing
description	structure
draft	struggling
editing process	to author
editor	to deliver
fact	to draft
fiction	to outline
former	to pen
guaranteed	to plot
mainland	to research
manuscript	to twist
massive	trainers
narrative	travel book
notes	twist
novel	uncool
original work	version

Word Plus

awe-inspiring
figure of fun
first-time writer
from a mile off
to face up to
to not mind admitting something
to relate to
to settle down

50 Could you be a writer? Use five words from the Word List and Word Plus to describe the kind of writer you would like to be. Explain your words to your partner.

Example: *I'd like to write an autobiography. I think I've had an interesting life and that's the easiest thing to write about.*

● ● ● Pronunciation

51 a Find all the words in the Word List with more than two syllables. Ignore the word *to* in the infinitives (e.g. *(to) deliver*). Put the words in groups depending on which syllable is stressed.

🔊 Check your answers by listening to Track 65.

b Find all the words in the Word List and Word Plus that have the sound /f/ and which are followed by a vowel sound. What vowel sounds follow /f/? Which four words have the same sound?

🔊 Check your answers by listening to Track 66.

52 Just a minute Work in groups. You have one minute to talk about one of the words from the Word List without pausing, or repeating nouns or verbs or going off the topic. If you pause or repeat a noun or verb or change the subject, the other members of the group can challenge you and *they* continue to speak on the topic. The winner is the person who is still talking at the end of one minute. One person keeps time and stops the clock every time there is a challenge.

Example: STUDENT A: *'Awe-inspiring' is a very interesting word that can be used to describe a lot of things. There are people who do great things, like ...*

STUDENT B: *Stop the clock. You repeated 'things'. Start the clock. I know a person who is awe-inspiring – this is my sister. I am amazed at the way she ...*

Crime and punishment

→ the passive voice
→ crime and criminals
→ making deductions

Listening: crime doesn't pay

1 Look at these pictures of true crimes that went wrong. Can you guess what happened?

2 Now listen to Track 67 to check your answers and match one story to each picture.

3 Listen to Track 67 again and fill in the table with the information you hear.

	a What went wrong?	b What was stolen?
Story 1		
Story 2		
Story 3		
Story 4		
Story 5		

4 What do these words from the news reports mean?

a armoured car
b getaway
c escape route
d handpicked
e without a hitch
f convicted
g sentenced
h appeal
i prosecuted
j shoplifting
k attempted
l in the course of
m shifted

5 **In pairs** Find a crime story in the newspaper, or one that you know about. Write the news item for it for an English-language news station.

Join with two other pairs and write a three-story news bulletin. Practise reading it. Make recordings.

Vocabulary: crime and criminals

6 **Word formation** Copy and complete this table with the names of crimes and criminals, and with crime verbs.

Crime	Criminal	Crime verb
a murder		
b	assassin	
c		to hack into a computer
d		to rob
e mugging		
f		to burgle
g	thief	
h pickpocketing		
i shoplifting		
j		to commit arson
k embezzlement		
l	kidnapper	
m		to evade taxes

Think of other crimes and add these to the table. Compare in groups.

7 Write your own definitions of the crimes.

Now test your partner.

Example: STUDENT A: *to assassinate*

STUDENT B: *That means to kill a famous person, usually a political figure or leader.*

8 **Dictionary work** Use your dictionary to find the correct preposition to complete these verb forms.

a to admit .... something
b to convict / be convicted .... something
c to charge / be charged .... something
d to confess .... something
e to sentence someone / be sentenced .... something
f to arrest someone / be arrested .... something
g to suspect someone / be suspected .... something
h to find someone guilty / be found guilty .... something
i to be wanted .... something

9 Now read about these notorious criminals on this page and page 136 and complete the texts with the appropriate verb or preposition.

Jack the Ripper

Jack the Ripper lived in England in the 19th century. From August to November 1888, he killed at least seven women and the police could not catch him. He even sent letters to the police, (a) .... the murders and taunting the police. The Ripper was never caught so he was never (b) .... any crime and the killings stopped as suddenly as they had started.

Al Capone

Born in Naples, Italy, but brought up in New York City, Al Capone (1899–1947) was a notorious gangster who moved to Chicago and became connected with organised crime there. He was (c) .... being involved in killings, but he was never arrested (d) .... murder. He was eventually (e) .... with not paying money that he owed to the government in 1931, he was found (f) .... the crime and was (g) .... 11 years in jail. He was set free in 1939 because of illness.

Bonnie and Clyde

Bonnie Parker (1911–1934) and Clyde Barrow (1909–1934) were infamous criminals who robbed banks and stores and were (h) .... their crimes in Texas, Oklahoma, New Mexico and Missouri between 1932 and 1934. Known for their love affair, they were always in the newspapers. Although they admitted (i) .... their crimes, they were never convicted (j) .... what they did, but were finally shot by the police while they were robbing a store. They were considered heroes by many and some people thought they did not deserve to die.

Compare your answers in groups. What were the crimes that they committed?

10 What other famous criminals from real life or the movies do you know? What were their crimes? What made them famous? Do you know what happened to them?

Speaking: Is crime ever justified? (discussion and role-play)

11 **In pairs** Read the three situations and decide how you would describe the crime in each case.

a Michael Trent was an unemployed construction worker. His wife was very sick and she needed an expensive medicine. He could not afford to buy her the medicine, so he broke into a drugstore at night and took the drugs that he needed.

b Maria (15) was from a poor family. At school they laughed at her because of her clothes. She stole from a department store to look nicer.

c Richard Moore needed good grades to get to university. He worked hard all the way through school, but a series of minor illnesses affected his grades in the final semester. His sister, Judy, was a computer expert and knew how to break into databases so she broke into the college database and got the answers to the exams.

12 **In groups** Read the situations again. What should the punishment be for each person?

13 **Role-play** Work in groups of five. Choose one of the stories (a–c) above and role-play the trial of the crime. Choose one of the following characters and read about your role in the Activity Bank.

Story a	Story b	Story c
Defendant	**Defendant**	**Defendant**
Michael Trent	Maria Metcalf	Judy Moore
Witness	**Witness**	**Witness**
Mrs Trent	Maria's best friend	Richard Moore
Judge	**Judge**	**Judge**
Prosecuting counsel	Prosecuting counsel	Prosecuting counsel
Defence counsel	Defence counsel	Defence counsel

DEFENDANT: look at Activity Bank 20 on page 165.

WITNESS: look at Activity Bank 24 on page 167.

JUDGE: look at Activity Bank 22 on page 166.

PROSECUTING COUNSEL: look at Activity Bank 23 on page 166.

DEFENCE COUNSEL: look at Activity Bank 25 on page 167.

Conduct the trial using the information and instructions that you found in the Activity Bank.

Functional language: making deductions

14 Listen to Track 68 and complete this audioscript with the words that you hear.

PHIL: Hey Mum! There's a man going into our neighbour's house.

MUM: It (**a**) .... their son, Jack. He's watching their place while his parents are away on holiday.

PHIL: It (**b**) .... their son. The man's too old. He's about 45.

MUM: Well, it (**c**) .... Jack's brother. He sometimes comes to stay.

PHIL: I'm sure it's not Jack's brother! He's looking around very suspiciously. (**d**) .... he's a burglar.

MUM: You and your imagination, Phil. It's probably a friend.

PHIL: I don't think so, Mum. I've never seen him before.

MUM: Well, we don't know all their friends. He (**e**) .... to feed the cat while they're away.

PHIL: He's (**f**) .... feeding the cat, Mum. He's climbing in the window.

MUM: What? Are you sure? Let me see.

PHIL: Look – over there.

MUM: You're right – there's (**g**) .... something going on. No doubt about it. Let's call the police.

PHIL: OK, Mum.

15 Each of these sentences (*a–n*) can be followed by one of the sentences *1–14* in the table. Choose the correct one in each case. The first one is done for you.

a Jake's mother is older than that woman.   12
b The diamonds were found in his house.
c Hannah's been working all day.
d I think I recognise that man.
e I think it was an accident.
f That woman put something in her pocket.
g It's impossible – he's not that smart.
h Stephen has darker hair, I believe.
i I feel very tired and my throat hurts.
j He's been in jail three times for robbery.
k I think my mother was there, but I'm not sure.
l I hear noises outside.
m She was found innocent.
n There's a tall man outside with dark hair.

Possibility (when you are not quite sure if something is true)	Certainty (when you are sure that something is true)	Certainty (when you are sure that something is *not* true)
A Present	**C Present**	**E Present**
1 It **might** be a cold.	8 She **must** be tired.	12 That **can't** be her.
2 She **could** be shoplifting.	9 He's **definitely** a criminal.	13 She's **definitely not** a criminal.
3 **Maybe** it's a friend from school.	10 **That'll be** my son.	
4 **I don't think** that's him.		
5 There **may** be someone walking around.		
B Past	**D Past**	**F Past**
6 He **might not have taken** the pen deliberately.	11 He **must have stolen** them.	14 He **couldn't have planned** the robbery.
7 She **may have seen** the crime.		

Which box (*A–F*) would you choose for phrases *a–g* from Activity 14?

16 Which box (a–f) in Activity 15 on page 137 would you place the following sentences in?

a I *reckon* she did it.
b *I don't know about you, but I think* he's a thief.
c *If you ask me, he probably* took the radio by accident.
d *I don't imagine that* it was someone who worked there who stole the money.
e *For all I know,* he might have come in when I was out and stolen my keys.

17 Make appropriate deductions about these situations. How many different possibilities can you come up with? What makes you sure or not sure?

a

b

c

d

e

●●●

●● ● **Pronunciation:** sentence stress in deductions

18 Listen to Track 69 and mark (') the stressed syllables.

a She might be a kidnapper.
b They can't be burglars.
c He could be an assassin.
d He may have come to deliver the newspaper.
e They must be going on vacation.

Now practise saying the sentences with the same use of stress.

19 Look at these sentences and mark the stressed syllables.

a She must be visiting her sister.
b They might have stolen the flowers.
c He might be a kidnapper.
d There may be a pickpocket.

Listen to Track 70 and check your answers.

●●●

20 In groups What do you know about this painting? Make notes of everything you know.

When you have finished, check Activity Bank 26 on page 167 and note any information that you have not already noted.

21 Did you know that the painting was once stolen? Read the story of the theft of the painting.

The theft of the Mona Lisa

On Monday, August 21, 1911, the Mona Lisa was stolen from the wall of the Louvre museum in Paris. No one noticed that it was stolen until the following day when Louis Béroud, a painter, went to see it. He saw it was missing and asked where it was. The painting was missing for two years before the case was solved.

22 In groups These are the different theories about who stole the Mona Lisa. Discuss the theories and discuss who you think stole the painting and why.

Theories

'The painting was accidentally destroyed so the museum is inventing the theft.'
Jules Bernard, owner of an art gallery

'Some German art collectors think of themselves as our cultural rivals. They are jealous of France and they want to make the French collectors feel bad so they have stolen the picture.'
Gaston Bologne, politician

'The Italians are still angry that the painting left Italy and they want it returned to Italy.'
Jacques Durand, historian

'The employees in the Louvre want to show how bad security is.'
Berthe Maupassant, ex-employee of the Louvre

'France has many problems. The theft of the painting will give people something else to think about.'
Sabine Clouthier, homemaker

Look at the true story in Activity Bank 27 on page 168. Were you surprised?

23 In groups Do you know any stories of mysterious events which have never been properly explained? Tell the other students.

Reading: When is a crime not a crime?

24 In groups What would you do if you suddenly found something very valuable like a wallet in the street which had a lot of money in it? Would you keep it? Would you try to return it? Would you tell anyone?

25 Read *either* 'Finders keepers' *or* 'Man 1 Bank 0'. Is your story happy or sad?

Finders keepers?

Joey Coyle wasn't doing too well. He was a dockworker by trade, but he had been unemployed for some time. He had a drug problem too and nothing went right for him. And even when it did, poor Joey managed to make a mess of it.

And then, on February 26 1981, Joey, aged 28, spotted a yellow box on the side of a road in Philadelphia. He looked around but there was nobody who might be the owner of such a box. He thought about it for a moment and then decided to pick it up and take it home. He reckoned it would make a good toolbox.

Before taking the box home, he opened it. He expected it to be empty. But it wasn't. Instead he found two bags inside with the words 'Reserve Bank' printed on them. With his pulse quickening, he pulled the bags open and found himself looking at over a million dollars in $100 bills. Joey stared and stared and then quickly put the bags into his car and drove away.

A few minutes later, an armoured money truck came roaring up to the place where the yellow box had been. The guards inside had realised that they had dropped the box out of the van and had come back to look for it. But of course it wasn't there and they were left wondering how to explain to their company that they had mislaid a million dollars in cash.

Joey made a mess of his windfall as you might expect. One moment he was experiencing the euphoria of being rich beyond his wildest dreams and the next, he was experiencing a bad case of paranoia about being discovered and having 'his' money taken away from him. He told everyone he met about his good luck and then swore them to secrecy. He had no idea what to do with the money, but his girlfriend put him in touch with gangster friends of hers who offered to help him invest his money and make it grow. In his confusion, Joey trusted them and within only a short time the money had gone.

Joey had lost all the money he had found, but that didn't mean he wasn't guilty of committing a crime. In the state of Pennsylvania, you are committing an offence if you do not try to return things with a value of more than $250. The police finally caught up with him and Joey was arrested and thrown in jail, but he was released when a jury found him not guilty because, they thought, he had become temporarily insane on finding the money.

Sometime later, Joey's story was made into a Hollywood movie called *Money for Nothing*, starring John Cusack. Perhaps the unemployed dockworker's luck was about to change. But it was too late for Joey Coyle. He died before the film was released.

Man 1 Bank 0

In 1995 Patrick Combs was living in San Francisco and trying desperately to make ends meet. He had just written a guide for college students called *Major in Success* and he was using the book to launch what he hoped would be a successful career as a motivational speaker, helping people to make the most of their talents and abilities. And no one needed his advice more than Patrick himself. Money had always been tight in Patrick's family and, at 28, he thought it was always going to be like that for him.

But you never know your luck! One day he found some junk mail that had been delivered to his mail box. He was going to throw it away, but instead he decided to give it a quick look before getting rid of it. He found himself looking at a letter promising that if he sent money to a certain company, he would soon be receiving huge cheques which would make him rich. And to prove it, the company had put a specimen cheque in with their letter – just to show their clients what riches would look like.

Patrick looked at the fake cheque despondently. It was a depressing reminder of how broke he was. But then he saw an opportunity for some fun. After all, he had nothing to lose. He thought it would be a funny joke to deposit the cheque in his account. He would give bank employees a laugh when they discovered that 'some idiot' had tried to cash a junk mail cheque. So he giggled as he wrote in the amount of the deposit, $95,093.35, on the deposit slip. 'I didn't think I was sticking money into the bank,' he says. He didn't even bother to endorse the back by signing it as you are supposed to do.

After ten days, much to his shock, he found that the cheque had been cleared and the money had been credited to his account. (As he later learned, the cheque met the nine criteria of a valid cheque – and even the words 'non negotiable' printed on the front did not negate it.) The junk mail company had succeeded in making the cheque look real – far too real. And to make matters worse for the bank, they had missed their own legal deadline to notify him that the cheque had bounced as a 'non-cash' item. With 'money' in his account, Patrick became obsessed. He couldn't think of anything else. 'It was an addiction,' he says, 'for two months I obsessed on whether I should take the money or give the money back.' After researching his own legal position long and hard, he discovered that he was not legally responsible for returning the money – he had committed no crime.

But in the end, Patrick decided to do the 'right' thing. He returned the money to the bank but only after he had insisted (and the bank had agreed) that the bank would write him a letter confirming that they had made a mistake in cashing the cheque. Patrick had by this time become a celebrity and he used the story to catapult his career as a motivational speaker. Today his money worries are over.

26 **Fact check** On your own, answer these questions about the story that you read.

a When and where did the story take place?
b What was the name, age and occupation of the person in the story?
c How much money did he get?
d How did he get it?
e Was he guilty of any crime?
f What happened to the money?
g What happened to the person in the story in the end?

27 Now find someone who read the other story. Use the *Fact check* questions in Activity 26 to find out everything about their story.

Find similarities and differences between the stories.

28 **Vocabulary** Match these meanings with the words in yellow from the two texts.

a in short supply
b accepted, recognised as valid
c sign and make official
d looked keenly at something
e lost
f the feeling that people are against you
g laughed happily
h promote very quickly
i driving fast and noisily

29 **Noticing language** Look at this example of a passive sentence and answer the questions.

A lot of the money was given away by the charity.

a Who or what is the agent (i.e. the person or thing who did the action – the 'doer')?
b Who or what is the object of the action (i.e. the person or thing that the action was 'done to')?

Look back at the stories in Activity 25 and find other examples of passive sentences. Decide who or what the 'doer' and the 'done to' are in each case.

Language in chunks

30 Combine the words from the two circles to make phrases from the two stories. Three phrases start with *to make*.

a beyond his
b he had nothing
c his luck was
d nothing went
e to make
f to put someone
g to swear someone
h with his pulse

1 a mess of something
2 about to change
3 in touch with somebody
4 quickening
5 right for him
6 the most of something
7 to lose
8 to secrecy
9 wildest dreams
10 matters worse

31 Now use the phrases (or parts of the phrases) in the following sentences. You may have to change tenses, adjectives (e.g. *his*) or pronouns (e.g. *he* or *him*).

a .... Jennifer realised that she might have found the treasure she had been searching for since last week.

b After he had won the competition, he found that he was rich ....

c After he left his job, he found that .... anymore and so he decided to go back home.

d After years of poverty, and even though he didn't yet know it, George's ....

e He .... He said he would tell the world when he was ready, but until then he didn't want anyone to know.

f One of the things I've enjoyed most is .... friends they haven't seen for years.

g People who .... of every opportunity are usually more successful than those who don't.

h She admitted that she had .... her exam paper. She was sure she'd failed.

i She burnt the toast and .... she spilt milk all over the kitchen floor.

j She thought she might as well try to escape from prison. After all she had ....

Now use at least four of the phrases in sentences of your own.

32 In groups Answer these questions.

a Who do you feel more sympathy for? Joey or Patrick? Why?

b What would you have done if you had been Joey?

c If you had been Patrick, what would you have done?

Grammar: the passive voice

33 Why is the passive voice used in these sentences? Read the possible reasons (*1–4*) below and match each sentence (*a–i*) with the best reason. You can use **13B in the Mini-grammar** to help you. The first one is done for you.

a My car was stolen yesterday. **1**
b When I got home, I found that the window had been broken.
c The prisoners are taken to their cells at 11 pm and the lights are put out at 11.30.
d The experiment was conducted under controlled conditions.
e People are often arrested at football matches.
f You will be fined if you park your car in this zone.
g His case is being reviewed at the moment.
h Oil was put into the jar and water was added.
i The rubbish was being collected when I pulled the car into the drive.

1 We do not know the person who did the action.
2 The identity of the person doing the action is obvious.
3 The action is what is important as part of a process, not who does it.
4 We are writing in formal language, such as for academic reports.

34 Complete these passive voice sentences using the correct tense of the verb in brackets. You can use **13A and 13B in the Mini-grammar** to help you.

a The results (take) .... from the survey and then we wrote a report.

b The mail (deliver) .... at about 11 am every day.

c When I arrived, the TV (move) .... to the living room. Everyone was helping because it was heavy.

d My PC (fix) .... at the moment. I'm going to get it from the shop tomorrow.

e The suspect (question) .... and we are now ready to charge him.

f When I arrived home, I was surprised to find my house (break into) ....

g Do you think the criminal (arrest) .... by now?

h That package should (deliver) .... by now.

i Later today, the defendant (sentence) ....

35 Read this police report. How could you re-write the sentences with verbs in blue in the passive (to make it more formal)? You may have to change the construction of the sentences the verbs occur in. You can use **13A–13E in the Mini-grammar** to help you.

We *followed* the suspect along Parker Street and waited as he paid the taxi driver. He *entered* the Wishbone Club and we *saw* him talking to two suspicious-looking young men, who were holding a baby. Someone came and *took* the baby away and then they left the young men to talk by themselves. At 2 pm, the two young men left the club and I *saw* them getting into a black car. There was a tall man with glasses who *was driving* the car. We *followed* the black car and it stopped outside the City Bank. Then we noticed that the two men were *wearing* masks. The two men entered the bank and at this point we *called* the officers who were waiting in the bank and they *sounded* the alarm. We ran into the bank and *arrested* the two men and *put* handcuffs on them. Then we put them in the car and we *took* them to the police station. They appeared in court last week and the judge *sentenced* them to six months in jail for attempted bank robbery.

36 Now complete this report about a 'reactions to crime' survey by writing the verb in brackets in the correct form.

Over 500 people (**a. interview**) .... in the survey conducted by the Society for the Prevention of Crime. It (**b. find**) .... that most people do keep their doors locked, but in rural areas many doors (**c. keep**) .... open. It (**d. hope**) .... that by making crime prevention a priority, more alarms (**e. install**) .... in houses. The full report on the survey (**f. publish**) .... this month in *Crime Prevention* magazine.

37 A puzzle Put the paragraphs in order to tell a story.

a But then, just after he had walked past a house, he heard the sound of raised voices, and then the sound of someone shouting out, 'Don't shoot me, John! Don't shoot!' This was the kind of thing that he was trained for so he turned back, but before he could get to the house he heard a gunshot.

b Without a second's thought, the policeman arrested the priest and charged him with murder.

c One summer evening, many years ago, a policeman was walking through the village where he had just been posted. He was looking forward to getting to know the various people who lived there. So far he knew none of their names.

d He realised something terrible had happened so he ran into the house. In the living room, he found himself face to face with a lawyer, a priest and an engineer. They were all standing over a dead body.

e He was whistling happily as he walked along. He could hear a car in the distance, and somewhere, someone was listening to the 6 o'clock news on the radio.

In pairs Did the policeman arrest the right person? How do you know? Re-tell the story as a news item. How many active and passive verbs do you need?

Writing: peer review

38 Copy and tick the table to show if you agree with what other students say.

	Agree	Disagree
I like to work by myself. I can find what I need in the dictionary.		
My classmates know things that I don't know and I know things that they don't know.		
Sometimes I learn wrong things from my classmates.		
My classmates sometimes show me mistakes in my writing that I didn't see.		

Compare your answers in groups.

39 Read this letter written by Juan Manuel, a student, and correct the mistakes in it. The parts which have the mistakes are highlighted in blue.

The Crime Page

Do you know of any famous or unusual crimes? We'd love to hear about them. Send the facts to famouscrimes@thisweek.com. If we publish your story, we'll send you a year's free subscription to our magazine.

Dear Editor,

I want ˄ tell you about a famous crime. This crime happen in my home town of Guadalajara five years ago. A little boy was kidnap. People was sure it was the family driver who did take the boy and the father get mad and fired the driver. But the mother of the boy knew he couldn't had done it. She trusted the driver. Then, sudenly, the father disappeared. Nobody knew where he did go. The police looked for man and they found him at the airport. He was trying leave the country with the boy. The police gave the boy back to his mother and the father went to the jail.

Juan Manuel Alvarez

Compare your work with a partner to see if you made the same corrections.

40 Read Juan Manuel's writing again. Copy and complete this form about it.

Name of writer: Juan Manuel Alvarez	
Checked by:	
a Is the writing interesting?	Yes / Not sure / No, not really
b Does the writing contain enough information?	Yes / Not sure / No, not really
c I think the writing could be improved by: • •	

41 Write about one of the following topics (after making notes individually or in groups).

- a famous crime
- a crime that went wrong
- an imaginary crime
- your favourite crime film or story

Swap papers with a partner. Use the questions from Activity 40 to comment on your partner's writing.

Review

42 Read the following newspaper crime report. Put the verb in brackets into the correct form of the active voice or passive voice. You can look at Activities 33–36 for help.

At Barton Crown Court today, a notorious local car thief (**a.** sentence) .... to a year in jail. Police officer Banks told the court that he (**b.** receive) .... a phone call on May 14th this year saying that a car (**c.** steal) .... About two hours later, the officer (**d.** alert) .... that the car (**e.** find) .... The car (**f.** immediately – claim) .... by the owner and the police officer (**g.** accompany) .... Kevin Bryant, the owner, to pick up the car. On arriving, it (**h.** discover) .... that the radio (**i.** steal) .... and the seats (**j.** vandalise) .... Before the car (**k.** abandon) .... , the thief (**l.** drive) .... it for about two hours. The fingerprints of the thief (**m.** find) .... all over the steering wheel and the thief (**n.** identify) .... quickly .... as Martin Merton, who (**o.** know) .... to the police. Mr Merton (**p.** arrest) .... and the radio (**q.** find) .... in his possession. At the trial today, he (**r.** plead) .... guilty to auto theft and the judge (**s.** sentence) .... him to 12 months in prison. Merton (**t.** not expect) .... to appeal the sentence.

43 Imagine you are a reporter. Read these notes about a trial that you observed and write the report for the newspaper.

Roger Bartlett and Simone Rogers (19 years old)

72-year-old lady – Mrs Edna Brooks

28 Feb last year – Bartlett and Rogers broke into her home (she was asleep)

stole some money and her TV set and DVD player

one of Mrs Brooks' grandchildren (Tom Brooks) studies with Bartlett and Rogers and heard them talking about the robbery in the cafeteria

Tom called the police – they went to Bartlett's house and found the stolen goods

judge ordered the young people (who seemed very sorry) to pay a fine and to do community service

Review: vocabulary

Word List

appeal	roaring
armoured car	shoplifting
arson	thief
assassin	tight
attempted	to burgle
(crime)	to catapult
cleared	to endorse
embezzlement	to giggle
escape route	to hack (into a
euphoria	computer)
getaway	to mug
handpicked	to prosecute
kidnapper	to rob
murder	to shift
paranoia	to stare
pickpocket	

Word Plus

beyond his wildest dreams
(his) luck was about to change
in the course of
nothing went right for (him)
to admit to something
to arrest someone / be arrested
   for something
to be wanted for something
to charge / be charged with
   something
to confess to something
to convict / be convicted of
   something
to evade taxes
to find someone guilty /
   be found guilty of something
to have nothing to lose
to make a mess of something
to make matters worse
to make the most of something
to put someone in touch with
   somebody
to sentence someone /
   be sentenced to something
to suspect someone /
   be suspected of something
to swear someone to secrecy
with his pulse quickening
without a hitch

44 In pairs Find five words or expressions that you like or you think are really useful. Explain why you like the words or think they are useful to your partner.

Example: STUDENT A: I think 'without a hitch' is a useful expression, because it's a way to describe something that went well without always saying 'it was no problem'. For example, if someone says to me, 'How was the meeting at work today?', I can say 'it went without a hitch'.

Pronunciation

45 Listen to Track 71 and find the words in the Word List. How many letters are 'silent'? Which letters can't you hear in the speakers' voices?

Are these letters always silent? Listen to Track 72 and hear two different speakers say the same words.

46 Find two words from the Word List and two words from Word Plus that you like the sound of best (don't worry about the meaning). Compare your words with other students. Have you chosen the same ones?

47 What's the word? Choose a word or expression from the Word List or Word Plus. Make a definition which does not include the word or expression itself. Read your definition or explanation to your partner, who must try to guess what the word or expression is. You can ask questions and explain the expression more, but don't use the word itself.

Example: STUDENT A: This expression means 'you do a thing badly'.
STUDENT B: You mean like you play basketball badly?
STUDENT A: No, like the one time you make a mistake and do something badly.
STUDENT B: Is it 'to make a mess of something'?
STUDENT A: Yes, that's right.

UNIT 14
Stories from the heart

→ direct and indirect speech
→ poetic effect
→ expressing likes and dislikes

Reading: stories in poems

1 **In groups** How do you feel about poetry? Find two things that everybody enjoys reading or writing *more* than poetry and two things that everybody enjoys reading or writing *less* than poetry.

2 Look at the three titles of poems. *Don't* look at the poems on the right yet. What words would you expect to see / hear in each poem?

Midsummer, Tobago

Derek Walcott

Like a Beacon

Grace Nichols

Handbag

Ruth Fainlight

 3 Listen to the poems being read on Track 73. Do you hear any of your words?

Now uncover the poems on the right and read them.

Midsummer, Tobago
Broad sun-stoned beaches.

White heat.
A green river.

A bridge,
scorched yellow palms

from the summer-sleeping house
drowsing through August.

Days I have held,
days I have lost,

days that outgrow, like daughters,
my harbouring arms.

Derek Walcott

Like a Beacon
In London
every now and then
I get this craving
for my mother's food
I leave art galleries
in search of plantains
saltfish / sweet potatoes

I need this touch of home
swinging my bag
like a beacon
against the cold

Grace Nichols

Handbag
My mother's old leather handbag,
crowded with letters she carried
all through the war. The smell
of my mother's handbag: mints
and lipstick and Coty powder.
The look of those letters, softened
and worn at the edges, opened,
read, and refolded so often.
Letters from my father. Odour
of leather and powder, which ever
since then has meant womanliness,
and love, and anguish, and war.

Ruth Fainlight

4 **In groups** Find at least two similarities and two differences between the three poems on page 145. What are they about? What feelings are the writers expressing?

5 Choose one of the boxes and ask another student to answer the questions you find there about the poems on page145.

Midsummer, Tobago	*Like a Beacon*	*Handbag*
a Explain the meaning of the following words and expressions. 1 broad 2 scorched 3 summer-sleeping house 4 drowsing 5 outgrow 6 harbouring **b** Explain how to get to the house from the beach, what the days are like and how Derek Walcott uses (and develops) the idea of 'days I have held ...'	**a** Explain the meaning of the following words and expressions. 1 craving 2 plantains 3 touch of home 4 swinging 5 beacon **b** Explain what it is the poet misses and how she compensates for this feeling.	**a** Explain the meaning of the following words and phrases. 1 crowded with letters 2 lipstick 3 powder 4 softened and worn at the edges 5 odour 6 womanliness 7 anguish **b** Explain what was in the handbag, who wrote the letters and what happened to them. Explain, in your own words, what the handbag makes the writer think of.

Now change pairs and answer questions about a different poem.

Change pairs again and ask or answer questions about the third poem.

6 Without looking back at the poems, tell their stories in your own words.

Vocabulary: poetic effect

7 Look at the evidence from the poems on page 145 and answer the questions.

The evidence	Broad sun-stoned beaches. White heat. A green river. scorched yellow palms the summer-sleeping house My mother's old leather handbag, crowded with letters The look of those letters, softened and worn at the edges
The questions	a Which 'sentences' do not have verbs? What is the effect of this? b Which sentences or phrases have more than one adjective before the noun? c Which adjectives are formed by joining words together? What is the effect of this? d What grammar form is used <u>after</u> the nouns to describe them?

Style note: Poets have the freedom to make the kind of compound adjectives (like *sun-stoned* and *summer-sleeping*) which we don't often use in speaking – until they become widely used and accepted.

8 Use the words in italics to make compound adjectives. The first two are done for you.

a A book with used pages like the *ears* of old *dogs* is a ......*dog-eared*...... book.

b A flower that *smells foul* is a ......*foul-smelling*...... flower.

c A boy with *brown hair* is a .... boy.

d A man who has *fair skin* is a .... man.

e A person who *loves fun* is a .... person.

f A pop star who *looks good* is a .... pop star.

g A rose that *smells sweet* is a .... rose.

h A suit that is *made* (al)*ready* is a .... suit.

i A woman who is '*built well*' (e.g. who has a big strong body) is a .... woman.

j An egg that has been *boiled* but is still *soft* is a .... egg.

k An egg that has been *boiled* until it is *hard* is a .... egg.

l An experience which *blows* your *mind* is a .... experience.

9 Use past participles to describe the nouns in blue. The first one is done for you.

a Someone picked a rose and gave it as a sign of love.

a rose, picked and given as a sign of love

b A criminal hatched (= made) a plan.

c The neighbours' noise finally drove the woman crazy.

d Someone fired a shot in anger.

e Someone wrote a letter in anger.

f Jealousy destroyed the actor's career.

g Someone painted a picture in a fit of creativity.

10 Poetic effect is often created by putting adjectives and nouns together in unexpected ways. Sometimes the words contradict each other; sometimes, together, they create a striking effect.

Examples: *white heat; unkind love; black summer*

What strong and / or contradictory images can you make by putting adjectives and nouns together? (You can use the words in the boxes or come up with your own ideas.)

> **Adjectives**
> black blue blunt cold dangerous
> desperate difficult easy empty
> full happy hot kind red sad
> selfish sharp white

> **Nouns**
> affection animal beach despair
> ghost hatred house letter
> love noise summer victory

11 Writing Choose one of the topics in the box below.

> a favourite place a good friend home
> the contents of someone's pockets

a Write down as many words as you can think of related to the topic.

b Write at least one phrase or sentence for each of the following categories (you can use your own phrases or phrases from Activities 8–10).
  • a compound adjective followed by a noun, e.g. *sun-stoned beaches, summer-sleeping house*
  • a noun followed by past participles, e.g. *a handbag, crowded with letters; letters, softened and worn at the edges*
  • strong / contradictory images formed by an adjective and a noun, e.g. *white heat, hateful love*

c Use your examples to write your own poem on the topic of your choice.

Listening: storyteller

12 Look at this picture. Where do you think this woman is from? What do you think she does?

Listen to Track 74. Were you right?

13 Listen to Track 74 again. In your own words, say what Jan thinks stories are for. Do you agree?

14 Read through the following questions and then say what you think Jan will say in Track 75.

    a What did Jan do at the age of 19?
    b Why did she go to a group called *Common Law*?
    c What three things did she have to do for her audition?
    d What story did she tell?
    e Where did she get the song and game from?
    f How did she learn it?
    g What happened when she told it?

Listen to Track 75. Were you right? Answer the questions.

15 Listen to Track 76 and answer these questions.

Who or what:
    a ... is *The Spitz*?
    b ... has a reputation for being late?
    c ... plays the drums?
    d ... said he was tired and had to lie down?
    e ... explained the stories five minutes before the show?
    f ... was on the edge of creativity?
    g ... weren't very enthusiastic at first?
    h ... spoke to the audience to encourage them?
    i ... had a fantastic experience?

Tell the story of Jan and Crispin's evening in your own words.

Language in chunks

16 Look at the Audioscript for Tracks 74–76 and find Jan's phrases (a–i). What do the phrases in italics mean? What was she talking about in each case?

    a *a tried and tested theory*
    b *Does that make sense?*
    c something ... *I can't put my finger on*
    d the opportunity *to delve deep* into your own consciousness
    e I couldn't learn the whole story *word for word*
    f from that moment *I haven't looked back*
    g I kind of *went through the sequence of events*
    h we were *on the edge* of our creativity
    i I'm slightly *off kilter*

17 Translate the phrases into your language so that they mean the same as they do in the context that Jan used them.

18 **Noticing language** Look at these phrases from Tracks 74–76 which contain direct and indirect speech. Find examples of things people actually said (direct speech) and of people reporting what other people said (indirect speech).

    a I said oh oh where can you earn some decent money then and she said oh as a storyteller so I said what's that and she said oh I'm a storyteller I think you'd be really good, I think you should come along to *Common Law* and you should audition.
    b ... and he was like Oh God my brain and the traffic's awful and just let me lie here for five minutes, and I said we're on in five minutes and he said er yeah just give me five minutes ...
    c I asked the audience to join in and sing it and they weren't giving us themselves and I said to them look you know, he was late, he was late ...

19 **Storytelling** When Jan told the story of *Why cat and dog are no longer friends*, she 'read that and read it and read it and read it and read it', before she told her story. Choose one of the following topics and then make notes about it. Think of ways to make it as exciting or funny as possible. Then write out a version as correctly as you can. Read it and read it and read it.

Without looking back at what you have written, tell your story to a neighbour. Now tell it to another neighbour, practise it and then tell it to the whole class.

Topics:
- my most embarrassing moment
- my favourite story from a book, TV or the movies
- my most memorable injury
- why I was late
- any other story from your life

Grammar: direct and indirect speech

20 How would you report the following if (a) you were there and you were telling someone about it on your cellphone, (b) if it happened yesterday and (c) if it happened yesterday and you wanted to give it maximum dramatic effect (especially if you were writing about it)? Use **14A–14C in the Mini-grammar** to help you.

Example:

Jane

(a) She says she's going to read her latest poem.

(b) She said she was going to read her latest poem.

(c) 'I'm going to read my latest poem,' Jane said.

21 Match the verb in the left-hand column with what was actually said in the right-hand column. The first one is done for you.

insist	m	a 'Let's go to the gallery.'
accept		b 'If I were you, I'd stay at home.'
apologise		c 'You just press the power button and put in a CD, then press play.'
deny		d 'Come here right now!'
refuse		e 'I did not steal the painting.'
compliment		f 'No, I won't do your homework.'
suggest		g 'Sure. I'll come to the movies with you.'
forgive		h 'I'm so sorry for losing your pen.'
complain		i 'It must have been George who broke the window.'
advise		j 'I'm the best artist in the world.'
order		k 'This painting is much too expensive.'
boast		l 'Your sculpture is beautiful.'
agree		m 'You must come with me. You'll really enjoy it.'
explain		n 'Forget about spilling the paint. It really doesn't matter.'
blame		o 'You're absolutely right. That's a great poem.'

Now report what was said. Use *he* or *she*.

Example: m He insisted that I went with him. He said I'd really enjoy it.

Look at 14E in the Mini-grammar. Do you want to change your answers?

22 **In pairs** Look at this picture of people at an art exhibition opening. What did the people say? You can use **14B–14F in the Mini-grammar** to help you.

a I hate coming to art exhibition openings. They're so boring.

b You're right. They're so tedious.

c Why don't we go and get a drink?

d This artist lived in Paris for five years.

e Was he trying a new technique when he did this?

f Don't bother coming to this – it's awful.

g I've told you before, Charlie, don't touch the paintings!

h This looks like a child painted it.

i I love the use of colour in your work.

j I'm experimenting with unconventional art.

Example: *The artist explained that he was experimenting with unconventional art. The young woman told the artist that …*

● ● ● **Pronunciation:** strong and weak forms (*was* and *were*)

23 Listen to Track 77 and read the sentences *a–h*. Copy the sentences and questions. Circle *was* or *were* if it is unstressed and underline it if it is stressed. The first two are done for you.

a Were Pedro and Amanda at home yesterday? – Yes, they <u>were</u>.
b Where (were) you when I called?
c They said they were going to the gallery.
d He told me he was doing a new piece for the exhibition.
e Was Marlene at the exhibition? – Yes, she was.
f She asked me if we were taking any art classes.
g They were at the gallery. I saw them there.
h I told her that I was taking a sculpture class.

Read the sentences using the same stress as the speakers on Track 77.

24 Change these sentences to indirect speech and say them using the correct pronunciation of *was / were*.

a 'I'm learning to paint,' said Fumiko.
b Brian said, 'We're going to the Picasso exhibition!'
c Maria asked, 'Are you enjoying the museum tour?'
d Wilton and Gaby said, 'We're very tired.'

● Speaking and writing: reporting conversations and events

25 Which sentence in each pair is an example of informal speech? Which is more like formal writing / grammar?

a 1 He's like 'that's cool' and I'm like 'well yeah!'
  2 He said that it was cool and I replied that it was.

b 1 So she goes 'that's ridiculous' and then goes red in the face.
  2 She said that it was ridiculous and then she went red in the face.

c 1 A man asked me where I was going and I asked him why he wanted to know.
  2 So this guy he asks me where I'm going and I'm like 'why do you want to know?'

d 1 He was about to lose control and so I suggested that he calmed down and he thanked me.
  2 So he's like about to completely lose it and I'm like 'calm down, OK' and he's like 'thanks, I needed that'.

e 1 We say 'hello' and they go 'what are you guys doing here?' and we go 'well you invited us didn't you?'
  2 We said 'hello' and they asked us what we were doing there. We said that they'd asked us.

26 Are these notes referring to *be like*, to *go*, or both?

a used for reporting conversations
b informal and used when talking
c used mainly in British English
d an informal phrase, used especially in American English
e can describe a situation too
f can describe an action too

Speaking: reading aloud

27 Choose the poem (*Small Boy*) or the story extract from *Space Station 5*
and complete the tasks which follow them.

Small Boy

He picked up a pebble
and threw it in the sea

And another and another
He couldn't stop

He wasn't trying to fill the sea
He wasn't trying to empty the beach

He was just throwing away
nothing else but

Like a kitten playing
he was practising for the future

when there'll be so many things
he'll want to throw away

if only his fingers will unclench
and let them go

Norman MacCraig

From *Space Station 5*

They had been up here for five years Five years for
five people cut off from Earth since World War IV
True the Moonshuttle came every six months with a
supply of food but it was pilotless They had not been
able to make contact with Moonbase for two years
Cathy said it was weird
    You say that three times a day Rosie answered
    Well it's true It's weird and I don't think I can
stand it much longer
    Oh for Jupiter's sake shut up Go and play eight-
dimensional death-chess and leave me alone You
drive me crazy!
    You shouldn't have spoken to me like that Cathy
said quietly and left the cabin The door hissed
behind her

a Copy the poem.
b Listen to Track 78 and write in the commas and
full stops in the poem, depending on how the
speaker reads it.
c Check your version in the Audioscript.
d Listen to Track 78 again and read along with
the speaker.
e Practise reading the poem.
f Read it to other students in the class who have
worked on Track 79.

a Copy the extract.
b Listen to Track 79 and write in commas, full
stops and inverted commas, depending on how
the speaker reads it.
c Check your version in the Audioscript.
d Listen to Track 79 again and read along with
the speaker.
e Practise reading the extract.
f Read it to other students in the class who have
worked on Track 78.

Functional language: expressing likes and dislikes

28 Look at the picture. Listen to Track 80 and write the words that you hear in the gaps.

A: Look at that sculpture!
B: What do you think of it?
A: I don't like it (a) .... It (b) ....
B: Oh really? I (c) .... it very much.
A: I was talking to my friend. She said she (d) .... either.
B: Did she really? That's too bad.
A: Who's the artist?
B: It's Philip Martin.
A: Oh that explains it. I (e) .... his work. I find it too abstract.
His sculptures aren't very convincing.
B: You really think so? I (f) .... his work a lot.
A: Well, we all have our different tastes, but all my friends tonight
said his piece was (g) .... !
B: Did they?
A: Yes, they did. Anyway, nice to meet you. What's your name?
B: Ummm. Philip Martin. Nice to meet you too.

29 Expressing likes and dislikes Say whether the following words and phrases are (a) positive comments, (b) opinions that have changed over time, or (c) negative comments.

Dali is *the best*.
I've *grown to like* Yoko Ono's work.
I *adore* surrealist paintings.
I *can't stand* (looking at) watercolours.
I *don't have anything against* modern art.
I *don't mind* sculpture.
I *loathe* modern art.
I'm *crazy about* Picasso.
I'm *keen on* modern art.
I've really *gone off* Michaelangelo.
I've *taken a liking* to the old masters.
Impressionism *doesn't do much for me*.
There's *nothing worse than* bad art.
You *can't beat* Van Gogh.
I'm *warming to* Frida Kahlo's painting.

a Which words are strongest in meaning?
b Which words suggest that something is taking or has taken quite a long time?
c Can you replace the words in red with words which have a similar meaning?
d Add more words to the categories (*a*, *b* and *c*) if you can.

30 Look at these three works of art and describe what you like and dislike about them. Imagine you are (a) talking to the artist, then (b) talking to a friend.

Example: STUDENT A: I like Amish Kapor's sculpture very much. You can't beat simple elegant shapes.

STUDENT B: Oh really? I can't stand abstract sculptures.

31 In groups Answer these questions.

a Do you think it is good to always give your true opinion? Explain your answer.
b Have you ever said that you liked or didn't like something and then regretted it? Are you prepared to tell your partner about it?

32 Questionnaires Choose one of the following four topics and make a list of things you know about it. Make a questionnaire about what people like and don't like. Go round the class asking the other students about their likes and dislikes.

Topics:
• art • music • food • sport

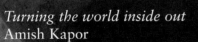

Turning the world inside out
Amish Kapor

Mother and child divided
Damien Hirst

My bed
Tracey Emin

Writing: films and music

33 Listen to the two pieces of music on Track 81. As you listen, write down what scene from a movie they might come from.

34 **In pairs** Look at these opening scenes from two different movies. What music would you expect to hear as you watched them?

Film A:

SCENE 1

Exterior. Night. Ten years ago. A small side street in a city. Pools of light from street lights. We see a figure walk through one of the light pools towards us. He or she (it is difficult to tell) has a hat pulled down over the side of their face. The camera follows the figure as he or she walks past us.

SCENE 2

Interior. The same night. A smoky café. Crowded. People sit at tables, talking furtively. They're all waiting for something perhaps. Edgy. The camera pans over the tables until it gets to the door. Which opens. Silhouetted in the street lamp from outside stands the figure we saw in Scene 1.

Film B:

SCENE 1

Exterior. Bright sunlight. Aerial shot. We see blue sky and then the camera pans down to glittering surf and a long tropical beach. White sand stretching for miles. Palm trees. The camera continues along the beach and we become aware of a figure running towards us, a man, dressed in shorts and a T-shirt. No shoes. As the camera passes him, we see his face. He is clearly running as fast as he can.

SCENE 2

Exterior. We are behind the runner. We can hear his heavy breathing. He looks over his shoulder back towards the camera as if he is expecting to see something. As he does so, he seems to trip and pitches forward into the sand.

What kind of films do you think the scenes come from? What will happen next?

35 In the scenes in Activity 34, what do you understand by the following words or phrases?

a exterior
b pools of light
c figure
d interior
e pans
f aerial shot
g glittering surf
h heavy breathing
i pitches forward

Some of the 'sentences' in the descriptions do not have verbs. Why is that? Is it acceptable here? When would it not be acceptable?

36 Choose one of the following film categories.

adventure   comedy
historical   horror   romance

Imagine the first scene of your film. Say:

a ... where the scene takes place.
b ... when the scene takes place (present day or historical, time of day, etc.).
c ... who is in the scene or comes into it.
d ... what the mood is.

37 Write the scene description in the same way as the examples in Activity 34. Say what music you would use in the background.

Review: grammar and functional language

38 Rewrite the following story using direct speech (the speakers' actual words). You can look at Activities 20–22 for help.

How they met

The artist and the gallery owner

At an exhibition of her paintings, a local newspaper reporter was just complimenting the artist, Tina Ferranti, on her use of colour when a young man (Graeme Wright) walked up to one of her self-portraits with a large bucket full of black paint. The reporter saw him and ordered him to put the bucket down, but the young man refused. The reporter advised him to do what he was told and when the man boasted that he wasn't afraid of anyone, the reporter insisted that he put down the bucket as otherwise the police would be called.

Reluctantly, the young man agreed and he tried to deny that he had intended to damage the painting. When Tina Ferranti suggested that people didn't usually approach paintings carrying buckets of black paint, Graeme Wright finally admitted that he had been intending to destroy one of her paintings because he wanted to get publicity for his own art show at a little gallery further down the street. Ms Ferranti forgave him and accepted his invitation to the show at his gallery.

Example: REPORTER: *I really like your use of colour.*

39 Complete the gaps in the following sentences with as many words or phrases as possible. You can look at Activities 28–32 for help.

a I .... the sound of the cello. It's my favourite instrument.
b I .... the music they play in shopping centres. It really gets on my nerves.
c I'm .... Paul Auster's novels. I just love them.
d I .... the stories in this book. I didn't like them at first, but now – well I'm an enthusiast.
e I've .... Eminem. He was OK for a bit, but not any more.
f Classical music .... I prefer something with a bit more beat.
g There's .... people who forget the punchline of a joke.
h I've .... poetry. I used to think I couldn't understand it, but I've suddenly realised how good some of it is.

Are any of these opinions similar to your own?

40 Conversation writing In pairs complete the following tasks.

a Fill in the gaps to create your own scene

A/an (*choose a profession*) .... meets a/an (*choose another profession*) .... at (*choose a location*) .... and they talk about (*choose a topic*) ....

b Write the conversation, using phrases from Activities 28–32.
c Act out your conversation for the class.
d Choose two of the conversations. How would the class report them?

Review: vocabulary

<table>
<tr><td rowspan="2">**Word List**</td><td>

aerial shot
anguish
beacon
broad
brown-haired
craving
crowded with
dog-eared
drowsing
edge
exterior
fair-haired
figure
foul-smelling
fun-loving
glittering
good-looking
harbouring
hard-boiled

</td><td>

interior
lipstick
mind-blowing
odour
plantain
pools (of light)
powder
ready-made
scorched
soft-boiled
softened
surf
sweet-smelling
swinging
to outgrow
to pan
well-built
womanliness
worn

</td></tr>
</table>

Word Plus

a tried and tested theory
heavy breathing
'I can't put my finger on' *
off kilter
on the edge of something
to delve deep into your own
  consciousness
to go through a sequence of
  events
to learn something word for
  word
to make sense (of something)
to not look back
to pitch forward
touch of home

*Conversational phrases.

41 Word auction Decide which words you want to 'buy'. Make a list. Don't tell anyone else.

You have £500. Bid against other students for words you really want. How many words can you buy (no one may bid more than £200 for any one word)?

● ● ● Pronunciation

42 Make a list of words from the Word List and Word Plus which you find difficult to pronounce. Compare your list with a partner.

a How many words are the same in both lists?
b What is difficult about the words you have selected: sounds or stress?
c What's the best way of improving your pronunciation of the 'difficult' words?

43 The diphthong challenge Copy the table and find words in the Word List for all the sounds (except the ones in yellow).

Check your answers by listening to Track 82.

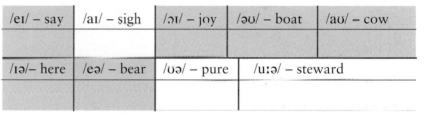

/eɪ/ – say	/aɪ/ – sigh	/ɔɪ/ – joy	/əʊ/ – boat	/aʊ/ – cow

/ɪə/– here	/eə/ – bear	/ʊə/ – pure	/uːə/ – steward

Who can add the most words to all the parts of the table in the shortest possible time?

And, in the end...

44 Now that you have finished *Just Right Upper Intermediate*, copy and complete the table about your progress.

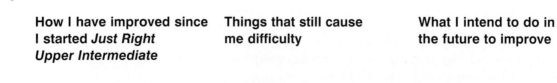

	How I have improved since I started *Just Right Upper Intermediate*	Things that still cause me difficulty	What I intend to do in the future to improve
Vocabulary			
Grammar			
Pronunciation			
Listening			
Speaking			
Reading			
Writing			

Activity Bank

1 [Unit 3]

Find five similarities and five differences between your picture and your partner's – but without looking at your partner's picture.

Now turn back to Activity 38 on page 36.

2 [Unit 3]

I'd like to start this composition by saying that I have enjoyed going to zoos and looking at animals in the past. It's always very exciting to look at creatures you have never seen before. <u>However,</u> many people say that zoos are not pleasant places <u>and furthermore</u> the animals are in cages and don't have their freedom. <u>Moreover,</u> if you deny animals their freedom and keep them in enclosed spaces they become ill and psychologically disturbed.

<u>On the other hand,</u> people who support zoos say that the animals are well looked after and fed, something that does not always happen to them in the wild. <u>Not only that, but</u> zoos have started many breeding programmes to save endangered species. <u>Therefore,</u> many animals that might have become extinct are now still alive.

If I had thought about it when I first went to see a zoo, I would have been unhappy about animals in cages, and I now think that is wrong. <u>In contrast,</u> some of the wildlife parks in various countries in the world give animals both security and freedom. <u>As a result,</u> those are the ones I approve of.

<u>In conclusion,</u> I think that zoos are often cruel places. Proper wildlife parks are a better way for man to preserve species whilst, at the same time, giving us all a chance to see animals in a natural habitat. <u>Nevertheless,</u> I am sure many families will still take their young children to visit zoos.

3 [Unit 5]

a Read the extract.

Are there anger types?

Psychologists have suggested a number of different personality types to explain why some people get angrier than others.

- *Absolutist thinkers* have a set of expectations and values which they require other people and events to conform to. They see the world in black and white, with no shades of grey, and if others don't give way to their demands, they become angry.

- *Ambitious anger* is the result of a personality that is driven, wants success and achievement very badly and gets furious with anyone who gets in their way. Such people are ruthless and fixated, and anger is one of their weapons either consciously or subconsciously.

- *Chronically angry* people have a deep-seated problem but cannot respond to the source of their unhappiness so they take their anger out on others. This kind of anger might be the result of a bad marriage or the death of a parent. 'The problem builds up over a long time, the person feels trapped and takes every opportunity to get at a weaker person.'

- *Situationally aggressive* people, in contrast, get angry when they get stressed by a particular situation and can't cope with it. When that situation goes away, so does their anger.

How angry are you? Personality questionnaire

Anger management – a growing trend

b Copy and complete the chart, using your own words.

Type	Description of type

c What's your reaction to the information here? Do you agree with it?

Now turn back to Activity 3 on page 51.

4 [Unit 5]

Suspect
- You are seventeen-and-a-half years old.
- You did steal the car, of course, but you don't think the police have any proof since you set the car on fire when you had finished having a good time with it.
- You want to know where the police got their information. When they ask you what you were doing last night, you'll say you were with a friend.
- You enjoy having fun by being cheeky to the police. You get angry when the lawyer tries to stop you doing this.

Now turn back to Activity 23 on page 55.

5 [Unit 5]

Police officer 1

- You and your police colleague are in charge of the interview. You decide who says what and when.
- The suspect was seen taking the car by two other criminals, Ben and Joey, but you can't tell the suspect this, because that would put Ben and Joey in danger. So the only thing you can do is keep asking the suspect different questions about what he or she was doing last night in the hope that he or she will get confused and in the end confess.
- You have had enough of kids taking cars for fun. It makes you really mad. Anyway, you want to get home. Unfortunately, you lose your temper rather quickly. You get especially irritated when your partner tells you to calm down.

Now turn back to Activity 23 on page 55.

6 [Unit 8]

Read your first lines. Can B give you answers which are funny?

First lines of jokes
a   Waiter! There's a fly in my soup!
b   What's this fly doing in my soup?
c   Hey watch out! Your thumb's in my soup!
d   Do you serve crabs here?
e   This egg is bad!
f   Waiter! Where's my honey?
g   Did you hear about the new restaurant on the moon?

Listen to B's first lines. Can you give answers which are funny?

Second lines of jokes
1   That must be the tea. The coffee tastes like glue.
2   Don't worry sir, it won't shrink.
3   No, sir, I always walk this way.
4   No, sir, that's a cockroach. The fly is on your steak.
5   Accidentally! I moved the lettuce and there it was.
6   About three or four inches, if you're lucky.
7   That's your sausage, sir.

7 [Unit 9]

Make sure you know the answers to the following questions about your text.

a   What two disadvantages did Diana Kayle find for blonde job applicants?
b   What might be the connection between blonde hair, youth and the bias against blonde women?

Recent research conducted by, among others, Diana Kayle at California State University reveals – amazingly – that while being blonde may boost your social life, it can also damage your career prospects. Blonde females are rejected for jobs more often than equally qualified brunettes. And where blondes and brunettes are given similar jobs, the darker-haired applicants are awarded higher salaries. It seems hardly credible that such changeable features as hair colour could so influence recruitment decisions but the research findings are unequivocal.

So what lies behind this remarkable bias? One theory is that blonde hair gives the appearance of youth. This is because people have lighter hair and skin when they are children than when they get older. So blonde people are treated (unconsciously – we are not aware we are doing it) as if they were less intelligent, more naïve, more vulnerable, less mature and less capable.

Find answers to the following questions from either Student B or Student C.

a What was Brian Bates' experiment and what did it show?
b What do men think of blondes?

Now turn back to Activity 17 on page 93.

8 [Unit 5]

a Read the extract.

Differences between men and women

Studies have long shown differences between the way men and women react, how they use anger and how anger affects them. However, this may be changing as society changes.

We do know that by the age of three, boys show three times as much aggressive behaviour as girls do and that high levels of testosterone (the male hormone) have been linked with increased anger patterns. So it does seem that men, in general, are 'angrier' than women.

Anger is also more acceptable in men than in women. Those women who show anger are often thought of as mad, bad, crazy and emotional. Studies suggest that many women in such situations suppress their anger or channel it in other ways such as eating disorders, for example. It is now thought that suppressing anger is extremely bad for people, especially women.

However, in the eyes of many researchers, the difference between the sexes may not be nearly as significant as changes in society which have led to an erosion of social skills in both men and women. In the modern world, we spend more time on the Internet or looking at the TV and not enough time talking to each other. We expect everything to happen quickly and as a result, we become frustrated very easily.

Women against anger
Shouting in the age of IT
Psychology Today

b Copy and complete the chart with notes in your own words.

Topic	Your notes
Anger in men and women	
The acceptability of anger	
The modern world	

c Do you agree with what you have read?

Now turn back to Activity 4 on page 51.

9 [Unit 5]

Police officer 2

- You and your police colleague are in charge of the interview. You decide who says what and when.
- The suspect was seen taking the car by two other criminals, Ben and Joey, but you can't tell the suspect this, because that would put Ben and Joey in danger. So the only thing you can do is keep asking the suspect different questions about what he or she was doing last night in the hope that he or she will get confused and in the end confess.
- You like your partner but you get really worried when he / she starts getting angry since this doesn't help in a police interview situation, so you try and calm your partner down. The only thing that makes you angry is when a suspect's mother or father tries to say that their child is not really to blame.

Now turn back to Activity 23 on page 55.

10 [Unit 7]

black	pink
blue	purple
brown	red
green	violet
grey	white
orange	yellow

11 [Unit 8]

Read your first lines. Can A give you answers which are funny?

First lines of jokes

a Waiter! There's a fly in my soup!
b Do you have frogs' legs?
c Waiter! There's a worm on my plate.
d How did you find your steak, sir?
e Waiter! Your tie is in my soup.
f This coffee tastes like soap!
g How long will my sausages be?

Listen to A's first lines. Can you give answers which are funny?

Second lines of jokes

1 Thanks for your concern, sir, but it's not that hot.
2 We serve *anyone* here, sir.
3 Don't blame me, sir. I only laid the table.
4 Yes – great food but no atmosphere.
5 She left last week, sir.
6 It looks like it's swimming, sir.
7 Don't worry, the spider on the bread will get it.

12 [Unit 9]

Make sure you know the answers to the following questions about your text.

a What were the business students given and what was different about the job applicants?
b What different treatment was given to blonde and brunette applicants?
c Why did the business students make the decisions they did?

Brian Bates did an experiment for a BBC television programme. Business students were given CVs for six job applicants. There were photos attached. Some of the candidates had brown hair, the others were blonde.

When they were asked whether the photos had affected their choices, the business students were convinced that hair colour had not influenced them. 'The picture for me didn't play a major part,' said one. 'I made a studious attempt to ignore the appearance of the applicants,' said another. 'I focused primarily on the CV,' insisted a third.

But the result revealed a different story. While they had appointed the blondes and the brunettes almost equally to the job, they had awarded the brunettes a higher salary.

Under close questioning, they revealed that the blonde stereotype had indeed affected their judgement. 'The woman with blonde hair is more of a wannabe – I would think she is probably an experienced secretary or something,' confessed one. 'She looks like a PA rather than a middle manager,' said another. 'The brunette does look more like one would imagine a middle manager would look.'

Find answers to the following questions from either Student A or Student C.

a What were the results of Diana Kayle's research?
b What, if any, are the differences between blue- and brown-eyed children, and what does this suggest?

Now turn back to Activity 17 on page 93.

13 [Unit 9]

Wordbank for Activity 34

a **Things you might complain to the doctor about:**

aches	earache, headache, neck ache, stomach-ache (tummy-ache), toothache
swollen ...	ankle, arm, ear, elbow, finger, foot, head, heel, knee, leg, neck, nose, shoulder, stomach, throat, thumb, toe, wrist
sore ... a pain in my ...	ankle, arm, back, big toe, collar bone, ear, elbow, eye, hand, heel, index finger, knee, leg, little finger, nose, stomach, throat, thumb, toes, tooth, wrist

b **What you might hear at the dentist's:**
Because you have a *cavity*, you might need a *filling*.

c **Things you might ask for at the hairdresser's:**

(blonde) highlights
a (centre) parting
a fringe
a trim
quite long / short at the front / back
to have your hair layered

Find out as many similarities as you can between Nigel Thomas and Student A's Neil Todd.

Example: When was Neil Todd born? (one similarity)

Name: Nigel Thomas
Date of birth: 23 / 10 / 75
Address: 26 Landsdowne Road, London SE3 4LR

Schools / Colleges attended:
1997 – 1999 Camelthorpe College of Further Education
1994 – 1997 University of Leeds
1986 – 1993 Parkridge Community College
1980 – 1986 Camelthorpe Primary School

Exams:

1993 'A' levels in
History (Grade A)
Art (Grade A)
English Literature (Grade B)

1991 GCSEs in:
Maths (Grade A)
History (Grade A)
Maths (Grade A*)
Biology (Grade A)
French (Grade A)
Music (Grade A*)
English (Grade A)
Art (Grade A*)
Physics (Grade A*)
Chemistry (Grade A*)

Qualifications:
Diploma in Journalism
BA (Hons) 2:1 History

Employment record (including holiday jobs):
2001 – present: reporter for the *Daily Mirror* newspaper
1997 – 2001: working for the *Camelthorpe Daily News*
1994 – 1997 (Christmas holidays): working for the Post Office sorting Christmas mail
2001 July and August: part-time working at MacDonald's
1993 – 1994: working at a secondary school in Tanzania for my gap year

Hobbies and interests:
I'm keen on football (I support London's Chelsea football team). I play tennis and I'm a keen amateur painter.

Anything else you wish to say to support your application:
I feel that my experience equips me perfectly for the job of Features Editor at the *Times* newspaper. The work I have done for the *Daily Mirror* (see enclosed documents) is exactly the kind that your advertisement is aiming for.
Colleagues at the Daily Mirror will tell you that I get on well with people and enjoy the atmosphere of a busy working newspaper.

References:

Morgan Peters
Editor
Daily Mirror
36 Farringdon Street
London EC4 2GY

Martha Galton
Editor
Camelthorpe Daily News
1 High Street
Camelthorpe CT54 5SG

Now turn back to Activity 36 on page 97.

a Read the extract.

Controlling anger

Here are some ways of dealing with anger.

Change what you expect. If you don't expect too much, you won't be too disappointed. If you are more flexible about what you want and need, you are less likely to become angry when the situation doesn't match up to your expectations.

Empathise with the other person – try and understand his or her position. Why are they behaving like that? How would you feel if you were in their shoes? Can you sympathise with their reasons for being angry? Once you see things from their perspective, your anger may be replaced by concern.

Learn how to be assertive rather than aggressive. Being able to state a point of view or hold down an argument is different from shouting at someone.

Monitor your thoughts for traces of cynicism and general discontent. Then, when they come along, you're ready for them and you can minimise their effects.

Stop the clock. When you get angry, take a deep breath and stop the thoughts that are making you that way. Think of something pleasant instead, something you like and enjoy. Your anger will gradually lessen.

Surround yourself with positive people. The more people around you show that they are calm and happier, the calmer and happier you become too.

Use your imagination, not your voice. Imagine doing something terrible to the person who is annoying you and channel all your anger into your imagination. That way, you are free to act calmly and rationally on the surface.

Anger control classes   How anger changed my life   Never angry again

b Copy and complete the chart with notes, using your own words.

Technique	How to do it
1	
2	
3	
4	
5	
6	
7	

c Do you think these methods of controlling anger are useful?

Now turn back to Activity 4 on page 51.

16 [Unit 5]

Lawyer
- It is your job to represent the interests of the suspect.
- You try to stop the police asking difficult questions – and you try to stop the suspect saying too much.

Now turn back to Activity 23 on page 55.

17 [Unit 5]

Suspect's parent
- You think your child is a good person and that if he or she has got into any trouble, it isn't his / her fault. It was difficult for the suspect when the other parent was sent to prison.
- If you think the police are being unfair to your child, you should tell them so – and make sure they realise it isn't really your child's fault.

Now turn back to Activity 23 on page 55.

18 [Unit 6]

In the year 2050, I'll be living on Mars. Even though I'll be 70 years old, I'll still be young, because scientists will have found a way for us to live forever. I'll get up when my robot comes to wake me and bring me coffee in bed and my breakfast. My breakfast will be just some pills. All food on Mars will be dehydrated, because nothing will grow there. I'll 'think up' (dial) my friends on earth and on the moon on my TPP (telepathy-phone) and we'll talk while I get ready for work.

19 [Unit 9]

Make sure you know the answers to the following questions about your text.

a What is the attitude of men to blonde and brunette women? Are they right?
b What is the difference between blue-eyed and brown-eyed children, according to Jerome Kagan?
c What 'common biological package' might exist, according to Jerome Kagan?

Men tend to rate blondes as more feminine but less intelligent than brunettes. Studies in Ireland confirmed that men rated blonde females as of significantly lower intelligence than brunettes and in America, job applicants were rated as less capable and assigned a lower salary than brunettes. In other words, blondes are seen as attractive but dumb.

Tests show, of course, that there is no difference in intelligence between blonde and brunette people. But there may be some character differences: American psychologist Jerome Kagan has investigated differences in temperament between blue- and brown-eyed infants and young children. He has discovered that children with blue eyes are far more likely to be shy and inhibited than dark-eyed children. Brown-eyed children are naturally bolder. He speculates that the genes for blonde hair, blue eyes and shyness may be a common biological package.

Find answers to the following questions from either Student A or Student B.

a What is the connection between blonde hair and youth – and what has this got to do with perceptions of intelligence?
b How did the blonde stereotype affect the judgement of the business students in Brian Bates' experiment?

Now turn back to Activity 17 on page 93.

20 [Unit 13]

Defendants

You need to prepare a good reason for why you committed the crime. You need to justify why you did it. Try to make the judge understand why you did it.

a **Michael Trent**
Last Friday, your wife was in a lot of pain and you could not bear to see her like that, so you broke into the drugstore to take the drug, because you could not afford to buy it. No one was hurt when you stole the medicine and you did not carry a gun.

b **Maria Metcalf**
You are a very quiet girl, but you want to do well at school so that you can become a doctor in the future – you would like to work with young children who are sick. You are very sorry for what you did, but you felt very bad at school when the other students made fun of you for not having new things.

c **Judy Moore**
You hated to see your brother do badly at school when you knew that it was because he had been sick. You decided to help him by getting the exam answers just once until he had time to catch up with his classmates. You are very sorry for what you did.

The defendants' language box

> guilty / not guilty
>
> I would like to explain why …
>
> Although I was wrong to … , I did it because …

Play your part in the trial using the information and instructions that you find here.

21 [Unit 11]

Students A and B, try to memorise all the information on the posters, tickets and schedule.

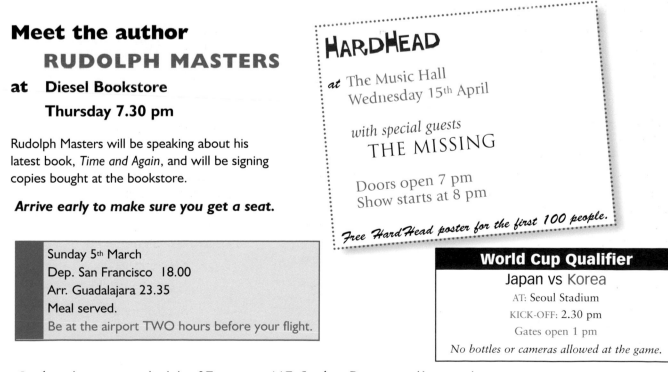

Meet the author
RUDOLPH MASTERS

at Diesel Bookstore

Thursday 7.30 pm

Rudolph Masters will be speaking about his latest book, *Time and Again*, and will be signing copies bought at the bookstore.

Arrive early to make sure you get a seat.

HARDHEAD
at The Music Hall
Wednesday 15th April

with special guests
THE MISSING

Doors open 7 pm
Show starts at 8 pm

Free HardHead poster for the first 100 people.

Sunday 5th March
Dep. San Francisco 18.00
Arr. Guadalajara 23.35
Meal served.
Be at the airport TWO hours before your flight.

World Cup Qualifier
Japan vs Korea
AT: Seoul Stadium
KICK-OFF: 2.30 pm
Gates open 1 pm
No bottles or cameras allowed at the game.

a Student A, return to Activity 27 on page 117. Student B, answer A's questions.
b Now change round. Student A can look at this page. B returns to Activity 27 on page 117.

22 [Unit 13]

Judge

You must listen carefully to what the defendant, the witness and the counsels say. At the end, you can ask questions until you decide if the defendant is guilty or innocent and what the punishment should be.

Questions to ask the defendant:
- Do you admit to the crime?
- Do you understand that what you did was wrong?
- Are you sorry for what you did?

The judge's language box

> Do you plead guilty or not guilty?
>
> I find you guilty / not guilty.
>
> I sentence you to X months / years in prison.

Conduct the trial using the information and instructions that you find here.

23 [Unit 13]

Prosecuting counsel

You must interview the defendant and the witness and try to get the defendant to admit to the crime. You want to show how bad the crime was.

Questions to ask:
- Where were you on the night / day of the crime?
- What exactly happened?
- Why did you do it?

The prosecuting counsel's language box

> I put it to you that you ... (= accusing someone)
>
> Do you really expect the court to believe that ... ?

Play your part in the trial using the information and instructions that you find here.

24 [Unit 13]

Witnesses

a **Mrs Trent**
   You have been very ill and you understand and appreciate why your husband did what he did, even though you don't agree with what he did.

b **Maria's best friend**
   You feel sorry for Maria and want to protect her, so you must try to justify why she stole. She is a good student and a good friend. She helps you with your homework when you have problems.

c **Richard Moore**
   You know your sister did it for you and you feel bad, but you don't want to be prosecuted yourself. You have to try to defend yourself and defend your sister.

Play your part in the trial using the information and instructions that you find here.

25 [Unit 13]

Defence counsel

You have to try to defend the actions of the defendant, by asking questions about the circumstances of the crime, so that the judge will understand and not give long sentences.

Questions to ask the defendant:
• Why did you commit the crime?
• Can you explain the circumstances very carefully?

Questions to ask the witness:
• Is the defendant a good person?
• Can you explain her / his behaviour?

The defence counsel's language box

> In mitigation, I would like to explain that my client …
> (*In mitigation* is a legal term to say that a crime is less serious because the guilty person was not responsible or had reasons for doing what he or she did.)

Play your part in the trial using the information and instructions that you find here.

26 [Unit 13]

The Mona Lisa, or *La Gioconda* as it is also called, is probably the most famous painting in the world. It was painted between 1503 and 1505 by Leonardo da Vinci, the famous Italian painter. It was probably sold to François I of France shortly before da Vinci died, when he was living in France. In 1800, Napoleon had the painting hanging in his bedroom, but it was placed in the Louvre museum in 1804.

The Mona Lisa was stolen by Vincenzo Perugia, an Italian. He had worked at the Louvre in 1908 so the guards knew him. He had walked into the museum and noticed that the guard was not there so he had stolen the picture by taking it from its frame and walking out with it hidden inside his painter's smock. He wanted the painting returned to Italy, because he felt it belonged in Italy.